Key	Description
Ctrl-B	Snap mode
Ctrl-D	Coordinate display
Ctrl-E	Next Isometric plane
Ctrl-G	Grid mode
Ctrl-O	Ortho mode
Ctrl-T	Tablet mode
Ctrl-V	Cycles thru active viewports

Scale object = 2

dimLFAC = .5

PEN WIDTHS

1	.002
2	.006
3	.002
4	.002
5	.015
6	.000
7	.008
9-11	.002
12 →	.000

SOLIDS-SECTION
SELECT OBJ
> points

- Zoom to desired obj in new vport
② SOL DRAW
  select obj.
① SOL VIEW
  - section
  - cut plane 2 ft
  - vis port
  - scale
  - view ctr
  - clip image
  - view name

The SYBEX Instant Reference Series

Instant References are available on these topics:

AutoCAD Release 11

AutoCAD Release 12

CorelDRAW 3

dBASE

dBASE IV 1.1 Programmer's

dBASE IV 1.1 User's

DESQview

DOS

DOS 5

DR DOS 6

Excel 4 for Windows

Harvard Graphics 3

Harvard Graphics
for Windows

Lotus 1-2-3 Release 2.3 &
2.4 for DOS

Lotus 1-2-3 for Windows

Macintosh Software

Microsoft Access

Norton Desktop for DOS

Norton Desktop for
Windows 2.0

Norton Utilities 6

OS/2 2.1

PageMaker 4.0
for the Macintosh

Paradox 3.5 User's

Paradox 4 Programmer's

Paradox 4 User's

Paradox for Windows User's

PC Tools 7.1

PC Tools 8

Windows 3.1

Word for Windows,
Version 2.0

WordPerfect 5

WordPerfect 5.1 for DOS

Computer users are not all alike.
Neither are SYBEX books.

We know our customers have a variety of needs. They've told us so. And because we've listened, we've developed several distinct types of books to meet the needs of each of our customers. What are you looking for in computer help?

If you're looking for the basics, try the **ABC's** series. For a more visual approach, select full-color **Quick & Easy** books.

Running Start books are two books in one: a fast-paced tutorial, followed by a command reference.

Mastering and **Understanding** titles offer you a step-by-step introduction, plus an in-depth examination of intermediate-level features, to use as you progress.

Our **Up & Running** series is designed for computer-literate consumers who want a no-nonsense overview of new programs. Just 20 basic lessons, and you're on your way.

SYBEX **Encyclopedias**, **Desktop References**, and **A to Z** books provide a *comprehensive reference* and explanation of all of the commands, features, and functions of the subject software.

Sometimes a subject requires a special treatment that our standard series don't provide. So you'll find we have titles like **Advanced Techniques, Handbooks, Tips & Tricks,** and others that are specifically tailored to satisfy a unique need.

You'll find SYBEX publishes a variety of books on every popular software package. Looking for computer help? Help Yourself to SYBEX.

For a complete catalog of our publications:

SYBEX Inc.
2021 Challenger Drive, Alameda, CA 94501
Tel: (510) 523-8233/(800) 227-2346 Telex: 336311
Fax: (510) 523-2373

SYBEX is committed to using natural resources wisely to preserve and improve our environment. This is why we have been printing the text of books like this one on recycled paper since 1982.

This year our use of recycled paper will result in the saving of more than 15,300 trees. We will lower air pollution effluents by 54,000 pounds, save 6,300,000 gallons of water, and reduce landfill by 2,700 cubic yards.

In choosing a SYBEX book you are not only making a choice for the best in skills and information, you are also choosing to enhance the quality of life for all of us.

AutoCAD® Release 12 for Windows™ Instant Reference

George Omura

B. Robert Callori

SYBEX®

San Francisco • Paris • Düsseldorf • Soest

Acquisitions Editor: Dianne King
Editors: Michelle Nance, Doug Robert
Technical Editors: B. Robert Callori, Laurence Sy
Series Designer: Ingrid Owen
Production Artist: Helen Bruno
Screen Graphics: Cuong Le, John Corrigan
Typesetter: Ann Dunn
Production Editor: Carolina Montilla
Indexer: Ted Laux
Cover Designer: Archer Design

Library of Congress Card Number: 93-83694

ISBN: 0-7821-1222-6

Manufactured in the United States of America

10 9 8 7 6 5 4 3 2 1

To my son, Arthur
— G.O.

To my Dad, Michael A. Callori, Sr.
—B.R.C.

Acknowledgments

It seems that the world is changing at an ever increasing rate. To keep up with those changes, I find that I must rely more heavily on the people with whom I work. I am grateful to the many people at Sybex who have been instrumental in creating this latest edition of the AutoCAD Instant Reference.

First, I'd like to thank Michelle Nance for those long hours and weekends making sure no stone was left unturned, and Bob Callori, who acted as coauthor as well as technical reviewer. I'd also like to thank the rest of the Sybex staff who worked on the book: Carolina Montilla, production editor; Ann Dunn, typesetter; Ingrid Owen, artist and book designer; and Cuong Le and John Corrigan, screen graphics. Thanks again to those who worked on the last edition: Doug Robert, editor; and Laurence Sy, technical editor.

Thank you to my friend Larry Knott at Autodesk for helping me sort out last minute details, Rob Fassberg in Technical Support for taking time to show me the new features, and Neele Johnston for his quick response to my incessant phone calls.

Introduction

This book is designed to give you quick and comprehensive answers to your questions about AutoCAD Release 12 for Windows functions and commands. Whether the command you've just issued does not work as you intended or you need a concise guide to using a feature you've never tried before, *AutoCAD Instant Reference* will help you solve the problem quickly so you can get on with your work. All of the main program's features are here—the basic commands as well as the built-in functions you may not use every day. (Auxiliary programs, like the Advanced Modeling Extension, are not covered.)

WHO SHOULD USE THIS BOOK

We designed this book for users who have some basic knowledge of AutoCAD—people who already have an idea of what they need to know but just aren't sure of the precise steps involved. It is equally useful for casual AutoCAD users who need basic information fast and experienced users who need a refresher on specific commands. All the information in the book is specific to AutoCAD Release 12.

If you are new to AutoCAD, read *Mastering AutoCAD Release 12 for Windows* (SYBEX, 1993), which offers a tutorial approach and contains a wealth of tips and techniques for both beginning and advanced users. The two books together make for a valuable pair.

HOW THE BOOK IS ORGANIZED

Besides the **Introduction**, which merely serves to acquaint you with the book's organizing principles, and the **Index**, to make it easy to find specific topics, this book consists of a single alphabetically arranged presentation of commands, features, and important filenames. Most entries present the following information:

1. The *name* of the command or feature appears as a header
    displayed graphically in a shaded box.

    *   If the command can be used *transparently*—that is, if
        you can enter it at the keyboard while another com-
        mand is being executed—the transparent version of
        the command is repeated below the header. (All you
        have to do to issue the command transparently is to
        preface the command with an apostrophe.)

    *   If a command can be selected from the *pull-down
        menu*, it also appears under the header, with ➤ sym-
        bols as necessary to indicate a sequence of cascading
        levels or picks. (In our experience we rarely use the
        "screen menus" at the side of the screen; for this
        reason we do not present selection sequences for
        these menus.)

2. A short paragraph or two follows explaining the
    command's *purpose*.

3. Unless the procedure is completely obvious, *instructions*
    on using the command follow a head that takes the form
    To Do Such-and-Such:. The instructions will usually walk
    you through the command-line prompts and/or dialog-
    box settings that AutoCAD displays requiring you to pro-
    vide additional information.

4. Commands that open dialog boxes or subdialog boxes re-
    quire you to respond by picking or checking special boxes
    or by entering data. Short descriptions of these options,
    and notes on how to select them as well, are presented in
    the **Options** section. (Later in this introduction you will
    find a presentation of the components of a typical
    AutoCAD dialog box.)

5. The **Notes** section describes command restrictions and in-
    teractions with other commands, and provides special tips
    or warnings.

6. **See Also** directs you to related entries for further information, and lists the command's system variables (which are themselves presented under the main entry "Setvar/System Variables").

We have also used the following typographic conventions throughout the different sections: **Boldface** for commands to be typed or otherwise selected, *Italic* for command options, system variables, and filenames, and a separate Prompt: typeface for AutoCAD prompts and miscellanous on-screen messages. The various boxes and buttons presented in dialog boxes are frequently the equivalent of the prompts that would be displayed at the command line if you weren't already taking advantage of the dialog-box system. Where the dialog-box item and the command-line prompt are virtually the same, we set them as prompts (that is, we use the prompt typeface); otherwise, we set the dialog-box item in italics.

WORKING WITH THE
COMMAND LINE OR WITH DIALOG BOXES

Most commands will either execute immediately or will prompt you for further information. These prompts appear on the Command: line at the bottom of the screen or in the command's dialog box which pops open on the screen. In many cases you can enter the necessary information using either method: typing your response at the command line or using the dialog box. Many times you may prefer using the command-line approach because the prompts come up automatically, saving you from having to move a pointer around inside a dialog box. Other times you will appreciate using a dialog box because it allows you to see at one time all the options necessary for the operation you want to perform.

All commands beginning with **Dd** (Dynamic Dialog) can open a dialog box. However, if the system variable *Filedia* or *Cmddia* is off (has a value of zero), the dialog box will not appear, and all prompts will be displayed at the command line. (A dialog box may also be prevented from opening if a script or AutoLISP/ADS program is active.) *Filedia* controls dialog boxes pertaining to file and directory management, and *Cmddia* controls all other commands. The default for both variables is ON (1). You may change *Filedia* as often as you wish according to how you want to work. To change

Filedia, simply type **Filedia** at the command line and enter a different value. If Filedia is off and you only wish to override it for the current command, type ~ (tilde) at a any prompt asking for a filename.

When a dialog box opens, the cursor changes from a crosshair to an arrow, which you then position on the item you want by moving and clicking a mouse (or some other point-and-click device) or by pressing the Tab key on your keyboard (which jumps directly from one item to the next). You can also press and hold the Alt key on your keyboard and type the letter that is underscored in the item you want to pick. For example, typing Alt-**P** will activate the **P**attern: edit box for keyboard entry.

How to Use AutoCAD Dialog Boxes:

The following dialog box operations are standard throughout the AutoCAD dialog box system.

- To make a cursor *pick*, click the arrow on the item you want to pick.

- To type information in an *edit box*, click the arrow inside the edit box to place the text insertion cursor where you want it.

- To move a *slide bar*, drag the arrow the direction you want (hold the mouse button down while moving the mouse).

- To toggle a *radio button* or *check box*, simply click on it.

- To expand a *popup list*, click on it twice quickly.

- To view an *image tile*, click on it twice quickly.

- To pick an *icon*, click on it twice quickly.

ABOUT

Transparent: **'About**

Menu: **Help ➤ About AutoCAD**

About identifies your AutoCAD version and serial numbers and displays the *Acad.MSG* message file.

To Access AutoCAD Information:

Issue the command.

Notes The *Acad.MSG* file can be customized using any word processor that saves files in the ASCII format.

ACAD -P

The -p Command Line Switch allows you to plot a drawing using a method called *freeplotting*, which offers only a limited set of AutoCAD commands.

To Freeplot a Script File:

Issue the command, appending the file name as follows:

acad -p *scriptfile.scr*

Notes The AutoCAD session invoked with this option does not penalize the number of licensed copy(s) installed.

See Also Environment Setting (Program Item Properties).

ACAD.INI

Acad.INI is an ASCII file that contains the settings made in the File ➤ Preferences... options. It also contains the macros stored in the toolbar buttons. You can edit Acad.INI using the Windows Notepad application. Other settings in this file include the size of the toolbar icons (16 or 24 square pixels) and the default size and location of the AutoCAD window.

See Also   Preferences, Toolbar.

ACAD.PGP

Acad.PGP is an ASCII file that contains information needed to launch a DOS program from within AutoCAD; it is also the location for command alias definitions. Most of the commands in the Utility-External Commands menu need this file. For example, if you use a word processor, specifying the alias in *Acad.PGP* allows you to execute it as an AutoCAD command.

Notes   Each external command has four to six parts (see FIG-URE 1). The first item in each entry is the command name to be entered at the AutoCAD command prompt. The second item is the actual command as it would be entered at the DOS prompt. Next is the amount of memory in bytes to allocate to the command. AutoCAD Release 12 does not use the value of this field — it is retained for compatibility with previous releases, and should be set to 0 for Release 12. The fourth item specifies the prompt, if there is any, that appears after the command is issued. An asterisk (optional) preceding the prompt tells AutoCAD to accept spaces within the user's response. The fifth part can be used to enter a statement, similar to **Files to delete:**, to clarify the prompt; if no prompt is

```
; acad.pgp - External Command and Command Alias definitions

; External Command format:
;   <Command name>,[<DOS request>],<Memory reserve>,[*]<Prompt>,<Return code>

; Examples of External Commands for DOS

CATALOG,DIR /W,0,File specification: ,0
DEL,DEL,        0,File to delete: ,4
DIR,DIR,        0,File specification: ,0
EDIT,EDLIN,     0,File to edit: ,4
SH,,            0,*OS Command: ,4
SHELL,,         0,*OS Command: ,4
TYPE,TYPE,      0,File to list: ,0
amp,C:\amp\ampro,450000,,4
am,c:\a\amext -oe,420000,,4
a1,1,4500000,,0
a7,7,4500000,,0
xtg,c:\xtg\xtg /ZS, 350000,,4
dbase,dbase/T,    127000,,4
rbase,rbase -R,   127000,,4
ne,ne,         127000,,4
wp,\wp51\wp,            350000,,4
FF,FF,30000,,0
ASGSHELL,,400000,*,4

; Command alias format:
;    <Alias>,*<Full command name>

; Sample aliases for AutoCAD Commands
; These examples reflect the most frequently used commands.
; Each alias uses a small amount of memory, so don't go
; overboard on systems with tight memory.

A,       *ARC
CI,      *CIRCLE
```

Figure 1: External command and command alias definitions

needed, this item can be blank. The last item is a return code, usually 0. The primary return codes are listed below:

0 = Screen remains in text mode.

1 = Loads the file *$cmd.DXB* when the command is terminated.

2 = Creates a block with the name from the prompt. Block entities will be taken from the file *$cmd.DXB*. This return code must be used in conjunction with return code 1.

4 = Restores previous screen mode (text or graphics).

The command alias format is simple. The first item is the alias. It is followed by a comma, a space, an asterisk, and the name of the command being aliased.

Use the **Reinit** command to reinitialize the *Acad.PGP* file if you edit it and want to activate those changes in the current drawing session.

See Also   Del, Dir, Edit, Type, Reinit.

ALIGN

Menu: **Modify ➤ Align**

Align relocates an object in two or three dimensions using up to three source and three destination points.

To Align Objects:

Issue the command, then provide the following information:

1.   Select objects: Pick objects to move.

2.   1st source point: Select first source point.

3.   1st destination point: Select first destination point.

4.   Either press ↵ to move the object directly from the source point to the destination point, or relocate the object in two or three dimensions by specifying the second and third pairs of points at the subsequent prompts.

• OPTIONS

2d   Rotations in 2D occur in the XY plane of the current UCS (user coordinate system).

3d   Rotations in 3D use the two destination points and the second source point defined by the first source and destination points.

APERTURE

Menu: **Settings ➤Object Snap ➤Aperture Size**

Transparent: **'Aperture**

Aperture sets the size of the Osnap (object snap) target box to your preference. The equivalent dialog box command is **Ddosnap**.

To Set the Size of the Osnap Target Box:

Issue the command, then provide the following information:

- Object snap target height (1-50 pixels) <10>: Enter
  desired size of Osnap target in pixels. Default settings may
  vary depending on your display.

See Also   Ddosnap, Osnap. *System Variables:* Aperture.

Menu: **File ➤ Applications...**

Appload displays a dialog box for loading AutoLISP files or loading and unloading ADS applications (see FIGURE 2).

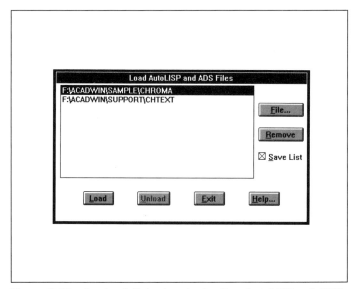

Figure 2: The Appload dialog box for loading AutoLISP and ADS
files

To Load AutoLISP Applications:

Issue the command as shown, or enter the following from the command line:

- **(load"<drive>:/path/filename")** ↵ **filename** ↵

● OPTIONS

File...   Displays a list of files to add to list box.

Remove   Deletes files from list box.

Load   Loads files from list box.

Unload   Removes ADS applications.

Save   Saves current applications shown in list box.

Notes   Files listed on DOS systems and Windows are limited to *.LSP*, *.EXE*, and *.EXP* file extensions.

See Also   AutoLISP.

ARC

Menu: **Draw ➤ Arc ➤ (preset options)**

Arc allows you to draw an arc using a variety of methods.

To Draw an Arc:

Issue the command, then provide the following information:

1.   Center/<Start point>: Use mouse to pick start point of arc or select **C** for more options.

2. Center/End/<Second point>: Pick second point of arc, or select **C** or **E** for more options.

3. End point: Pick end point of arc.

● OPTIONS

Angle   Enters an arc in terms of degrees or current angular units. You are prompted for the Included angle:. You can enter an angle value or use the cursor to visually select an angle.

Center   Enters the location of an arc's center point. At the prompt Center:, enter a coordinate or pick a point with your cursor.

Direction   Enters a tangent direction from the start point of an arc. At the prompt Direction from start point:, either enter a relative coordinate or pick a point with your cursor.

End   Enters the end point of an arc. At the prompt End point:, enter a coordinate or pick a point with your cursor.

Length   Enters the length of an arc's chord. At the prompt Length of chord:, enter a length or drag and pick a length with your cursor.

Radius   Enters an arc's radius. At the prompt Radius:, enter a radius or pick a point that defines a radius length.

Start point   Enters the beginning point of an arc.

Notes   If you press ⏎ at the first prompt of the Arc command, AutoCAD uses the most recent point entered for a line or arc as the first point of the new arc. It then prompts you for a new end point. An arc is drawn tangent to the last line or arc drawn.

If you select Arc from the pull-down menu, the Arc cascading menu appears, with ten preset arc options. For example, *S,E,D* allows you to select the start point, the end point, and the direction of the arc. FIGURE 3 illustrates how these options draw arcs.

You can convert arcs to polyline arcs with the **Pedit** or **Bpoly** command.

See Also   Change, Elev, UCS.

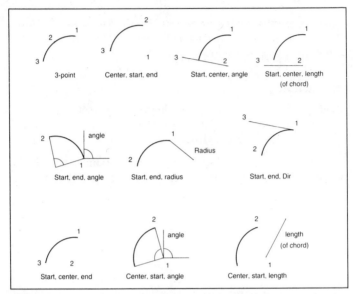

Figure 3: The Arc menu options and their meanings

AREA

Menu: **Assist ➤ Inquiry ➤ Area**

Area carries out an area calculation based on dimensions that you specify by defining line segments, by selecting lines and polylines, or both.

To Calculate an Area:

Issue the command, then provide the following information:

1.   <First point>/Entity/Add/Subtract: Pick first point or enter option.

2.   Next Point: Pick the next point.

3. Continue picking points until you have defined the area, then press ↵ to display the calculated area and perimeter in the following format:

Area = <Calculated area>, Perimeter = <Perimeter>

● OPTIONS

Next point   Continues selecting points until you have defined the area to be calculated. Once you have defined the area, press ↵ at the Next Point: prompt.

Entity   Selects a circle or polyline for area calculation. If you pick an open polyline, AutoCAD will calculate the area of the polyline as if its two end points were closed.

Add   Keeps a running count of areas. Normally, Area returns you to the command prompt as soon as an area has been calculated. If you enter the Add mode, you are returned to the Area command prompt once an area has been calculated, and you can continue to add area values to the current area.

Subtract   Subtracts areas from a running count of areas.

RETURN   Exits the command.

Notes   Area does not calculate areas for arcs. To find the area of a shape that includes arcs, you must convert the arc areas into polylines (see **Pedit**) before you issue the Area command. Then issue the command, select the *Entity* option, and pick the polyline—Area calculates the area of the polyline. Add all the polyline areas to rectangular areas to arrive at the total area.

Setting Retain Boundaries in the Advanced Options... subdialog box creates a closed polyline automatically.

Area only calculates areas in a plane parallel to the current user coordinate system.

See Also   Bhatch, Dblist, List, Bpoly, Pedit. *System Variables:* Area, Perimeter.

ARRAY/ARRAY 3D

Menu: **Construct ➤ Array** or **Construct ➤ Array 3D**

Use Array to make multiple copies of an object or group of objects in a row-and-column matrix, a single row or column, or a circular array (to form such objects as teeth in a gear or the numbers on a circular clock).

To Create Object Arrays:

Issue the command, then provide the following information:

1. Select objects: Pick objects to array.

2. Rectangular or Polar array (R/P): Enter desired array type.

If you enter **R** at the Rectangular or Polar array: prompt, you are given the following series of prompts:

a. Number of rows (---) <1>: Enter the number of rows.

b. Number of columns (| | |) <1>: Enter the number of columns. If you use Array 3D, you are also prompted for the number of levels.

c. Unit cell or distance between rows (---): Enter the numeric distance between rows or depth of cell (see *Unit cell* option below).

d. Distance between columns (| | |): Enter numeric distance between columns.

If you enter **P** at the Rectangular or Polar array: prompt, you are given the following prompts:

a. Center point of array: Pick the center of rotation.

b. Number of items: Enter number of items in the array, including the originally selected objects.

c. Angle to fill <360>: Enter the angle the array is to occupy. Use a negative value to indicate a clockwise array.

d. Rotate objects as they are copied? <Y>: Enter **N** if the arrayed objects are to maintain their current orientation.

● OPTIONS

Rectangular   Copies the selected objects in an array of rows and columns. You are then prompted for the number of rows and columns and the distance between them.

Polar   Copies the selected objects in a circular array. You are prompted first for the center point of the array and then for the number of items in the array. You are asked whether you want to rotate the objects as they are copied. If you press ↵ without entering a value at the Number of items: prompt, you will be prompted for the angle between items.

Unit cell Enter the size of rectangular unit cell by picking two points dynamically or with an Osnap mode. After picking the first point, you are prompted to select Other corner: of the unit cell.

Notes   Usually, row-and-column arrays are aligned with the X and Y axes of your current user coordinate system. To create an array at any other angle, set the **Snap** command's *Rotate* option to the desired angle. Rectangular arrays will be rotated by the snap angle (see FIGURE 4). The *Snapang* system variable also allows you to set the cursor rotation angle.

The order in which you select the two points for the *Unit cell* option determines the direction of the array.

See Also   Minsert, Snap/Rotate, Select, 3D array. *System Variables:* Snapang.

ASE

ASE is an application that links AutoCAD to external database files. You can modify database files from within AutoCAD and link AutoCAD objects to database records. Use ASE to access dBase III

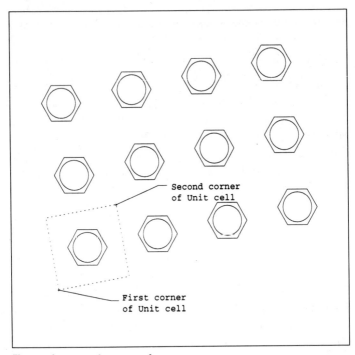

Figure 4: Rotated rectangular array

Plus, dBase IV, Informix, Oracle, and Paradox files.

Notes   Before you can use ASE, you must first initialize it. To do this, either click on **File ➤ ASE ➤ Initialize**, or enter **(xload "ase")** ↵ at the command prompt.

● OPTIONS

The following options appear in the **File ➤ ASE** menu. The Menu options are shown first, followed by the command equivalent in parentheses.

Set Row... (asesetrow)   sets the current database record or row.

Make Link (asemakelink)   connects a selected object with the current database table row.

Quick Link... (aseqlink)   lets you set the current row and then link the row to an object.

Quick View... (aseqview)   lets you simultaneously set and view the current row.

Quick Edit... (aseqedit)   simultaneously sets the current row and allows you to edit it.

Make DA... (asemakeda)   creates a drawing note that shows the value of the current row.

Quick Make DA... (aseqmakeda)   simultaneously sets the current row and creates a drawing note that shows its value.

Reload DA (asereloadda)   updates a drawing note created by Make DA or Quick Make DA after the associated database row has been changed.

SQL Edit... (asesqled)   allows the entry of SQL statements.

Select (aseselect)   lets you select objects on the basis of their database link.

Set ➤ Table (asesettable)   selects a database file.

Set ➤ DB (asesetdb)   selects the database. The database can be an alias set to a directory on your hard disk containing the database files. Set the alias by using the DOS Set command.

Set ➤ DBMS (asesetdbms)   selects the database file format.

Link ➤ View... (aseviewlink)   lets you view the link of an object, if a link exists.

Link ➤ Edit... (aseeditlink)   lets you edit a link to an object.

Link ➤ Delete (asedellink)   deletes a link to a database.

Row ➤ View... (aseviewrow)   lets you view the current row.

Row ➤ Edit... (aseeditrow)   lets you edit the current row.

Row ➤ Add... (aseaddrow)   lets you add a row to the current table.

Row ➤ Delete (asedelrow)   deletes the current row from the current table.

Utility ➤ *Export* (aseexport)   exports entity link information to an SDF, CDF, or native DBMS file format.

Utility ➤ *Make Report* (asemakerep)   lets you generate a report using the DBMS report making facility.

Utility ➤ *Post* (asepost)   synchronizes the drawing with its database. This is useful if a linked object has been deleted without using Asedellink.

Utility ➤ *Erase* ➤ *Table* (aseerasetable)   erases a table from the control database. Use this option with caution.

Utility ➤ *Erase* ➤ *DBMS* (aseerasedbms)   closes all open databases associated with the current DBMS. All links to the DBMS are lost when you use this option, so use it with caution.

Utility ➤ *Erase* ➤ *DB* (aseerasedb)   closes the specified database and deletes all links to it. Use this option with caution.

Utility ➤ *Erase* ➤ *All* (aseeraseall)   closes all open databases and unloads all database drivers. All links are lost when you use this option, so use it with caution.

Terminate (aseterm)   unloads the ASE application.

ATTDEF

Menu: **Draw ➤ Text ➤ Attributes ➤ Define**...

Attdef creates an attribute definition that allows you to store textual and numeric data with a block. When you insert a block containing an attribute definition into a drawing, you are prompted for the data that is to be stored with the block. Later, you can use the **Ddatte**, **Ddattdef**, **Ddedit**, or **List** command to view the data and edit attributes. The **Attext** or **Ddattext** command extracts it into an ASCII text file. You can control the format of the extracted file for easy importation to a database manager, spreadsheet, or word processing program.

To Create an Attribute Definition with Attdef:

Issue the command, then provide the following information:

1. Attribute modes—Invisible:N Constant:N Verify:N Preset:N Enter (ICVP) to change, RETURN when done: Enter **I, C, V,** or **P** to toggle an option on or off, or press ⏎ to go to the next prompt.

2. Attribute tag: Enter the attribute name.

3. Attribute prompt: Enter the prompt to be displayed for attribute input.

4. Default attribute value: Enter the default value for attribute input.

5. Justify/Style/<Start point>: Enter coordinates or pick with the cursor to indicate the location of attribute text, or select an option to determine orientation or style of the attribute text.

6. Height (2.000): Enter the attribute text height. This prompt appears only if the current text style height is set to 0.

7. Rotation angle <0>: Enter the angle of the attribute text.

• OPTIONS

Invisible   Makes the attribute invisible when inserted.

Constant   Gives the attribute a value that you cannot change.

Verify   Allows review of the attribute value after insertion.

Preset   Automatically inputs the default attribute value on insertion. Unlike the Constant option, it lets you change the input value of a preset attribute by using the **Ddatte** or **Attedit** commands. See **Text** for *Attdef* options related to location, style, and orientation of attributes.

Notes   Use **Change**, **Chprop**, or **Ddedit** to edit the attribute definition before making the attribute into a block. When inserting a block with attributes, the prompt sequence is determined by the order selected during creation of the block.

See Also   Attedit, Attdisp, Attext, Block, Change, Chprop, Ddatte, Ddattext, Ddedit, Insert, Text, Xdata/Xdlist. *System Variables:* Attdia, Attreq, Aflags.

ATTDISP

Transparent: '**Attdisp**

Attdisp allows you to control the display and plotting of all attributes in a drawing. You can force attributes to be displayed according to their display mode, or made invisible.

To Set Attribute Display Using Attdisp:

Issue the command, then provide the following information:

- Normal/ON/OFF <Normal>: Enter **ON**, **OFF**, or ⌐ for your selection.

• OPTIONS

Normal   Hides attributes that are set to be invisible. All other attributes are displayed.

ON   Displays all attributes, including those set to be invisible.

OFF   Hides all attributes, whether or not they are set to be invisible.

Notes   If autoregeneration is on (see **Regenauto**), your drawing will regenerate when you complete the command, and the display of attributes will reflect the option you select. If autoregeneration is off, the drawing will not regenerate until you issue **Regen**.

See Also   Attdef, Regen, Regenauto. *System Variables:* Aflags, Attmode.

ATTEDIT

Menu: **Draw ➤ Text ➤ Attributes ➤ Edit**...

Attedit edits attribute values after you have inserted them in a drawing. You can edit attributes individually or globally.

To Edit Attribute Values with Attedit:

Issue the command, then provide the following information:

1. Edit attributes one at a time? <Y>: Enter **Y** for individual or **N** for global attribute editing. Depending on your response, you may see one or more additional prompts before the Block name: prompt below. These prompts are self-explanatory; respond to them to move on to the following.

2. Block name specification <*>: Press ↵, or enter a block name to restrict the attribute edits to a specific block, or enter a wildcard filter list to limit it to a group of blocks.

3. Attribute tag specification <*>: Press ↵, or enter an attribute tag to restrict attribute edits to a specific attribute, or enter a wildcard filter list.

4. Attribute value specification <*>: Press ↵, or enter a value to restrict attribute edits to a specific attribute value, or enter a wildcard to filter a list.

5. In most cases, the next prompt asks you to select an attribute. Pick the attributes you want to edit. If you elected in Step 1 to edit the attributes one at a time, an X appears on the first attribute to be edited, and you will see the following prompt:

- Value/Position/Height/Angle/Style/Layer/Color/ Next/<N>: The options in this prompt are discussed below.

● OPTIONS

Y (at first prompt)   Allows you to edit attribute values one at a time, and change an attribute's position, height, angle, text style, layer, and color.

N (at first prompt)   Allows you to modify attribute values globally. If you select this option, you are asked whether you want to edit only visible attributes.

Value   Changes the value of the currently marked attribute(s).

Position   Moves an attribute.

Height   Changes the height of attribute text.

Angle   Changes the attribute angle.

Style   Changes the attribute text style.

Layer   Changes the layer that the attribute is on.

Color   Changes the attribute color. Colors are specified by numeric code or by name. See *Color*.

Notes   If you choose to edit attributes individually and answer all of the prompts (you select *Y* at the first prompt), you are prompted to select attributes. After you have made your selection, an X marks the first attribute to edit. The default option, *Next,* will move the marking X to the next attribute.

By entering **V** at the Value/Position/Height... prompt, you can proceed to either change or replace the attribute value. If you choose *Replace,* the default option, you are prompted for a new attribute value. The new attribute value replaces the previous one and you return to the Value/Position/Height... prompt. If you choose *Change,* you are prompted for a specific string of characters to change and for a new string to replace the old. This allows you to change portions of an attribute's value without having to enter the entire attribute value.

If you choose to edit only visible attributes (after entering **N** at the first prompt), you are prompted to select attributes. You can then visually pick the attributes to edit. You are next prompted for the string to change and the replacement string. Once you have answered the prompts, AutoCAD changes all the selected attributes. If you enter **N** at the prompt Visible attribute:, you won't be prompted to select attributes. Instead, AutoCAD assumes you want to edit all the attributes in the drawing, regardless of whether they are visible. The Select attribute prompt: is skipped and you are sent directly to the prompt Change string:.

When answering the attribute specification prompts, you can use wildcard characters (the question mark, the asterisk, and a few others) to "filter" a group of attribute blocks, tags, or values.

To restrict attribute edits to attributes that have a null value, enter \ (a backslash) at the Attribute value specification <*>: prompt.

The Ddatte attribute dialog box limits editing to attribute values only.

See Also   Ddatte, Ddattdef, Ddattext, Attedit, Attext, Select, Wildcards.

ATTEXT

Menu: **Draw ➤ Text ➤ Attributes ➤ Extract**...

Attext converts attribute information into external ASCII text files. You can then bring these files into database or spreadsheet programs for analysis. Attext allows you to choose from three standard database and spreadsheet file formats.

To Do an Attext Conversion:

Issue the command, then provide the following information:

1.   CDF, SDF or DXF Attribute extract (or Entities)? <C>:
Enter format of extracted file or ↵ to select specific attributes for extraction.

2.   If the *Filedia* system variable is set to 1, the Select Template File dialog list box will appear to pick a template file, and the Create Extract File dialog list box will then open to name the extract file.

If the Filedia system variable is set to 0, the command-line prompts are as follows:

Template file <filename.txt>: Enter the name of the external template file.

Extract file name <drawing name>: Enter the name of the file to hold the extracted information.

● OPTIONS

CDF (comma delimited format)   Creates an ASCII file using commas to delimit fields. Each attribute is treated as a field of a record, and all the attributes in a block are treated as one record. Character fields are enclosed in quotes. Some database programs such as dBASE III, III Plus, and IV can read this format without any alteration.

SDF (space delimited format)   Creates an ASCII file using spaces to delimit fields. Each attribute is treated as a field of a record, and all attributes in a block are treated as one record. The field values are given a fixed width, and character fields are not given special treatment. If you open this file using a word processor, the attribute values appear as rows and columns (the rows are the records and the columns are the fields).

DXF (data exchange format)   Creates an abbreviated AutoCAD DXF file that contains only the block reference, attribute, and end-of-sequence entities. Entities prompts you to select objects. You can then select specific attributes to extract. Once you are done with the selection, the Attribute extract: prompt reappears.

Notes   Before you can extract attribute values with Attext, you need to create a *template* file, an external ASCII file containing a list of attribute tags you wish to extract. Template files, which have the extension .*TXT*, also contain a code describing the characteristics of the attributes associated with each tag. The code denotes character and numeric values as well as the number of characters for string values or the number of placeholders for numeric values. For example, if you expect the value entered for a numeric attribute whose tag is *cost* to be five characters long with two decimal places, include the following line in the template file:

cost   N005002

The N indicates that this attribute is a numeric value. The next three characters indicate the number of digits the value will hold. The last three characters indicate the number of decimal places the number will require. If you want to extract a character attribute, you might include the following line in the template file:

name   C030000

The C denotes a character value. The next three characters indicate the number of characters you expect for the attribute value. The last three characters in character attributes are always zeros, because character values have no decimal places.

Follow the last line in the template file by a ↵, or you will receive an error message when you try to use the template file.

You can also extract information about the block that contains the attributes. TABLE 1 shows the format you use in the template file to extract block information. A template file containing these codes must also contain at least one attribute tag, because AutoCAD must know which attribute it is extracting before it can tell what block the attribute is associated with.

See Also   Attdef, Attedit, Ddattdef, Ddattext. *System Variables:* Filedia.

Table 1: Template Tags and Codes for Extracting Information

Tag	Code	Description
BL:LEVEL	N*xxx*000	Level of nesting for block
BL:NAME	C*xxx*000	Block name
BL:X	N*xxxxxx*	X value for block insertion point
BL:Y	N*xxxxxx*	Y value for block insertion point
BL:Z	N*xxxxxx*	Z value for block insertion point
BL:NUMBER	N*xxx*000	Block counter
BL:HANDLE	C*xxx*000	Block handle
BL:LAYER	C*xxx*000	Name of layer block is on
BL:ORIENT	N*xxxxxx*	Block rotation angle
BL:XSCALE	N*xxxxxx*	Block X scale
BL:YSCALE	N*xxxxxx*	Block Y scale
BL:ZSCALE	N*xxxxxx*	Block Z scale
BL:XEXTRUDE	N*xxxxxx*	X value for block extrusion direction
BL:YEXTRUDE	N*xxxxxx*	Y value for block extrusion direction
BL:ZEXTRUDE	N*xxxxxx*	Z value for block extrusion direction

Note: Italicized x's indicate adjustable numeric variables.

AUDIT

Use Audit to check a drawing file for errors or corrupted data. If errors are detected, AutoCAD will optionally correct them.

To Use Audit:

Issue the command, then provide the following information:

- Fix errors detected? <N>: Select **Y** to correct any errors found. Selecting **N** reports errors but will not fix them.

If no errors are detected, a screen display like the following will appear:

```
4       Blocks audited
Pass 1 4 entities audited
Pass 2 4 entities audited
total errors found 0 fixed 0
```

Notes Audit creates an ASCII file that contains a report of the audit and any action taken. The file has the extension *.ADT*. The information presented by the Audit command may not be important to most users. However, it may help your AutoCAD dealer or Autodesk's product support department to diagnose a problem with a file.

See Also Recover. *System variables:* Auditctl.

AUTOLISP

AutoLISP is a programming language embedded in AutoCAD. It allows you to automate repetitive tasks and add your own custom commands to AutoCAD. AutoLISP enables you to link applications written in C to AutoCAD. Several AutoLISP programs are provided with AutoCAD, and others can be obtained from computer bulletin boards such as the Autodesk forum on CompuServe.

To Use AutoLISP:

1. Enter your AutoLISP program code directly through the command prompt, or write your code with a word processor and store it as an ASCII file with the file name extension *.LSP*.

2. If you save your program code as a file on disk, use the AutoLISP *Load* function to load your program while in the AutoCAD drawing editor or issue the **Appload** command as described in Step 3. The following example shows the syntax for the *Load* function at the command line:

    (load "drive/directory/filename") ⏎

    You can leave off the drive and directory information if either your DOS path or the *Acad* environment variable points to the directory that holds the AutoLISP programs.

3. You can also open the Appload dialog box and save the LISP file in the list box, then activate it by selecting *Load*. (The **Alias** command describes this in more detail.)

4. Once a program file is loaded, you can use it by entering its name through the keyboard, just like a standard AutoCAD program. You don't have to load the file again while in the current editing session.

Notes You can combine your favorite AutoLISP programs into a single file called *Acad.LSP*. Place this file in your AutoCAD directory. It will be loaded automatically every time you open a drawing file. AutoLISP code can also be embedded in the AutoCAD menu system. TABLE 2 describes some of the AutoLISP files supplied with AutoCAD. For a detailed discussion of AutoLISP, you may want to purchase *ABC's of AutoLISP* by George Omura (SYBEX, 1990). For information on how to edit an AutoCAD menu file, consult *Mastering AutoCAD Release 12 for Windows* by George Omura (SYBEX, 1993) or *Advanced AutoCAD* by Robert M. Thomas (SYBEX, 1992).

See Also Appload.

Table 2: AutoLISP Commands and Descriptions

Command	Description
3D	Creates 3D wire frame objects.
3Darray	Creates multiple copies of an object or set of objects in a three-dimensional matrix or array.
3Dface	Allows you to draw a 3Dface in three-dimensional space. 3Dfaces are surfaces defined by four points in space picked in circular fashion. Though they appear transparent, 3Dfaces are treated as opaque when you remove hidden lines from a drawing. After the first face is defined, you are prompted for additional third and fourth points, which allow the addition of adjoining 3Dfaces.
3Dmesh	Draws a three-dimensional surface using coordinate values you specify. 3Dmesh is designed for programmers who want control over each node of a mesh.
3Dpoly	Allows you to draw a polyline in three-dimensional space using X, Y, and Z coordinates or object-snap points. Three-dimensional polylines are like standard polylines except that you can't give them a width or use arc segments. Also, you cannot use the Pedit command's Fit curve option with 3Dpoly. To create a smooth curve using three-dimensional polylines, use the Spline Pedit option.
Align	Relocates entities in 3D space. (Pick Modify ➤ Align from the pull down menu.)

Table 2:   AutoLISP Commands and Descriptions (continued)

Command	Description
Asctext	Imports ASCII text files into your drawing. Asctext has options with which you can control the text's appearance, such as underlining, line spacing, and columns.
Attredef	Redefines a block that contains attributes. Attredef automatically updates the location, angle, and style of existing attributes.
Axrot	Allows you to rotate an object or set of objects about the X, Y, or Z axis.
Cal	Cal is an on-line calculator. It stores calculated values as variables that can be recalled any time during the current editing session.
Chblock	Changes the X, Y, or Z scale of a block, a block's insertion point, or a rotation angle.
Cht	Changes text wording, justification, height, width, location, rotation angle, and style.
Cl	Draws a pair of center lines through an arc or circle.
Dellayer	Erases all entities on a specified layer.
Dline	Draws double lines and arcs along a path. This is handy for drawing walls in a floor plan. (Draw ➤ Line ➤ Double Lines from the pull-down menu.)
Edge	Turns the visibility of a 3Dface edge on or off.
Fact	Finds the factorial of an integer.
Lload	Eases loading of AutoLISP and ADS (AutoCAD Development Systems) utilities and applications.

Table 2: AutoLISP Commands and Descriptions (continued)

Command	Description
Mface	Mface is an alternative to the Pface command. It simplifies the construction of a polylface mesh by automatically making adjacent Pface edges invisible.
Mvsetup	Sets up the Paperspace of a drawing including viewports, drawing scale, and sheet title block.
Project	Offers a choice of two projection types—Project1 and Projects—to create a two-dimensional drawing from a three-dimensional model. Use Project1 to project entities onto the current UCS and Project2 for projecting entities from the current UCS onto a user-defined construction plane.
Ptext	Simplifies the input and editing of text paragraphs. It has a word-wrap capability and lets you control justification. The Edit option lets you edit text by placing a cursor on exact text locations.
Rectang	Simplifies the drawing of a rectangle. (Draw ➤ Rectangle from the pull down menu.)
Rpoly	Generates a smooth convex polygon from a random polygon. It does this by repeatedly drawing new polygons. Each new polygon uses the midpoints of the previous polygon as its vertices.
Rotate3D	Rotates entities about an arbitrary 3D axis.
Spiral	Draws a spiral.
Ssx	Allows you to select objects by their properties.

Table 2: AutoLISP Commands and Descriptions (continued)

Command	Description
Tables	Lists the layers, line types, view, blocks, styles, UCS, and viewports of a drawing. It demonstrates the Tblnext and Tblsearch functions of AutoLISP.
Xplode	Lets you explode multiple objects and blocks with scale factors having the same values (for example: 3, −3, and 3), as well as control their color, layer, and line type.
Xrefclip	Lets you add an Xref file to the current drawing and "clip" the Xref's display.

BASE

Transparent: **'Base**

When you insert one drawing into another, Base sets the drawing's *base point,* a point of reference for insertion. You select the base point in relation to the WCS (world coordinate system). The default base point for all drawings is the WCS origin point at coordinate 0,0,0.

To Set a Base Point:

Issue the command, then provide the following information:

- Base point <0.0000,0.0000,0.0000>: Enter the coordinates of a point or pick a point.

See Also Block, Insert, Ddinsert, Select, Wblock. *System Variables:* Insbase.

BHATCH

Menu: **Draw ➤ Bhatch**

Bhatch opens a dialog box (FIGURE 5) with hatching options. It enables you to fill an enclosed boundary defined by lines, arcs, circles, and polylines with a predefined pattern or a simple hatch pattern by pointing to it. The pattern can also be previewed before being applied.

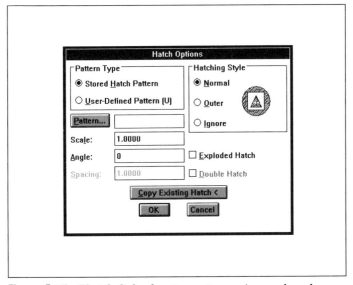

Figure 5: The Bhatch dialog box to create, preview, and apply hatch patterns

To Use the Bhatch Dialog Box:

Issue the command. Then pick the appropriate options from the Bhatch dialog box.

• OPTIONS

Hatch Options...   Opens the Hatch Options subdialog box. You can set a *Pattern Type* using Stored hatch patterns from the *Acad.PAT* file or User-Defined single line patterns. The greyed *Double Hatch* box becomes active when the *User-Defined Pattern* radio box is selected, allowing you to draw lines at 90 degrees. *Hatching Style* can be set to Normal, Outer, or Ignore as displayed in the tile box. *Pattern...* opens the Choose Hatch Pattern subdialog box and displays a slide or icon of each pattern. Selecting the icon activates that pattern in the edit dialog box adjacent to the *Pattern...* button. You can *Copy Existing Hatch* patterns, insert *Exploded Hatch* patterns, or view the existing *Scale, Angle*, and *Spacing*.

Pick Points   Prompts you to pick a point within the bounded area. Selecting text contained within a bounded area creates an imaginary rectangle around the text and prevents it from being hatched.

Select Objects   Select entities or use **Osnap** modes to determine area to be hatched.

View Selections   Highlights boundaries and entities selected for the hatching area, then returns you to the dialog box.

Preview Hatch   Displays an advanced view of hatch pattern, then returns you to the dialog box.

Advanced Options   Allows you to control the method AutoCAD uses to define the boundary set or to make a new boundary set. *Ray Casting* determines how AutoCAD finds the enclosed border for the hatch pattern when you pick a point. You can also *Retain Boundaries* as a polyline; if you don't choose this option, it is erased after the hatch pattern is created.

Apply   Applies the selected pattern to the bounded area.

Another   Allows you to pick another hatch pattern by opening the Hatch Options subdialog box if you haven't defined a pattern.

Notes   You cannot copy a hatch pattern created with an earlier version of AutoCAD. Hatched boundaries can be defined by a line, arc, circle, 2D or 3D polyline, 3D face, and viewport entities. Areas in nested blocks can also be hatched.

See Also   Hatch. *System Variables:* Hpang, Hpdouble, Hpname, Hpscale, Hpspace.

BLIPMODE

Transparent: **'Blipmode**

When you draw with AutoCAD, tiny crosses called blips appear wherever you select points. These blips are not part of your drawing; they merely help you locate the points that you have selected. You can use Blipmode to suppress these blips if you don't want them or if you have written a macro that does not require them.

To Reset Blipmode:

Issue the command, then provide the following information:

*   ON/OFF <current setting>: Enter **ON** or **OFF**.

• OPTIONS

ON   Displays blips when you enter points.

OFF   Suppresses blips when you enter points.

See Also   *System variables:* Blipmode.

BLOCK

Menu: **Construct ➤ Block**

Block groups a set of drawing objects together to act as a single object. You can then insert, copy, mirror, move, rotate, scale, or save the block as an external file.

To Create a Block:

Issue the command, then provide the following information:

1. Block name (or ?): Enter the name for the block. Enter a question mark to list existing blocks.

2. Insertion base point: Enter a coordinate value or pick a point to set the base point of the block.

3. Select objects: Pick objects to include in the block. The objects you select will disappear, but you can restore them as individual objects by issuing the **Oops** command.

Notes   Blocks exist only within the drawing in which they are created. However, you can convert them into drawing files with the **Wblock** command.

Blocks can contain other blocks. You can include attributes in blocks to allow the input and storage of information with the block; see **Attdef**.

If you attempt to create a block that has the same name as an existing block, you will see the prompt:

Block \<name> already exists.
Redefine it? \<N>

To redefine the existing block, enter **Y**. The Block command proceeds as usual and replaces the existing block with the new one. If the existing block has been inserted into the drawing, the new block appears in its place. If **Regenauto** has been turned off, the new block will not appear until you issue a **Regen** command.

To insert an exploded block into a drawing, preface the block name with an asterisk.

See Also   Attedit, Attdisp, Attext, Ddatte, Insert, Regen, Regenauto, Wildcards.

BPOLY

Bpoly works like the **Bhatch** command, but displays a dialog box to automatically create a polyline boundary from enclosed entities by picking a point within the area. No hatch pattern is drawn.

To Create an Enclosed Polyline:

Issue the command and click on the pick points, then provide the following information:

- Select internal point: Selecting a point within the connected entities first highlights the boundary, then joins the entities into a polyline.

Notes The Polyline Creation dialog box displayed by this command is the same as the Advanced Options subdialog box of the **Bhatch** command.

Use **3Dpoly** to draw a three-dimensional polyline with straight line segments. The **Pedit** command edits 3D polylines.

See Also Bhatch, Pedit, 3Dpoly, Area, Polygon.

BREAK

Menu: **Modify ➤Break ➤ (Preset Options)**

Break erases a line, trace, circle, or arc, or a two-dimensional polyline between two points.

To Use Break:

Issue the command, then provide the following information:

1. Select object: Pick an object to be broken.

2.   Enter second point (or F for first point): Pick second point of break or enter **F** to specify first and second points.

Notes   If you use the cursor to pick the object, the "pick" point becomes the first point of the break. Pick the second point of the break or enter **F** to specify a different first break point. If you selected the object using a window, crossing window, wpolygon, cpolygon, fence, or a *Last* or *Previous* option, you are automatically prompted for a first and second point.

Break does not work on blocks, solids, text, shapes, three- dimensional faces, or three-dimensional polylines.

You can only break objects that lie in a plane parallel to the current UCS (user coordinate system). Also, if you are not viewing the current UCS in plan, you may get the wrong result. Use the **Plan** command to view the current UCS in plan.

When breaking circles, you must use the proper break-point selection sequence. A counterclockwise sequence causes the break to occur between the two break points. A clockwise sequence causes the segment between the two points to remain and the rest of the circle to disappear.

See Also   Trim, Change, UCS.

CHAMFER

Menu: **Construct ➤ Chamfer**

Chamfer joins two nonparallel lines with an intermediate line, or adds intermediate lines between the line segments of a two-dimensional polyline.

To Use Chamfer:

Issue the command, then provide the following information:

1.   Polyline/Distance/<select first line>: Pick first line.

2.   Select second line: Pick second line.

● OPTIONS

Polyline   Allows you to chamfer all line segments within a polyline. This option prompts you to select a two-dimensional polyline. All the joining polyline segments are then chamfered.

Distance   Allows you to specify the length of the chamfer. This option prompts you for the first and second chamfer distance. These are the distances measured from the intersection point of the two lines to the beginning of the chamfer.

Notes   You can chamfer only objects that lie in a plane parallel to the current user coordinate system (UCS). Further, if you are not viewing the current UCS in plan, you may get the wrong result. Use the **Plan** command to view the current UCS in plan, then use the Chamfer command.

The two lines meet when the chamfer distances are set to 0 (the default value).

See Also   Fillet. *System Variables:* Chamfera, Chamferb.

CHANGE

Menu: **Modify ➤ Change ➤ Points**

Change can alter several properties of an object. You can change all the properties of lines. Move line end points by selecting a point at the first prompt. If you select several lines, all of the end points closest to the selected point are moved to the new point. If the Ortho mode is on, the lines become parallel and their end points align with the selected point.

You can change the color, layer, or line type of arcs, circles, and polylines. You can also change the rotation angle or layer assignment of a block.

To Change the Properties of an Object:

Issue the command, then provide the following information:

1. Select objects: Select objects to be changed.

2. Properties/<Change point>: Enter **P** to change the property of the selected object(s).

3. Change what property (Color/Elev/LAyer/LType/ Thickness) ?: Enter the desired option.

4. Depending on what you have selected to change, some or all of the following prompts will appear:

- Enter text insertion point: Pick new location for text.
- New style or RETURN for no change: Enter style for text. The style must have previously been created using the **Style** command.
- New height <height>: Enter new height.
- New rotation angle <0>: Enter new rotation angle.
- New text <text>: Enter new text.
- New tag <tag name>: Enter new attribute tag name.
- New prompt <prompt>: Enter new attribute prompt.
- New default value <value>: Enter new attribute value.

● OPTIONS

Color   Prompts you for color to change selected objects to.

Properties   Changes the color, elevation, layer, line type, or thickness of an object.

Elev   Prompts you for a new elevation in the object's Z axis.

LAyer   Prompts you for a new layer.

LType   Prompts you for a new line type.

Thickness   Prompts you for a new thickness in the object's Z axis.

Notes   The *Thickness* option will extrude a two-dimensional line, arc, circle, or polyline into the Z axis. This option does not work on blocks, however.

Elev changes an object's location in the Z axis. This option does not work on objects that are not in a plane parallel to the current UCS.

When you change an object's color, the object no longer has the color of the layer on which it resides. This can be confusing in complex drawings. To make an object the same color as its layer, enter **Bylayer** at the *Color* prompt.

See Also Color, Elev, Chprop, UCS, Select.

CHPROP

Chprop works like the **Change** command except that Chprop allows you to change the properties of all object types regardless of their three-dimensional orientation. However, the *Elev* option is not offered—use the **Move** command instead. The equivalent dialog box command is **Ddchprop**.

To Change an Object's Properties:

Issue the command, then provide the following information:

1. Select objects: Select objects whose properties you wish to modify.

2. Change what property (Color/LAyer/LType/Thickness)?: Enter the option.

• OPTIONS

Color   Prompts you for a color to which selected objects will be changed.

LAyer   Prompts you for a new layer.

LType   Prompts you for a new line type.

Thickness   Prompts you for new thickness in the object's Z axis.

See Also Ddchprop, Change, UCS, Elev, Color, Select.

CIRCLE

Menu: **Draw ➤ Circle ➤ (Preset Options)**

Circle offers several methods for drawing circles, the default being to choose a center point and enter or pick a diameter or radius.

To Draw a Circle:

Issue the command, then provide the following information:

- Circle 3P/2P/TTR/<Center point>: Pick a center point, then provide a diameter or radius by dynamically picking or entering a value.

● OPTIONS

3P   (3 Point) Allows you to define a circle based on three points. Once you select this option, you are prompted for a first, second, and third point. The circle will be drawn to pass through these points.

2P   (2 Point) Allows you to define a circle's diameter based on two points. Once you select this option, you are prompted to select the first and second point. The two points will be the opposite ends of the diameter.

TTR   (Tangent, Tangent, Radius) Allows you to define a circle based on two tangent points and a radius. The tangent points can be on lines, arcs, or circles.

COLOR/COLOUR

Transparent: **'Color** or **'Colour**

Menu: **Settings ➤ Entity Modes ➤ Color…, Color button on the toolbar**

Color sets the color of objects being drawn. Once you select a color, all objects will be given the selected color regardless of their layers, unless you specify *Bylayer* as the color. Objects you drew before using the Color command are not affected.

To Set the Color of Objects:

Issue the command, then provide the following information:

- New entity color <current default>: Enter the color.

When using the pull-down menu, you will get a dialog box with a subdialog color input box labeled **Select Color**... (FIGURE 6). Picking a color from the palette makes that number and color current as they appear in the color box.

● OPTIONS

Bylayer   Gives objects the color of the layer on which they are placed. It is the default color setting.

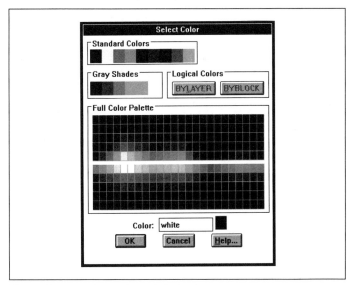

Figure 6: The Select Color subdialog box

Byblock Works on objects used in blocks. If such an object is assigned the Byblock color, it will take on the color of the layer in which the block is placed.

TABLE 3 contains the color names that AutoCAD recognizes, and their number codes. You can enter any of these names or numbers—in fact, you can enter any number from 1 to 255. The color that is displayed depends on your display adapter and monitor, but the first seven colors are the same for most display systems.

Notes Assign colors carefully, especially if you use them to distinguish different layers.

The Color... subdialog box is accessible only through the pull-down menu or dialog boxes (including Ddchprop, Ddemodes, Ddlmodes).

Selecting the Color button on the toolbar opens the Entity Creation Modes dialog box.

See Also Layer, Change, Chprop, Ddemodes.

Table 3: Color Names Recognized by AutoCAD

Color Name	Color Number
Red	1
Yellow	2
Green	3
Cyan	4
Blue	5
Magenta	6
White	7
Bylayer	Color of the layer on which the object is located
Byblock	Color of the layer on which the block is located

COMPILE

Menu: **File ➤ Compile**

You can create your own text fonts and shapes by compiling a shape/font description file. This file is an ASCII file that uses a special system of codes to describe your fonts or shapes. Compile displays a dialog box listing ASCII files with .SHP or .PFB extensions for converting into a form that lets AutoCAD read the descriptions and include them in a drawing.

To Compile Your Own Text Fonts:

Issue the command.

- When the *Filedia* system variable is set to 1, Compile opens the Select Shape or Font File dialog box, displaying .SHP extensions for Shape files or .PFB extensions for PostScript files. Enter a Shape/Font filename into the *File:* box to compile into a .SHX extension.

- When *Filedia* is set to 0, and Compile is entered at the command line, the following prompt appears:

  - Enter NAME of shape file: Enter the shape or font filename.

CONFIG

Menu: **File ➤ Configure**

Use Config to configure AutoCAD for specific input and output devices and display systems. You can also control plotting optimization and aspect ratio, screen aspect ratio, network capabilities, the location of temporary files, and much more.

To Configure AutoCAD:

Issue the command, then provide the following information:

1. A screen appears showing the current configuration. Press ↵ to go to the Configuration menu.

2. Enter the number of the configuration option you wish to access.

3. After you have gone through the configuration, you are returned to the Configuration menu. You can enter the number of another configuration option or enter **0** to exit the Configuration menu and return to the main menu.

4. After you enter 0, you are prompted to save the configuration changes you have just made. Press ↵ to accept the changes or enter **N** to cancel the changes and return to the previous settings.

● OPTIONS

0. Exit to drawing editor   Lets you exit the Configuration menu. You are then asked whether you want to save your configuration changes.

1. Show current configuration   Displays the current configuration.

2. Allow detailed configuration   Gives you access to more detailed configuration options. These include plotter optimization and the control of the display colors on color systems.

3. Configure video display   Lets you control the aspect ratio of your drawing editor screen. You can also turn on or off the various parts of the drawing editor screen. You can control the colors shown in the drawing editor if you select option 2 before picking this option.

4. Configure digitizer   Lets you control the sensitivity of your pointing device. If you use a digitizer, you can change the puck configuration. Port assignments can also be controlled through this option.

5. Configure Plotter Allows multiple configurations displaying a menu to add, delete, change, or rename a plotting or printing device. Lets you adjust the plotter output aspect ratio and change post assignments. If you use option 2 before issuing this option, you can also control pen optimization. Most of the other options can also be changed using the **Plot** command. To adjust the aspect ratio, draw a square that measures 5 units by 5 units. Use this square to help adjust the plotter aspect ratio.

When the *Cmddia* system variable is set to 1, the Plot command displays a Device and Default Selection... subdialog box that allows you to view, save, get, or change configurations prior to plotting.

6. Configure system console This option is not applicable to IBM-type computers.

7. Configure operating parameters Lets you control a variety of default settings and network features, as follows:

- *Alarm on error* Turns on a beep sound when errors occur.

- *Initial drawing setup* Lets you use a prototype drawing file other than the standard *Acad.DWG*.

- *Default plot file name* Lets you specify a plot-to-file filename extension.

- *Plot spooler directory* Lets you specify a directory in which to store your plot files. (Some plot-spooling software can periodically check a directory and automatically plot new files that appear there.)

- *Placement of Temporary Files* Lets you specify where AutoCAD is to place temporary files. For non-386 versions, directing AutoCAD to store temporary files in a RAM disk can improve overall speed. This option is also useful in networks.

- *Network node name* Lets you segregate temporary files by specifying a unique filename extension. This is useful when several people are working on files in the same directory of a network server.

- *Automatic save feature*   Lets you save your drawing to a name of your choice for set time intervals.

- *Full-time CRC (Cyclic Redundancy Check) validation* Lets you control an error-checking mechanism built into AutoCAD.

- *Automatic auditing after IGENSIN, DXFIN, or DXBIN* Controls the auditing of imported files of the DXF, DXB, or IGES file type (see **Audit**).

- *Release 11 hidden line removal*   Lets you select between AutoCAD's release 11 or 12 algorithm.

- *Login name*   Used to specify the default login name of AutoCAD nodes on a network, or stand-alone station.

- *Server authorization and file locking*   Lets you control the file-locking function of AutoCAD and allows updating of server authorization codes when network nodes are added.

Notes   When you first install AutoCAD, you are asked to specify a video display, pointing device, and plotter. If you change your display or input/output hardware, you must run the appropriate configuration option to inform AutoCAD of the change.

See Also   Plot.

COPY

Menu: **Construct ➤ Copy**

Copy copies a single object or a set of objects.

To Copy:

Issue the command, then provide the following information:

1. Select objects: Select objects to be copied.

2. <Base point or displacement>/Multiple: Pick the reference or "base" point for copy or enter **M** for multiple copies. The M option instructs AutoCAD that you wish to make several copies and prompts you for the base point again.

3. Second point of displacement: Pick the copy distance and direction in relation to the base point or enter the displacement value.

● OPTIONS

Multiple   Allows you to make several copies of the selected objects. The second point prompt is repeated until you press ↵ or Ctrl-C.

Notes   AutoCAD assumes you want to make copies within the current UCS (user coordinate system). However, you can make copies in three-dimensional space by entering **0,0,0** as the base point and the desired X,Y,Z coordinates as the second point or by using the **Osnap** overrides to pick objects in three-dimensional space.

If you press ↵ at the Second point of displacement: prompt without entering a point value, the selected objects may be copied to an area that is off your current drawing. To recover use the **Undo** command.

For multiple copying using grips, see **Move**.

See Also   Array, Grips, Move, Multiple, Select.

CUT AND PASTE

Menu: **Edit ➤ Copy Image, Edit ➤ Copy Vectors, Edit ➤ Paste, Edit ➤ Paste Command**

The Cut and Paste facility allows you to export vector and bitmap graphics from AutoCAD to other programs that accept graphics from the Clipboard. It also lets you exchange graphics between multiple AutoCAD sessions, or to import text to AutoCAD from a text-based application.

● OPTIONS

Copy Image   lets you transport a bitmap version of an AutoCAD drawing to the Windows Clipboard.

Copy Link/Copy Imbed   lets you use the object linking and imbedding feature of Windows. See OLE for more information.

Copy Vectors   lets you transport a vector-based version (Windows Metafile) of an AutoCAD drawing to the Windows Clipboard.

Paste   lets you paste a vector image (usually from another AutoCAD session) from the Clipboard into an AutoCAD drawing.

Paste Command   lets you import text to the command prompt. If you issue the Dtext command just before using this option, you can import text into your drawing.

See Also   OLE.

DBLIST

Dblist lists the properties of all objects in a drawing.

Notes When you invoke Dblist the screen switches to Text mode and the list of objects pauses at each screen of text. Press Ctrl-C to cancel the listing. Dblist is similar to the **List** command.

See Also ID, List.

DDATTDEF

Menu: **Draw ➤ Text ➤ Attributes ➤ Define**...

Ddattdef opens the Attribute Definition dialog box that lets you create attribute definitions that can store textual and numeric data with a block. The equivalent command-line prompt is **Attdef**.

To Use the Attribute Definition Dialog Box:

Issue the command, then provide information as needed in the dialog or subdialog box(es).

● OPTIONS

Mode Sets Invisible, Constant, Verify and Preset modes.

Attribute Sets Tag name, input Prompt, and default Value.

Insertion Point Allows you to Pick Point or enter the XYZ coordinates.

Text Options Sets text Justification, Text Style, Height, or Rotation.

Align below previous attribute Locates an attribute tag below a previously defined attribute.

Notes   Use **Change** or **Ddedit** to edit the attribute definition. Attribute tags are always displayed in upper case.

See Also   Attdef, Change, Ddedit.

DDATTE

Menu: **Draw ➤ Text ➤ Attributes ➤ Edit...**

Ddatte displays the Edit Attributes dialog box that lets you view and edit the attribute values of a single block. The equivalent command-line prompt is **Attedit**.

To Edit Attribute Values:

Issue the command, then provide the following information:

1. Select block: Pick the block containing the attribute(s) to edit.

2. The Edit attributes dialog box appears containing the attribute prompts and values. You can edit the existing attribute text by positioning the cursor at the appropriate location, deleting text, and typing your correction.

Notes   If you need to edit or browse through several attributes, you can use Ddatte together with the **Multiple** command. (At the command prompt type **Multiple**, then **Ddatte**.) Every time you finish editing or browsing through one block, AutoCAD will prompt you to select a block rather than return you to the command prompt. To exit the Multiple Ddatte command, press Ctrl-C.

See Also   Attedit, Attdef, Attext, Ddattdef, Ddattext, Multiple.

DDATTEXT

Menu: **Draw ➤ Text ➤ Attributes ➤ Extract**...

Ddattext displays an Attribute Extraction dialog box allowing you to convert attributes into external ASCII text files. These files can then be imported into database or spreadsheet programs. The equivalent command-line prompt is **Attext**.

To Convert Attributes to ASCII:

Issue the command, then provide the following information:

1. File Format: Pick *CDF*, *SDF*, or *DXF* format for the extracted file.

2. Select Objects: Temporarily exits the dialog box, allowing you to select the attribute entities.

3. Template File...: Opens the standard file dialog box, displaying a list box showing all .TXT files from which to make a selection for the corresponding edit box. A .TXT file extension is automatically assigned to the filename in the edit box if you don't enter an extension.

4. Output File...: Opens the Output File subdialog box, displaying a list box showing all .TXT files from which to make a selection for the corresponding edit box. When a template file name is selected, the current drawing filename is automatically assigned to the file name in the edit box but with a .TXT extension. Entering **Con** as a filename in the edit box will output the extract on the text screen. Entering **Prn** sends the extract to your printer.

Notes   The *Template File...* button is disabled when the DXF format is active.

See Also   Attedit, Attdef, Attext, Ddattdef, Multiple.

DDCHPROP

Menu: **Modify ➤ Change ➤ Properties**...

Ddchprop opens the Change Properties dialog box that lets you change properties of all object types. The equivalent command-line prompt is **Chprop.**

To Change an Object's Properties:

Issue the command, then provide the following information:

- Select objects: Select the object(s) whose properties you wish to modify.

● OPTIONS

Color...   Opens the Select Color dialog box to set entity colors. (See **Color.**)

Layer Name...   Opens the Select Layer dialog box, displaying a list of layer names to make selection.

Linetype...   Opens the Select Linetype dialog box, displaying *Bylayer*, *Byblock*, and a list of line types to make selection.

Thickness: Edit box to change an object's 3D thickness.

See Also   Change, Chprop, Color, Ddemodes, Ddlmodes, Layer, Linetype, Thickness.

DDE

Menu: **Edit ➤ DDE**

DDE (Dynamic Data Exchange) is a Windows function that allows two programs to communicate with each other and to exchange data dynamically. AutoCAD's DDE application lets you link AutoCAD to Microsoft Excel or Lotus 1-2-3 for Windows. You can link entire drawings, or limit the link to drawing attributes.

• OPTIONS

The following options appear in the Edit ➤ DDE cascading menu. The command equivalents are shown in parentheses.

Export Selection Set (ddesset)   starts up the spreadsheet program and exports a selected set of entities.

Export Blocks (ddeblocks)   starts up the spreadsheet program and exports all blocks in a drawing.

Export Drawing (ddedrawing)   starts up the spreadsheet program and exports the entire drawing.

Import Changes (ddeupdate)   allows manual update of data from a spreadsheet to a drawing.

Dialog… (ddedialog)   lets you specify the spreadsheet program to link with.

No Filters (ddeformat 1)   turns off entity filtering and causes the Export options to export all drawing data.

Attribute Filter 1 (ddeformat 2)   causes the Export options to export only the attribute entities.

Attribute Filter 2 (ddeformat 3)   causes the Export options to export only attribute tags and values.

Unload DDE ((xunload "ddeads"))   unloads the DDE application.

NOTES   To use the DDE options from the command line, first load the Ddeads application by entering **(xload "ddeads")** ↵ from the command prompt. If you select any of the options from the pull-down menu, the Ddeads application is loaded automatically.

DDEDIT

Ddedit changes a text or attribute definition. Ddedit displays a line of text in a dialog box for editing and viewing. You can position a cursor to delete single characters, make corrections, or add to the text. The equivalent command-line prompt is **Change**.

To Edit Text Objects:

Issue the command, then provide the following information:

1. <Select a TEXT or ATTDEF object>/Undo: Pick the line of text or attribute definition to edit.

2. Depending upon your entity selection, the Edit Text dialog box will open (with a *Text* edit box) or the Edit Attribute Definition dialog box will open (with the *Tag*, *Prompt*, and *Default* edit boxes).

● OPTIONS

Text   Edit box for revising text.

Tag   Edit box to change the tag name.

Prompt   Edit box to change the attribute prompt.

Default   Edit box to change the attribute value.

Notes   Every time you finish editing one line of text, AutoCAD will then prompt you to select another text or Attdef object rather than return you to the command prompt. To exit the Ddedit command, press ↵ twice (do not enter any text at the last Text: prompt).

See Also   Attdef, Change, Chtext (AutoLISP), Ddattdef, Ddmodify.

DDEMODES

Transparent: '**Ddemodes**

Menu: **Settings ➤ Entity Modes, Color Button on the toolbar**

Ddemodes opens the Entity Creation Modes dialog box that sets several entity creation modes including default color, line type, elevation, and thickness of objects being drawn, as well as the current default layer. You can also use the equivalent **Color**, **Linetype**, **Elev**, **Layer**, and **Style** commands to set these modes individually.

To Open the Ddemodes Dialog Box:

Issue the command, then provide information as needed in the dialog or subdialog box(es).

• OPTIONS

Color Opens the Select Color dialog box to set the current default color for objects being drawn. (See **Color**.)

Layer name Opens the Layer Control subdialog box to set the current layer, displaying a list of layer names to make a selection.

Linetype Opens the Select Linetype subdialog box displaying linetypes to set the current default line type for objects being drawn.

Text Style Opens the Select Text Style subdialog box to show and set the current default text style. A list box appears with the currently loaded text styles. You cannot create new text styles in this dialog box; you must use the **Style** command to create a text style. The *Show All...* button displays the entire symbol set. The text font, height, width, obliging angle, and orientation are also identified.

Elevation Edit box used to set the current default elevation of objects being drawn. This elevation value is the distance in the Z axis from the XY plane of the current user coordinate system (UCS).

Thickness   Edit box used to set the default thickness of objects being drawn. This value is a distance along the Z axis of the object.

Notes   The default value for the color and line type setting is Bylayer, which sets an object color or line type to that of the layer in which it is placed.

See Also   Color, Linetype, Elev, Layer, Change.

DDGRIPS

Transparent: **'Ddgrips**

Menu: **Settings ➤ Grips...**

Ddgrips displays the Grips dialog box (FIGURE 7) for controlling selection methods, grip color, and size. Grips allows you to determine the selection-set sequence by first entering the entities or the command.

To Open the Grips dialog box:

Issue the command, then provide information as needed in the dialog or subdialog box(es).

● OPTIONS

Select Settings   Lets you *Enable Grips* to pick objects for editing using a grip box. *Enable Grips Within Blocks* determines whether one grip appears for the block or multiple grips appear for the entities in the block.

Grip Colors   Opens the Select color dialog box to define a color for *Unselected* grips that are not filled in or for *Selected* solid grips.

Grip Size   Controls grip size using a slider bar and adjacent tile box.

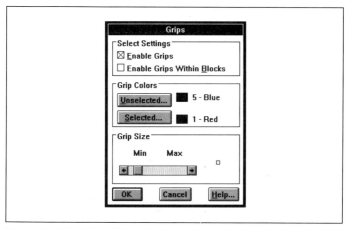

Figure 7: The Grips dialog box

Notes Grips can be set with their specific system variables and are associated with specific AutoCAD commands, including **Stretch**, **Move** (multiple copy), **Rotate**, **Scale**, and **Mirror**.

See Also *System Variables:* Gripblock, Gripcolor, Griphot, Grips, Gripsize.

DDIM

Transparent: 'Ddim ...

Menu: **Settings ➤ Dimension style**...

Ddim displays the Dimension Styles and Variables dialog box (FIGURE 8) for dimension and extension line settings, arrow type and size, text location and format, measurement units, dimension text appearance, and colors.

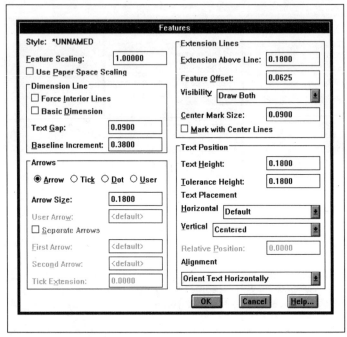

Figure 8: The Ddim Features dialog box

To Control Dimension Styling:

Issue the command, then provide the following information:

1. Dimension Styles: This list box contains the names of all the dimension styles that were created for the current drawing. To activate a style, pick it from the list box with your cursor and the style will appear in the *Dimension Style* edit box.

2. Dimension Variables: Choose one of the following to call up a subdialog box to determine specific dimension qualities:

- **Dimension Line**…
- **Extension Lines**…
- **Arrows**…

- **Text Location**…
- **Text Format**…
- **Features**…
- **Colors**…

• OPTIONS

There are two settings common to all the subdialog boxes: *Feature Scaling* and *Use Paper Space Scaling*. These are explained directly below. All other options are grouped by subdialog name.

Feature Scaling   Sets the overall scale factor of your drawing by specifying size, distances, or offsets and storing it in the *Dimscale* variable.

Use Paper Space Scaling   AutoCAD calculates the scale factor based on scaling between the current model-space viewport and paper space. Selecting Use Paper Space Scaling deactivates Feature Scaling and converts the *Dimscale* value to 0.0.

• OPTIONS: DIMENSION LINE…

Use Dimension Line Color to assign a color to your dimension lines, arrowheads, and dimension line leaders. The selected or entered value is stored in the variable *Dimclrd*. You can Force Interior Lines to occur between the extension lines (*Dimtofl* and *Dimsoxd* variables) or create a box around the basic dimension text as a Reference Dimension. An edit box is provided for setting the Text Gap, determining the distance to keep clear around the text. Text Gap and Reference Dimension share the same *Dimgap* variable. The Baseline Increment edit box sets the *Dimdli* system variable for off-setting consecutive Baseline and Continue dimensions.

• OPTIONS: EXTENSION LINES…

Use the Extension Line Color edit box to assign a color name or number to extension lines. This edit box also lets you designate extension line color Byblock or Bylayer. The value is then stored in the *Dimclre* variable. Extension Above Line provides an edit box to determine how far the dimension line should be from the end of the extension line. This value is stored in the *Dimexe* variable. Control the suppression of extension lines by picking the arrow adjacent to the Feature Offset edit box and choosing one of the four available options. Line suppression is adjusted by the *Dimse1* and *Dimse2* dimension variables. The **Center**, **Diameter**, and **Radius** Dimension subcommands can place a cross or centerline within a circle determined by Center Mark Size. Pick Mark with Center Line to draw a centerline mark or enter a positive number for the *Dimcen* variable value.

● OPTIONS: ARROWS...

Set or alter the arrow sizes drawn at the ends of dimension lines using the options in this dialog box. Both arrows and Dimension Line Color assignment can be altered from the edit box. Four radio buttons provide options to draw an *Arrow*, *Tick*, a *Dot*, or a *User*-defined arrow whose Arrow Size is set using an edit box. When the Arrow, Dot, or User button is selected, the value is stored in the *Dimasz* variable and automatically changes the *Dimtsz* to 0. When you pick the User radio button to place a customized arrow (*Dimblk* variable) at the ends of your dimension lines, you must enter a name for it in the User Arrow edit box. With the User button activated you can also select Separate Arrows, automatically turning the *Dimsah* variable on, and then enter names for the First Arrow and Second Arrow. The corresponding arrow dimension variables used are *Dimblk1* and *Dimblk2*. When you use AutoCAD Arrow to Appear as Tick Marks, we can adjust how far the dimension line will extend from the extension line using the Tick Extension edit box. This tick extension length is stored in the *Dimdle* variable.

● OPTIONS: TEXT LOCATION...

Use this subdialog box to manipulate text height, placement, and orientation. If text style is set to 0, you can enter a dimension Text Height, which will be stored in the *Dimtxt* variable. Tolerance values can be inserted adjacent to dimensioned text and modified from the Tolerance Height edit box. A ratio of the tolerance height and dimension text height is calculated and stored in the *Dimtfac* variable. Horizontal text placement shows a popup listing choices for *Default*, *Force Text Inside* and *Text, Arrows Inside*. Vertical shows a listing for *Centered*, *Above*, and *Relative*. These settings use the variables *Dimtix* and *Dimsoxd* for horizontal control, and *Dimtad* for vertical control. When using default settings (*Dimtix* and *Dimsoxd* are off), linear and angular dimensions place text inside the extension lines; radius and diameter dimensions place it outside. The grayed Relative Position becomes active when selecting Relative in the Vertical popup list. This allows you to determine the distance that dimension text will be placed above or below its dimension line. The entered value is stored in the *Dimtvp* variable. An Alignment popup list offers options for aligning text for linear, radius, and diameter dimensions. Each selection affects the variables *Dimtih* and *Dimtoh*, allowing you to Orient Text Horizontally or to have text Align With Dimension Line, Aligned When Inside Only or Aligned When Outside Only.

● OPTIONS: TEXT FORMAT...

Basic Units This section of the Text Format subdialog box includes edit boxes for the following: Length Scaling, which specifies a global scale factor for dimension length—useful when working in metric units—and can be used with Scale in Paper Space Only when dimensioning in paper space. Both items store their values in the *Dimlfac* variable. Checking the Paper Space box forces the Length Scaling factor to accept the Zoom Scale factor of entities in a model-space viewport. You can Round Off dimension distances (*Dimrnd* variable) to a specified unit, and add a Text Prefix or Text Suffix to the default dimension text by entering labels in each edit box or by using *Dimpost*. The Ddunits dialog box also contains settings that affect precision in rounding off dimensions.

Zero Suppression This section of the Text Format subdialog box contains check boxes for setting the appearance of Feet and Inches as well as suppressing Leading and Trailing zeros in dimension text (using the *Dimzin* variable).

Tolerances This section allows you to append dimension tolerances, with radio buttons to set *None*, *Variance*, and *Limits*. The variables *Dimtol, Dimlim, Dimtp*, and *Dimtm* are used to store values for this section.

Alternate Units This section displays bracketed alternate unit dimensioning. It offers edit boxes to enter numbers for Decimal Places and Scaling Factors and labels for a dimension text Suffix. The *Dimalt, Dimaltd, Dimaltf*, and *Dimpost* variables are all manipulated in this section.

● **OPTIONS: FEATURES...**

Use this subdialog box to review all the settings for the Ddim command. It includes sections for Dimension Line, Arrows, Extension Lines, and Text Position.

● **OPTIONS: COLORS...**

The Colors subdialog box offers edit boxes allowing you to enter values for Dimension Line Color, Extension Line Color, and Dimension Text Color while viewing its corresponding color swatch. Selecting the swatch box opens the standard Color dialog box.

See Also   Dim/Dim1, Ddunits, Units.

DDINSERT

Menu: **Draw ➤ Insert**...

Ddinsert opens the Insert dialog box (FIGURE 9) for inserting a block into your drawing. You can preset the block's insertion point, scale, and rotation angle, or insert the block as an exploded block. The equivalent command-line prompt is **Insert**.

To Insert a Block:

Issue the command, then provide information as needed in the dialog or subdialog box(es).

● **OPTIONS**

Block...   Opens the Blocks Defined in this Drawing subdialog box offering an alphabetical list of the blocks that have been defined in your drawing. Select from this list for a block to insert. The *Pattern* edit box can be used as a query with wildcards to filter block names. Picking a block name from the list with your cursor duplicates the block name in the *Selection* edit box.

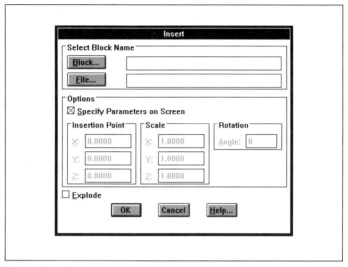

Figure 9: The Insert dialog box

Files... Opens the Select Drawing File subdialog box showing a list of *Directories* and drawing *Files*. Queries can be made using the *Pattern* edit box, with the results displayed in the *File* edit box. During the process the *Type it* and *Default* buttons are disabled.

Specify Parameters on Screen Allows you to specify the block's insertion point from the command line or by picking a point on the screen. When enabled, you can avoid prompts by preselecting *Insertion Point*, *Scale*, and *Rotation* by recording that information in their appropriate edit boxes. When the *Attdia* variable value is 1, an Attribute Edit dialog box appears during block insertion.

Explode Inserts an exploded version of the block into your drawing. The equivalent command-line procedure requires an asterisk before the block name:

```
Insert
Block name (or ?): <*block name>
```

See Also Ddatte, Insert. *System variables:* Attdia, Attreq, Base, Dragmode, Insbase.

DDLMODES

Transparent: 'Ddlmodes

Menu: **Settings ➤ Layer Control…, Layer toolbar button**

Ddlmodes displays the Layer Control dialog box (FIGURE 10) for control of layers. The equivalent command-line prompt is **Layer**.

To Invoke Ddlmodes Layer Control:

Issue the command, then provide information as needed in the dialog or subdialog box(es).

● OPTIONS

Current Layer   Identifies the current layer.

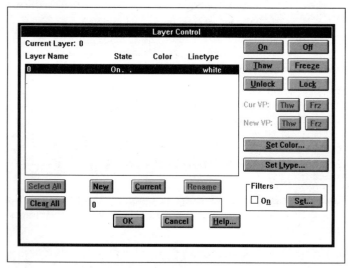

Figure 10: The Layer Control dialog box

Layer Name/State/Color/Linetype   Displays a list box with an alphabetized list of layer names, including their status, color, and line type.

Select All   Highlights all layers in the list box.

Clear All   Deselects all layers in the list box.

New   Enter new layer name or names (separating each with a comma) in the edit box below before picking New to add them to the list box.

Current   Highlight the desired layer in the list box for display in the edit box before picking Current to change the current layer name at the top of the dialog box.

Rename   First highlight the layer in the list box for editing in the edit box. Pick Rename to confirm revised layer name for the list box and enter its new name.

On   Highlight layers with cursor in list box, then pick On to change the assignment adjacent to each layer name, turning selected layers on.

Off   Highlight layers with cursor in list box, then pick Off to change the assignment adjacent to each layer name, turning selected layers off.

Thaw   Highlight layers with cursor in list box, then pick Thaw to change the assignment adjacent to each layer name, thawing selected layers.

Freeze   Highlight layers with cursor in list box, then pick Freeze to change the assignment adjacent to each layer name, freezing all selected layers.

Unlock   Highlight layers with cursor in list box, then pick Unlock to change the assignment adjacent to each layer name, unlocking all selected layers.

Lock   Highlight layers with cursor in list box, then pick Lock to change the assignment adjacent to each layer name. Locking selected layers preserves entities on that layer from editing. However, their color and line type can be changed, turned on/off, and thawed/frozen.

• OTHER OPTIONS

When *Tilemode* is set to 0 (off) you are in paper space and can manipu-late layers in model-space viewports or paper space as follows:

Cur VP: Thw   Highlight layer with cursor in list box, then pick Thw to change the assignment with "." adjacent to the layer name in current active model-space viewport or paper space.

Cur VP: Frz   Highlight layers with cursor in list box, then pick Frz to change the assignment with **C** adjacent to layer name in current active model-space viewport or paper space. Freezing or thawing layers from the *Cur VP:* boxes overrides global setting.

New VP: Thw   Highlight layers with cursor in list box, then pick Thw to change the assignment with "." adjacent to the layer name, thawing layers in new viewports.

New VP: Frz   Highlight layers with cursor in list box, then pick Frz for assignment of **N** adjacent to layer name, freezing layers in new viewports.

Set Color...   Displays the Select Color subdialog box to choose color for selected layers. (See **Color**.)

Set Ltype...   Opens the Select Linetype subdialog box to choose line type for selected layers. (See **Linetype** for loading layers.)

Filters   Opens the Set Layer Filters subdialog box using a popup list to assist in grouping portions of common layer names to turn *On/Off*, *Freeze/Thaw*, *Lock/Unlock*, in *Current Vport* or *New Vports*. Wildcards can be used in edit boxes to search *Layer Names*, *Colors*, and *Ltypes*. *Reset* cancels the filtering process. Picking *On* toggles the visibility of the filtered layers in the list box.

Notes   You can set the current layer by selecting it from the Popup list next to the Layer button on the toolbar.

See Also   Color, Layer, Rename, Linetype, Mspace, Pspace, Viewports, Mview, Vplayer. *System Variables:* Tilemode.

DDMODIFY

Menu: **Modify ➤ Entity**

Ddmodify opens a dialog box specific to the entity selected, including 3dfaces, arc, attribute definitions, block (FIGURE 11), circle, dimension, external reference, line, point, polyline, shape, solid, trace, text or viewport. The upper portion of each dialog box contains a Properties section to modify color, line type, layer name, thickness, and handle number.

To Modify an Entity:

Issue the command, then provide information as needed in the dialog or subdialog box(es).

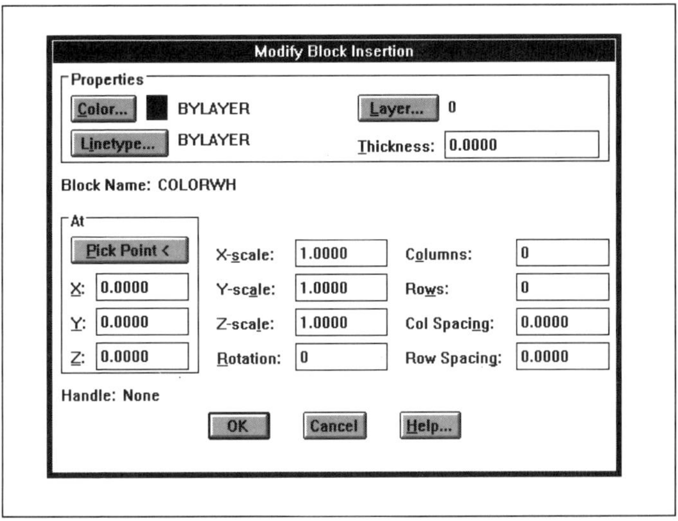

Figure 11: The Modify Block Insertion dialog box

• OPTIONS

The following controls are common to all the Modify dialog boxes:

Color... Picking this button or its adjacent swatch color displays the Select Color subdialog box to change a layer color. (See **Color**.)

Linetype... Opens the Select Linetype subdialog box to change line type for selected layers. (See Linetype for loading layers.)

Layer... Opens the Select Layer subdialog box to change an entity's layer by highlighting it in the *Layer Name* list box or entering it in the *Set Layer Name* edit box.

Thickness An edit box to enter an entity's thickness value.

• OTHER OPTIONS

The following controls are found in one or more of the Modify dialog boxes:

X,Y,Z Edit boxes for relocating an entity's initial coordinates.

Pick Point If you are using the current UCS (user coordinate system), you can temporarily exit the dialog box to pick a new point on the screen, using your cursor or entering coordinates from the command line.

Scale and Rotation Edit boxes to update the entity's XYZ scale and rotation.

Justify Opens a popup list of text justifications.

Style Opens a popup list of text styles currently defined in your drawing by the **Style** command. Additional check boxes are included to toggle *Text* as Right Side Up/Upside Down or Forward/Backward, and to select *Mode* as Invisible, Constant, Verify, and/or Preset.

Radius and Angle Edit boxes to change an arc angle's *Radius*, *Start Angle,* and *End Angle* while displaying Total Angle and Arc Length.

Tag Edit box to change an attribute's tag value.

Prompt Edit box to modify an attribute's prompt label.

Default   Edit box to alter an attribute's default assignment.

Height, Rotation, Width Factor and Obliquing   Edit boxes to change each property.

Size, Rotation, Width Factor and Obliquing   Edit boxes to change each property using the current UCS to define angles and points.

Columns and Rows   Edit boxes to create a rectangular array of a block.

Col Spacing and Row Spacing   Edit boxes to set the columns and row spacing for a rectangular array of a block. This feature duplicates the **Minsert** command.

Radius   Edit box lets you enter a new radius while displaying the Diameter, Circumference, and Area of a circle.

Columns and Rows   Edit boxes to create a rectangular array of an external reference (xref).

Vertex Listing   Lists successive vertices of coordinate X, Y, and Z values for polylines.

Fit/Smooth   Offers radio buttons for changing the type of line or surface curve fitting from None to Quadratic, Cubic, Bezier, or Curve Fit.

Mesh   Provides toggles to set Closed or Open mesh in the M or N direction for polylines. Also provides boxes accepting a range between 2 and 200 to control the accuracy of surface approximation in the M and N directions when using surface fit for a 3D polyline mesh. The edit boxes store the system variables *Surfu* and *Surfv*.

Polyline   Displays check boxes to confirm a Closed polyline and to establish an LT Gen (line type generation) pattern.

Visibility   Toggles to make a 3Dface's edges invisible. Assigning the system variable *Splframe* to 1 makes all edges visible regardless of the visibility settings.

See Also   Layer, 3D Face, Arc, Attdef, Ddattdef, Block, Circle, Dim/Dim1, Xref, Line, Point, Pline, Shape, Solid, Trace, Text, Dtext, Viewport.

DDOSNAP

Transparent: **'Ddosnap**

Menu: **Settings ➤ Object Snap...**

Ddosnap displays the Running Object Snap dialog box allowing you to have multiple object snap modes active while picking specific geometric points on an object and to set the target box size for your graphics cursor crosshairs. To override a running osnap, enter the specific osnap at the command line. The equivalent command-line commands are **Osnap** and **Aperture**.

To Invoke the Ddosnap Osnaps:

Issue the command, then provide information as needed in the dialog or subdialog box(es).

● OPTIONS

Select Settings   Activating one or more pick boxes in this section lets your pick location determine the osnap modes applied. For example, if both the Endpoint and Midpoint boxes are checked, AutoCAD automatically selects the mode based on which point is closer to the target box. Each mode can be overridden at the command line by entering the uppercase letters shown:

ENDpoint   Picks the endpoint of objects.

MIDpoint   Picks the midpoints of lines and arcs.

CENter   Picks the center of circles and arcs.

NODe   Picks a point object. (See **Ddptype**.)

QUAdrant   Picks a main point on an arc or circle.

INTersection   Picks the intersection of objects.

INSertion   Picks the insertion point of blocks and text.

PERpendicular   Picks the point on an object perpendicular to the last point.

TANgent   Picks a tangent point on a circle or arc.

NEArest   Picks the point on an object nearest to the cursor.

Quick   Shortens the time it takes AutoCAD to find an object snap point. Quick does not work in conjunction with INTersect.

Aperture Size   This section lets you adjust the aperture box size by moving the slider bar and viewing it at the adjacent tile box.

Notes   Cancel all osnap modes from the dialog box by deselecting all pick boxes. Entering **Osnap** at the command line and pressing ↵ at the Object snap modes: prompt will also cancel all osnap modes.

See Also   Aperture, Osnap. *System Variables:* Aperture, Osmode.

DDPTYPE

Transparent: '**Ddptype**

Menu: **Settings ➤ Point Style…**

Ddptype opens the Point Style dialog box (FIGURE 12) to select and control the appearances of points and to place point entities in your drawing, using the **Node Osnap** override. Points also appear as markers for the **Divide** and **Measure** commands.

To Set a Point Style:

Issue the command, then provide information as needed in the dialog or subdialog box(es).

• OPTIONS

The dialog box offers 16-point mode image tiles. Pick the desired tile, then use the *Point Size* edit box to adjust point size.

Point Size   Edit box for setting point size. Selecting a radio button changes the size specifications from Relative to Absolute as described below.

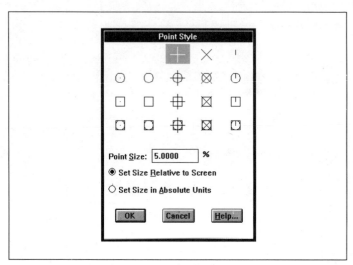

Figure 12: The Point Style dialog box

Set Size Relative to Screen   Radio button to set point size as per-centage of screen size.

Set Size in Absolute Units   Radio button to set actual point size based on absolute units.

See Also   Point. *System Variables:* Pdmode, Pdsize.

DDRENAME

Ddrename opens the Rename dialog box to change the name of a block, dimension style, layer, line type, text style, named view, user coordinate system, or viewport configuration.

To Activate the Rename Dialog Box:

Issue the command, then provide information as needed in the dialog or subdialog box(es).

• OPTIONS

Selecting the object from the Entity Type list box registers associated names in the Items list box. Pick the item to be renamed and it will appear in the *Old Name* edit box, then enter the new name in the *Rename To:* edit box.

Old Name Enter item to be renamed or pick from Items list box. Use wildcards for renaming groups of entities with common characters.

Rename To: Enter new name of item(s) shown in the *Old Name* edit box, using wildcards for groups of entities with common characters, then pick the *Rename To* box. The renamed entities will appear in the Items list box.

See Also Rename.

DDRMODES

Transparent: **'Ddrmodes**

Menu: **Settings ➤ Drawing Aids…**

Ddrmodes opens the Drawing Aids dialog box (FIGURE 13) to change several mode settings by accessing the functions for **Ortho**, **Fill**, (Solid Fill), **QText**, **Blipmode**, **Snap**, **Grid**, **Isoplane**, and the system variable *Highlight*.

To Open the Ddrmodes Dialog Box:

Issue the command, then provide information as needed in the dialog or subdialog box(es).

• OPTIONS

When you issue Ddrmodes, the following options appear as checkboxes in which you can either select an option or enter a distance value.

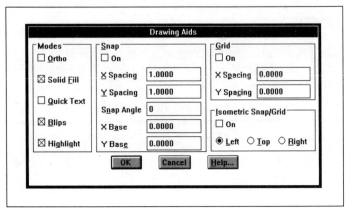

Figure 13: Drawing Aids dialog box

Modes   Pick boxes to toggle *Ortho* mode, *Solid Fill*, *Quick Text*, *Blips*, and *Highlight*. Ortho mode forces lines to be drawn vertically or horizontally following the orientation of the crosshairs. The **Fill** command makes areas solid for solids, traces and polylines. Quick Text uses the **Qtext** command to temporarily replace text with rectangles to reduce drawing regeneration. Blips are toggled on or off with the **Blipmode** command placing tiny crosses on the screen when you select points. The *Highlight* system variable controls the ghosting appearance of entities when selected.

Snap   Picking *On* sets the Snap mode while the *X Spacing, Y Spacing*, and *Snap Angle* edit boxes let you adjust the spacing and angle of the X and Y axis. *X Base* and *Y Base* edit boxes let you enter a Snap basepoint's X and Y coordinates. The F9 function key or the Ctrl-B combination performs the same toggle function as the Snap pick box. *Snap Angle* values determine the orientation of crosshairs on the screen.

Grid   Picking *On* toggles Grid mode on and off, to display a series of reference dots on the screen. Edit boxes for *X Spacing* and *Y Spacing* allow you to set the same intervals for your Grid and Snap distances.

Isometric Snap/Grid   Picking *On* switches your drawing to an isometric view. Radio buttons set the cursor orientation for *Left, Top*, and *Right* drawing planes.

See Also Fill, Ortho, Snap, Grid, Ortho, Isoplane, Blipmode, Qtext, Dtext. *Snap System Variables:* Snapang, Snapbase, Snapisopair, Snapmode, Snapstyl, Snapunit. *Grid System Variables:* Gridmode, Gridunit. *Ortho System Variables:* Orthomode. *Isoplane System Variables:* Snapisopair.

DDSELECT

Transparent: 'Ddselect

Menu: **Settings ➤ Selection Settings**…

Ddselect opens the Entity Selection Settings dialog box to define your method for selecting entities.

To Set Entity Modes:

Issue the command, then provide information as needed in the dialog or subdialog box(es).

● OPTIONS

Selection Modes Multiple settings can be configured from this section. Noun/Verb Selection: adds a target box to the graphics cursor for selecting entities prior to issuing specific commands, thus permitting the cursor to function as a pickbox. TABLE 4 shows the commands that support noun/verb selections.

The Selection Modes section also offers the following combinations for entity selection methods: Use Shift to Add: This toggle allows you to select or deselect multiple entities for Noun/Verb Selection sets. Press and Drag: This permits you to hold down the pick button, drag, then release, creating a selection window. Implied Windowing: This enables you to use a selection window by picking from left to right or use a crossing window by picking from

Table 4: Commands Allowing You to Use the Cursor as a Pick Box

• Array	• Dview	• Move
• Block	• Erase	• Rotate
• Change	• Explode	• Scale
• Chprop	• Hatch	• Stretch
• Copy	• List	• Wblock
• Ddchprop	• Mirror	

right to left at the Select objects: prompt. Default Selection Mode: returns the Selection Mode settings to their original Noun/Verb Selection and Implied Windowing.

Pickbox Size   This section furnishes a slider bar with an image tile to dynamically alter your pickbox size.

Entity Sort Method...   This pick box opens the Entity Sort Method subdialog box and lets you rearrange the following sort methods for entities in your database:

- Object Selection
- Object Snap
- Redraws
- Slide Creation
- Regens
- Plotting
- PostScript Output

See Also   Ddgrips, Grips. *System Variables:* Noun/Verb Selection-Pickfirst; Use Shift to Add-Pickadd; Press and Drag-Pickdrag;Implied Windowing-Pickauto; Pickbox Size-Pickbox.

DDUCS

Menu: **Settings ➤ UCS ➤ Named UCS**...

Dducs opens the UCS Control dialog box to rename, set current, list, or delete any existing UCS (user coordinate system).

To Open the Dducs Dialog Box:

Issue the command, then provide information as needed in the dialog or subdialog box(es).

● OPTIONS

Current   Select the UCS to be made current from the UCS Names list box.

Delete   Deletes a highlighted UCS from the list box.

List...   Opens the UCS Origin Point and Axis Vectors subdialog box to show X, Y, and Z coordinates for Origin, and direction of its X Axis, Y Axis, and Z Axis.

Rename To: Highlight layer in list box for editing in the edit box, then pick *Rename To:* to confirm new UCS name in the list box.

Notes   The list box always contains the *World* Coordinate System name. Entries for *Previous* and *No Name* may also appear.

See Also   UCS, Elev, Thickness, Vpoint, Dview, Plan, Rename. *System Variables:* Ucsfollow, Ucsicon, Ucsname, Ucsorg, Ucsxdir, Ucsydir, Worlducs.

DDUCSP

Menu: **Settings** ➤ **UCS** ➤ **Presets**…

Dducsp opens the UCS Orientation dialog box (FIGURE 14) display-ing image tiles to restore a specific UCS (user coordinate system).

To Invoke the Dducsp Dialog Box:

Issue the command, then provide information as needed in the dialog or subdialog box(es).

● OPTIONS

(Image tiles)   For the following UCS orientations: World, Top, Back, Left, Front, Right, Current View, Bottom and Previous.

Relative to Current UCS   Radio button to change current UCS based on an associated image tile.

Absolute to WCS   Radio button to change UCS based on an as-sociated image tile.

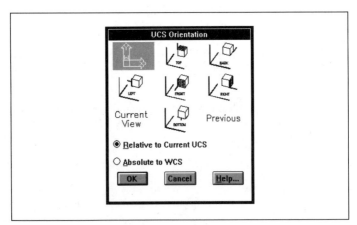

Figure 14: UCS Orientation dialog box

See Also Dview, UCS, Vpoint, View, Plan, Ucsicon. *System Variables:* Ucsfollow, Ucsicon, Ucsname, Ucsorg, Ucsxdir, Ucsydir, Worlducs

DDUNITS

Transparent: **'Ddunits**

Menu: **Settings ➤ Units Control**…

Ddunits opens the Units Control dialog box to set up the drawing's units of measure, angle measurement and direction.

To Display the Ddunits Dialog Box:

Issue the command, then provide information as needed in the dialog or subdialog box(es).

● OPTIONS

Units This section includes the following radio buttons for setting units of measure: Scientific, Decimal, Engineering, Architectural, and Fractional.

Angles This section provides the following radio buttons to set angle measurement: Decimal Degrees, Deg/Min/Sec, Grads, Radians, and Surveyor.

Direction… *Direction…* opens a Direction Control subdialog box with radio buttons to indicate the direction of angles: East, North, West, and South. An *Other* radio button enables a *Pick* button and *Angle* edit box as options.

Precision Popup list displays default values for units and angles.

DDVIEW

Menu: **Render ➤ Views, View➤Set View➤Named View...**

● PURPOSE

Ddview opens the View Control dialog box (FIGURE 15) to make, delete, and restore views.

To Invoke the Ddviews Dialog Box:

Issue the command, then provide information as needed in the dialog or subdialog box(es).

● OPTIONS

Views   Displays view names with Pspace or Mspace.

Restore   Pick button to restore view by highlighting view name from the list box.

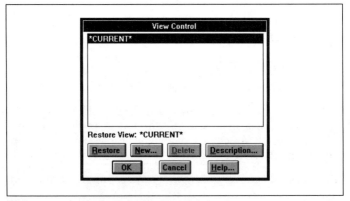

Figure 15: The Viewpoint Presets dialog box

New... Opens the Define New View subdialog box for saving a new view. Radio buttons allow you to save the Current Display as a view or to *Define Window*. Assign a *New Name* in the edit box, then use the *Window* button to temporarily exit dialog box for creating the view. Pick the *Save View* button to exit. Display boxes identify X and Y coordinates for the *First Corner* and *Other Corner*.

Delete Pick button to delete view by highlighting view name from the list box.

Description... Opens the View Description subdialog box specifying data on the highlighted view.

See Also View.

DDVPOINT

Menu: **View ➤ Set View ➤ Viewpoint ➤ Presets**

Ddvpoint opens the Viewpoint Presets dialog box (FIGURE 16) for establishing a 3D view by dynamically picking an angle from the X axis in the XY plane.

To Set a 3D View:

Issue the command, then provide information as needed in the dialog or subdialog box(es).

● OPTIONS

The Viewpoint Presets dialog box provides pick buttons to *Set Viewing Angles* Absolute to WCS or Relative to UCS. An image tile box rotates a white arm to preset viewing angles with your cursor when picking outside the circle and to specific angles when picking within the circle. The designated angle then appears in the edit box for X Axis and XY Plane.

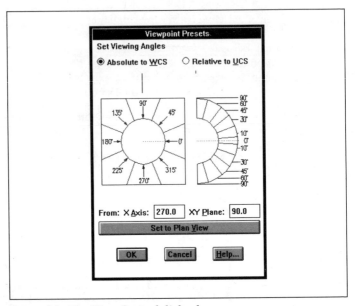

Figure 16: The View Control dialog box

DEL

Del deletes files from a specified disk and directories. You can also delete files from Files▶Utilities ...▶File Utilities dialog box.

To Delete a File:

Issue the command, then provide the following information:

- **File to delete:** Enter any drive letter, directory and file name.

See Also   Copy, Files.

DELAY

Transparent: **'Delay**

Delay lets you set a designated time period for viewing a slide in a script file.

To Delay a Slide:

Issue the command, then provide the following information:

- Delay time in milliseconds: Enter a number.

See Also   Script, Mslide, Vslide, Rscript.

DIM/DIM1

Menu: **Draw➤Dimensions➤(Preset Options)**

Dim and Dim1 let you add dimensions to a drawing. Once you issue either of these commands, you can issue any dimensioning subcommand.

To Issue a Dimensioning Subcommand:

Issue the command, then issue any of the dimensioning subcommands.

Notes   AutoCAD generally uses the same types of dimensions and dimension label components as standard drafting. FIGURE 17 gives examples of the five types of dimensions possible in AutoCAD drawings: linear, angular, diametric, radial, and ordinate.

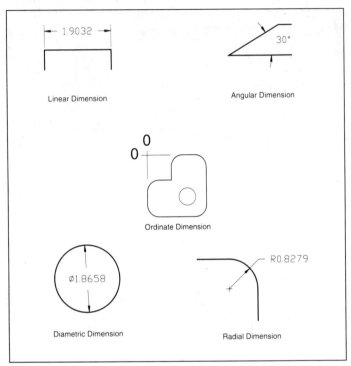

Figure 17: Types of dimensions

Dimension labels consist of the elements illustrated in FIGURE 18.

TABLE 5 describes variables that control the way AutoCAD draws dimensions. These variables control extension line and text location, tolerance specifications, arrow styles and sizes, and much more.

You can enter these subcommands at the Dim: prompt or pick specific subcommands from the **Draw ➤ Dimensions** pull-down menu. Since they are actually system variables, you can also set them using the **Setvar** command.

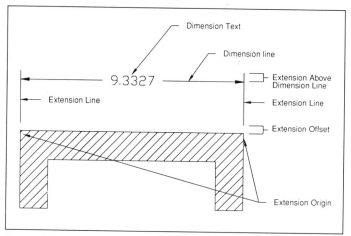

Figure 18: Components of dimension labels

Table 5: The Dimension Variables

Variable	Description
Dimalt	When on, dimension texts for two measurement systems are inserted simultaneously (**alt**ernate). Dimaltf and Dimaltd must also be set appropriately. The alternate dimension is placed within brackets. Angular dimensions are not affected. This variable is commonly used when inches and metric units must be displayed at the same time in a dimension. The default setting is off.
Dimaltd	When Dimalt is on, Dimaltd controls the number of decimal places the alternate dimension will have (**alt**ernate **d**ecimal places). The default value is 2.

$\emptyset = \%\%c$

Table 5: The Dimension Variables (continued)

Variable	Description
Dimaltf	When Dimalt is on, Dimaltf controls the multiplication factor for the alternate dimension (**alt**ernate **f**actor). The value held by Dimaltf will be multiplied by the standard dimension value to determine the alternate dimension. The default value is 25.4, the number required to display metric units.
Dimapost	When Dimalt is on, you can use Dimapost to append text to the alternate dimension (**a**lternate **post**). For example, if Dimapost is given the value "mm," the alternate dimension will appear as valuemm instead of just value. The default value is nul. To change a previously set value to nul, enter a period for the Dimapost new value.
Dimaso	When on, dimensions will be associative (**asso**ciative). When off, dimensions will consist of separate drawing entities with none of the associative dimension properties. The default is on.
Dimasz	Sets the size of dimension arrows or Dimblks (**a**rrow **s**ize). If set to 0, a tick is drawn in place of an arrow. (See Dimblk). The default value is .18 units.
Dimblk	You can replace the standard AutoCAD dimension arrow with one of your own design by creating a drawing of your symbol and making it a block. You then give Dimblk the name of your symbol block. This block must be drawn corresponding to a one-by-one unit area and must be oriented as the right side arrow. The default value is nul.

Table 5: The Dimension Variables (continued)

Variable	Description
Dimblk1	With Dimsah set to on, you can replace the standard AutoCAD dimension arrows with two different arrows using Dimblk1 and Dimblk2. Dimblk1 holds the name of the block defining the first dimension arrow while Dimblk2 holds the name of the second dimension arrow block.
Dimblk2	See Dimblk1.
Dimcen	Sets the size of center marks used during the Center, Diameter, and Radius dimension subcommands. A negative value draws center lines instead of the center mark cross, while a 0 value draws nothing. The default value is 0.09 units.
Dimclrd	Lets you specify colors for dimensions lines, arrowheads, and dimension leader lines.
Dimclre	Sets color for dimension extension lines.
Dimclrt	Sets color for dimension text.
Dimdle	With Dimtsz given a value greater than 0, dimension lines can extend past the extension lines by the amount specified in Dimdle (**d**imension **l**ine **e**xtension). This amount is not adjusted by Dimscale. The default value is 0.
Dimdli	Sets the distance at which dimension lines are offset when you use the Baseline or Continue dimension subcommands (**d**imension **l**ine **i**ncrement). The default is 0.38 units.
Dimexe	Sets the distance the extension lines are drawn past the dimension lines (**ex**tension line **e**xtension). The default value is 0.18 units.
Dimexo	Sets the distance between the beginning of the extension line and the actual point selected at the Extension line origin: prompt (**ex**tension line **o**ffset). The default value is 0.0625 units.

Table 5: The Dimension Variables (continued)

Variable	Description
Dimgap	Sets the distance between the text and the dimension line and lets you enclose text within a box by assigning it a negative value. The default value is 0.09.
Dimlfac	Sets the global scale factor for dimension values (length factor). Linear distances will be multiplied by the value held by Dimlfac. This multiple will be entered as the dimension text. The default value is 1.0. This can be useful when drawings are not drawn to scale.
Dimlim	When set to on, dimension text is entered as two values representing a dimension range rather than a single value. The range is determined by the values given to Dimtp (plus tolerance) and Dimtm (minus tolerance). The default value is off.
Dimpost	Automatically appends text strings to dimension text. For example, if Dimpost is given the value "inches," dimension text will appear as value inches instead of just value. The default value is nul. To change a previously set value to nul, enter a period for the Dimpost new value. If you use Dimpost in conjunction with appended dimension text, the Dimpost value is included as part of the default dimension text.
Dimrnd	Sets the amount to which all dimensions are rounded. For example, if you set Dimrnd to 1, all dimensions will be integer values. The number of decimal places affected depends on the precision value set by the Units command. The default is 0.

Table 5: The Dimension Variables (continued)

Variable	Description
Dimsah	When set to on, allows the separate arrow blocks Dimblk1 and Dimblk2 to replace the standard AutoCAD arrows (**separate arrow heads**). If Dimtsz is set to a value greater than 0, Dimsah has no effect.
Dimscale	Sets the scale factor for dimension variables that control dimension lines and arrows and text size (unless current text style has a fixed height). If your drawing is not full scale, you should set this variable to reflect the drawing scale. For example, for a drawing whose scale is ¼" equals 1′, you should set Dimscale to 48. The default value is 1.0.
Dimse1	When set to on, the first dimension line extension is not drawn (**suppress extension 1**). The default is off.
Dimse2	When set to on, the second dimension line extension is not drawn (**suppress extension 2**). The default is off.
Dimsho	When set to on, dimension text in associative dimensions will dynamically change to reflect the location of a dimension point as it is being moved (**show dimension**). The default is off.
Dimsoxd	When set to on, dimension lines do not appear outside of the extension lines (**suppress outside extension dimension lines**). If Dimtix is also set to on and the space between the extension lines prohibits the display of a dimension line, no dimension line is drawn. The default is off.
Dimstyle	Identifies the current dimension style. Use the Save and Restore dimensioning commands for alternate Dimstyles. The default is *UNNAMED.

Table 5: The Dimension Variables (continued)

Variable	Description
Dimtad	When set to on and Dimtih is off, dimension text in linear dimensions will be placed above the dimension line (text above dimension line). When off, the dimension line will be split in two and text will be placed in line with the dimension line. The default value is off.
Dimtfac	Sets the scale factor for text height of tolerance values based on Dimtxt, the dimension text height variable. Use Dimtfac to display the plus and minus characters when Dimtol is on and Dimtm does not equal Dimtp, or when Dimlim is on. The default is 1.0.
Dimtih	When set to on, dimension text placed between extension lines will always be horizontal (text inside horizontal). When set to off, text will be aligned with the dimension line. The default value is on.
Dimtix	When set to on, dimension text will always be placed between extension lines (text inside extension). The default value is off.
Dimtm	When Dimtol or Dimlin is on, Dimtm determines the minus tolerance value of the dimension text (tolerance minus).
Dimtofl	With Dimtofl on, a dimension line is always drawn between extension lines even when text is drawn outside (text outside—forced line). The default is off.
Dimtoh	With Dimtoh on, dimension text placed outside extension lines will always be horizontal (text outside—horizontal). When set to off, text outside extension lines will be aligned with dimension line. The default is on.

Table 5: The Dimension Variables (continued)

Variable	Description
Dimtol	With Dimtol on, tolerance values set by Dimtp and Dimtm are appended to the dimension text (**tol**erance). The default is off.
Dimtp	When Dimtol or Dimlim is on, Dimtp determines the plus tolerance value of the dimension text (**t**olerance **p**lus).
Dimtsz	Sets the size of tick marks drawn in place of the standard AutoCAD arrows (**t**ick **s**ize). When set to 0, the standard arrow is drawn. When greater than 0, tick marks are drawn and take precedence over Dimblk1 and Dimblk2. The default value is 0.
Dimtvp	When Dimtad is off, Dimtvp allows you to specify the location of the dimension text in relation to the dimension line (**t**ext **v**ertical **p**osition). A positive value places the text above the dimension line while a negative value places the text below the dimension line. The dimension line will split to accommodate the text unless the Dimtvp value is greater than 1.
Dimtxt	Sets the height of dimension text when the current text style height is set to 0. The default value is 0.18.
Dimzin	Determines the display of inches when Architectural units are used. When set to 0, zero feet or zero inches will not be displayed. When set to 1, zero feet and zero inches will be displayed. When set to 2, zero inches will not be displayed. When set to 3, zero feet will not be displayed.

Dimensioning and Drawing Scales:

Take care when dimensioning drawings at a scale other than 1-to-1. If the *Dimscale* dimension variable is not set properly, arrows and text will appear too small or too large. In extreme cases, they may not appear at all. If you enter a dimension and arrows or text do not appear, check the Dimscale setting and make sure it is a value equal to the drawing scale.

Starting the Dimensioning Process:

To add dimension labels to a drawing from the keyboard, enter **Dim** or **Dim1** at the command prompt. At this point, the prompt changes to Dim: and you can enter any dimensioning subcommand. These and the transparent commands (see **Transparent**) are the only AutoCAD commands you can enter while in the dimensioning mode.

When you have finished entering dimensions under the Dim command, issue the **Exit** command or press Ctrl-C to return to the standard AutoCAD prompt. If you want to enter only a single dimension, use **Dim1**. The 1 tells AutoCAD to return you automatically to the command prompt after you enter one dimension.

You can invoke any dimension command by entering just the abbreviated form shown after the slash in the following headings. For example, you can enter **Dia** instead of **Diameter**.

See Also   Ddim. *System Variables:* Dimaso, Dimscale.

DIM: ALIGNED/AL

Menu: **Draw ➤ Dimensions ➤ Linear ➤ Aligned**

Aligns a dimension with two points or an object. The dimension text appears in the current style. FIGURE 19 illustrates the difference between aligned and rotated dimensions. Dimension settings are modified with the Ddim dialog box.

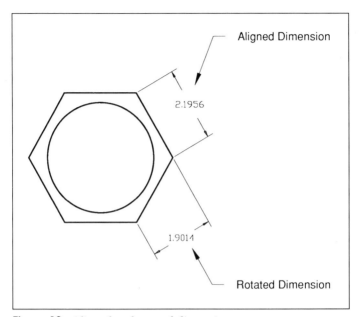

Figure 19: Aligned and rotated dimensions

To Align a Dimension:

Issue the command, then provide the following information:

1. First extension line origin or RETURN to select: Pick one end of object to be dimensioned or press Return.

2. If you pressed Return, you will be prompted to select an object. If you entered coordinates for an extension line, you will be prompted for the following:

- Second extension line origin: Pick the other end of the object.

3. Dimension line location (Text/Angle): Drag your cursor and pick a point, or enter a coordinate for the location of the dimension line as the extension line with text appears.

4. Dimension text <default dimension>: Press ↵ to accept the default dimension, or enter dimension value.

● OPTIONS

Text   This option will allow you to override the default value specified at the prompt Dimension text <default text>:

Angle   Text will be placed horizontally (0 degrees) unless you specify a dimension text orientation to the prompt Enter text angle:

See Also   Ddim, Ddunits, Dim/Dim1, Setup, Units.

DIM: ANGULAR/AN

Menu: **Draw ➤ Dimensions ➤ Angular**

Creates a dimension label showing the angle described by an arc, circle, or two lines, or by a set of three points. An arc with dimension arrows at each end is drawn and the angle value is placed using current text style. Dimension settings can be modified with the Ddim dialog box, or from the **Status** subcommand by selecting each individual Dim variable.

To Create an Angle Dimension Label:

Issue the command, then provide the following information:

1.   Select arc, circle, line, or RETURN: Pick an object as indicated by the prompt or press↵ to indicate angles using your cursor.

2.   If you pressed ↵ and selected a line, continue with Step 3. If you selected an arc or a circle, continue to steps 6, 7, and 8.

3.   Angle vertex: Pick a point using an osnap mode indicating the center angle vertex.

4.   First angle endpoint: Pick a point using an osnap mode indicating the first angle.

5.   Second angle endpoint: Pick a point using an osnap mode indicating the second angle.

6.   Dimension arc line location (Text/Angle): Drag your cursor and pick a point, or enter a coordinate for the location of the dimension line as the extension line with text appears.

7.   Dimension text <default dimension>: Press ↵ to accept default angle, or enter angle value.

8.   Enter text location (or RETURN): Pick the location for the beginning of the dimension text, or press ↵ and accept the default of text centered on the arc.

● OPTIONS

Text   This option will allow you to override the default value specified at the prompt Dimension text <default text>:

Angle   Text will be placed horizontally (0 degrees) unless you specify a dimension text orientation to the prompt Enter text angle:

Notes   At the Dimension text: prompt, you can append text to the default value. See next section.

See Also   Ddim, Ddunits, Dim/Dim1, Setup, Units.

DIM—APPENDING DIMENSION TEXT

At the Dimension text: prompt, you can append text to the default dimension text.

To Enter Dimension Text:

Issue the command, then provide the following information:

● Dimension text <default text>: Place <> signs where you want the text to appear, then enter the text.

See Also   Ddim, Dim/Dim1, *Dimension Variables:* Dimapost, Dimpost.

DIM—AUTOMATIC DIMENSIONING

At the First extension line or RETURN to select: prompt or the Select arc, circle, line or RETURN: prompt, you can let AutoCAD dimension a line, arc, or circle automatically.

To Use Automatic Dimensioning:

Issue the command, then provide the following information:

- First extension line or RETURN to select: Press ↵.
- Select arc, circle, line or RETURN: Pick the entity to be dimensioned.

Notes   After selecting a line, circle, or arc, you may drag your cursor and the dimension text and then pick a location point.

DIM: BASELINE/B

Menu: **Draw ➤ Dimensions ➤ Linear ➤ Baseline**

Continues a dimension string using the first extension line of the most recently inserted dimension as its first extension line. You are prompted only for the second extension line origin. The dimension is placed above, and is parallel to, the last dimension.

To Continue a Dimension from the Baseline:

Issue the command, then provide the following information:

1.   Second extension line origin: Pick a point indicating the extension line origin for a continuing dimension.

2.   Dimension text <default dimension>: Press ↵ to accept the default dimension text, or enter new text.

Notes   To continue a dimension from the baseline of an old dimension, use the dimension subcommand **Update** before using Baseline.

See Also   *Dimension Variable:* Dimdli.

DIM: CENTER/CE

Menu: **Draw ➤ Dimensions ➤ Radial ➤ Center Mark**

Center places a cross at the center point of a selected arc or circle. To choose center lines instead of a center cross, use the *Dimcen* dimension variable.

To Mark the Center of an Arc or Circle:

Issue the command, then provide the following information:

- Select arc or circle: Pick an arc or circle and the mark will appear.

See Also *Dimension Variables:* Dimcen

DIM: CONTINUE/CO

Menu: **Draw ➤ Dimensions ➤ Linear ➤ Continue**

Continues a dimension string by using the second extension line of the most recently inserted dimension as its first extension line. You are only prompted for the second extension line origin. The dimension is placed in line with and is parallel to the last dimension.

To Continue a Dimension:

Issue the command, then provide the following information:

1. Second extension line origin or RETURN to select: Pick a point indicating the extension line origin for a continuing dimension. The second extension line of the last dimension entered will be used as the first extension line.

2. Dimension text <default dimension>: Press ↵ to accept the default dimension text, or enter new dimension text.

Notes To continue a dimension from the last extension line of an old dimension, use the dimension subcommand *Update* before using Continue.

See Also *Dimension Variable:* Dimdli.

DIM: DIAMETER/DI

Menu: **Draw ➤ Dimensions ➤ Radial ➤ Diameter**

Adds a diameter dimension to arcs and circles.

To Dimension an Arc or Circle Diameter:

Issue the command, then provide the following information:

1. Select arc or circle: Pick the arc or circle as appropriate.

2. Dimension text <default dimension>: Press ↵ to accept the default dimension text, or enter dimension text.

3. Enter leader length for text: As the leader line extends in a dragging mode from the arc or circle, pick a point that indicates the location of the text. The direction of the leader is toward the center point. A center mark is also placed at the center of the arc or circle.

Notes   The point at which you pick the arc or circle determines one end of the dimension arrow. If you want the dimension to be in a horizontal or vertical orientation, use the **Quadrant Osnap** override. Pick the left or right quadrant for a horizontal dimension; pick the top or bottom quadrant for a vertical dimension. If the *Dimtix* dimension variable is set to on, the dimension is placed inside the circle starting at your pick point.

See Also   Dimcen, Dimtix.

DIM: DIMSTYLE

Finds the current dimension style.

To Change a Dimension Style:

Issue the command. The current dimension style appears on the prompt line as follows:

    Current value <(Style name)>

See Also   Restore, Save.

DIM: EXIT/E

Exits the Dim command and returns you to the standard command prompt.

Notes You can press Ctrl-C or type **E** in place of Exit. If you entered **Dim1** to begin dimensioning, Exit is not needed.

DIM: HOMETEXT/HOM

Menu: **Modify ➤ Edit Dimensions ➤ Dimension Text ➤ Home Position**

Moves the text of a dimension back to its default position after it has been moved using the **Stretch** command. Hometext works only with associative dimensions that have not been exploded.

To Return Dimension Text to Position:

Issue the command, then provide the following information:

- Select object: Pick the dimensions that need text to be moved to the default position.

See Also *Dimension Variables:* Dimaso

DIM: HORIZONTAL/HOR

Menu: **Draw ➤ Dimensions ➤ Linear ➤ Horizontal**

Creates a horizontal dimension regardless of the extension line origins or the orientation of the object picked.

To Create Horizontal Dimensions

Issue the command, then provide the following information:

1. First extension line origin or RETURN to select: Pick one end of object to be dimensioned or press Return.

2. If you pressed Return, you will be prompted to select an object. If you entered coordinates for an extension line, you will be prompted for the following:

- Second extension line origin: Pick the other end of the object.

3.   Dimension line location (Text/Angle): Drag your cursor and pick a point, or enter a coordinate for the location of the dimension line as the extension line with text appears.

4.   Dimension text <default dimension>: Press ↵ to accept the default dimension, or enter dimension value.

● OPTIONS

Text   This option will allow you to override the default value specified at the prompt Dimension text <default text>:

Angle   Text will be placed horizontally (0 degrees) unless you specify a dimension text orientation to the prompt Enter text angle:

Dim: Leader/L

Menu: **Draw ➤ Dimensions ➤ Leader**

Adds notes with arrows to drawings.

To Add Leaders:

Issue the command, then provide the following information:

1.   Leader start: Pick a point to start the leader. This is the point where the arrow will be placed.

2.   To point: Pick the next point along the leader line or continue to pick points as you would in drawing a line. When you are finished, press ↵. You can enter **U** to Undo the last drawn line segment.

3.   Dimension text <default dimension>: Press ↵ to accept the default, or enter new dimension text.

Notes   The distance between the Leader start point and the next point must be at least twice the length of the arrow, otherwise an arrow will not be placed.

If the last line segment of the leader is not horizontal, a horizontal line segment is added, as illustrated in FIGURE 20.

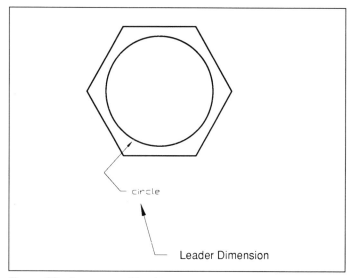

Figure 20: A segmented leader

Leadered text does not take on the properties of associative dimensioning.

You can append text to the default dimension value. The default value is usually the last dimension entered. See Dim—Appending Dimension Text.

See Also   *Dimension Variables:* Dimasz, Dimscale.

DIM: NEWTEXT/N

Menu: **Modify ➤ Edit Dimensions ➤ Dimension Text ➤ Change Text**

Edits associative dimension text in several dimensions at once.

To Change Associative Dimension Text:

Issue the command, then provide the following information:

1.   Enter new dimension text: Enter text. Type < > to append text to the current text.

2. Select objects: Pick the dimensions to be edited, select-ing one or several dimensions. All associative dimensions selected will be changed to the new text.

DIM: OBLIQUE /OB

Menu: **Modify ➤ Edit Dimensions ➤ Oblique Dimension**

Skews existing dimension extension lines to an angle other than 90 degrees to the dimension line.

To Skew Extension Lines:

Issue the command, then provide the following information:

1. Select objects: Pick the dimensions to be edited.

2. Enter obliquing angle (RETURN for none): Enter the desired angle for extension lines.

Notes   If the dimension being edited has a dimension style set-ting, then this setting is maintained. If no style is associated with the dimension, the current dimension variable settings are used to up-date the obliqued dimension.

DIM: ORDINATE/OR

Menu: **Draw ➤ Dimensions ➤ Ordinate ➤ Automatic/X-datum/ Y-datum**

Draws an ordinate dimension string based on a datum or origin point.

To Create Ordinate Dimensioning:

Use the **UCS** command to create a UCS with its origin at the datum location. Then issue the Dim command to access the Ordinate dimension subcommand. Then provide the following information:

1. Select Feature: Pick the location of the feature to be dimensioned.

2. Leader endpoint (X-datum/Y-datum): Indicate the orientation of the dimension leader or enter X or Y to specify the axis along which the dimension is to be taken, then pick endpoint of leader line.

3. Dimension Text <default dimension>: Press ⏎ to accept the default dimension text, or enter dimension text.

Notes   If you pick a point at the first Leader endpoint: prompt, then AutoCAD selects the dimension axis based on the angle defined by the points you pick during the Select Feature: and Leader endpoint: prompts.

See Also   UCS.

DIM: OVERRIDE/OVE

Changes an individual associative dimension's properties, such as its arrow style, colors, scale, text orientation, etc. Also modifies a dimension style by allowing you to alter the dimension variable settings associated with a dimension or dimension style.

To Change an
Associative Dimension's Properties:

Issue the command, then provide the following information:

1. Dimension variable to override: Enter dimension variable name.

2. Current value <(variables value)> New value: Enter new value.

3. Dimension variable to override: Enter another dimension variable name, or ⏎ to continue.

4. Select objects: Select dimension(s) to change. If the selected dimension is associated with a dimension style, the following prompt appears:

Modify dimension style "style name"? <N>: Enter **Y** for yes, or ⏎. If you enter **Y**, the style indicated by the prompt will be updated with the new setting(s). If you enter **N** or ↵, only the selected associative dimension(s) will change.

See Also Dimstyle, Restore.

DIM: RADIUS/RA

Menu: **Draw ➤ Dimensions ➤ Radial ➤ Radius**

Adds a radius dimension to arcs and circles.

To Add a Radius Dimension:

Issue the command, then provide the following information:

1. Select arc or circle: Pick the arc or circle. The point at which you pick the arc or circle determines one end of the dimension arrow.

2. Dimension text <default radius>: Press ↵ to accept the default radius, or enter text.

3. Enter leader length for text: Pick a point by dragging the leader length and dimension text.

Notes Step 3 does not occur if the *Dimtix* variable is On.

See Also *Dimension Variables:* Dimcen.

DIM: REDRAW/RED

Allows you to refresh the screen in the current viewport.

See Also Redraw

DIM: RESTORE/RES

Makes an existing dimension style the current default style.

To Use Restore:

Issue the command, then provide the following information:

- Current dimension style: (Style name) ?/Enter dimension style name or RETURN to select dimension: Enter **?** to list available dimension styles, or enter the name of a known dimension style (wildcard characters are accepted), or press ↵ to pick a dimension whose dimension style you want to make current.

Notes To select a dimension style, either pick an associative dimension that is associated with the desired style, or enter the name of the style.

The tilde (~) can also be used to compare styles. To find the differences between the current dimension style and another style, enter a dimension style name preceded by a tilde (~) at the prompt Dimension style(s) to list <*>:. Differences are displayed in a list of dimension variable settings.

See Also Save, Wildcards.

DIM: ROTATED/ROT

Menu: **Draw ➤ Dimensions ➤ Linear ➤ Rotated**

Measures and places a dimension at a specified angle regardless of the dimensioned object's orientation. The dimension text is in the current text style. As illustrated in previously in FIGURE 19, a rotated dimension measures a distance at the specified angle.

To Rotate a Dimension:

Issue the command, then provide the following information:

1. Dimension line angle <0>: Enter an angle for the dimension line.

2. First extension line origin or RETURN to select: Pick one end of object to be dimensioned, or ↵ to select an angle, line, or circle.

3. If you pressed Return, you will be prompted to select an object. If you entered coordinates for an extension line, you will be prompted for the following:

> Second extension line origin: Pick the other end of the object.

4. Dimension line location (Text/Angle): Drag your cursor and pick a point, or enter a coordinate for the location of the dimension line as the extension line with text appears.

5. Dimension text <default dimension>: Press ↵ to accept the default dimension, or enter the dimension value.

● OPTIONS

Text   This option will allow you to override the default value specified at the prompt Dimension text <default text>:

Angle   Text will be placed horizontally (0 degrees) unless you specify a dimension text orientation to the prompt Enter text angle:

Dim: Save/Sav

Saves the current dimension variable settings as a dimenion style that can later be restored using the Dim: Restore subcommand. You can save multiple dimension styles.

To Save Dimension Settings:

Issue the command, then provide the following information:

- ?/Name for new dimension style: Enter a new dimension style name. If you enter **?**, the following prompt appears:

  - Dimension style(s) to list <*>: Enter a name specification using wildcards.

Notes   The tilde (~) can also be used to compare styles. To find the differences between the current dimension style and another style, enter a dimension style name preceded by a tilde (~) at the prompt Dimension style(s) to list <*>:. Differences are displayed in a list of dimension variable settings.

See Also   Override, Restore, Ddim.

DIM: STATUS/STA

Displays the current Dimension variable settings and descriptions.

See Also   Ddim. *Dimension Variables:* Dimsen.

DIM: STYLE/STY

Specifies a text style for the dimension text. Once the text style is changed, any subsequent dimensions will contain text in the new style. Existing dimension text is not affected.

To Specify a Text Style:

Issue the command, then provide the following information:

   1.   New text style <current style>: Press ↵ to accept the current style, or enter a new style name. The new style will then be the current text style.

   2.   If you enter the name of a style that does not exist, you receive the message: No such text style. Use the main STYLE command to create it.

See Also   Ddim, Style. *Dimension Variables:* Dimtxt.

DIM: TEDIT/TE

Menu: **Modify ➤ Edit Dimensions ➤ Dimension Text ➤ Move Text**

Modifies the placement, justification, and rotation angle of associative dimension text.

Sequence of Steps:

Issue the command, then provide the following information:

   1.   Select dimension: Pick a single dimension.

2. Enter text location (Left/Right/Home/Angle): Enter an option or pick a new location for the dimension text. You can drag the text to the next location with the cursor. If you move the text to a position in line with the dimension line, the dimension will automatically join to become a continuous line.

● OPTIONS

Left   Justifies text to the left on linear, radius, and diameter dimensions.

Right   Justifies text to the right on linear, radius, and diameter dimensions.

Home   Places text in its default dimension. This has the same effect as the **Hometext** subcommand.

Angle   Changes the angle for text. At the prompt Text angle:, enter an angle value, or indicate an angle by picking two points.

Notes   When **Tedit** is used on a dimension the style is updated to the current dimension style setting. If no style is associated with the dimension, then current dimension variable settings are used.

The pull-down menu offers the following text edit options: *Change Text, Home Position, Move Text,* and *Rotate Text*.

See Also   Hometext. *System Variables:* Dimaso, Dimsho.

DIM—TRANSPARENT COMMANDS

Transparent commands defined as aliases in your *Acad.PGP* file can be used as valid Dim subcommands.

Notes   Entering the abbreviated command at the Dim: prompt identifies the command's execution with >> (double angle brackets). Any transparent alias sharing the same abbreviation as the dimension subcommand is ignored.

See Also   Transparent Commands, Alias, Acad.PGP.

DIM: TROTATE/TR

Menu: **Modify ➤ Edit Dimensions ➤ Dimension Text ➤ Rotate Text**

Changes the rotation angle of associative dimension text.

Sequence of Steps:

Issue the command, then provide the following information:

1. Enter new text angle: Enter the angle value, or indicate the angle by picking two points.

2. Select objects: Pick the associative dimensions that you want to change.

Notes If you enter 0 for the rotation angle, the text returns to its default angle. Trotate updates the dimension to the current settings for its associated dimension style. If no style is associated with the dimension, then the current dimension variable settings are used.

See Also Restore, Save. *Dimension Variables:* Dimtih, Dimtoh.

DIM: UNDO/U

Rescinds a dimension you decide you do not want, as long as you are still in the dimension mode. If you issue Undo during the **Leader** command, the last leader line segment drawn will be undone.

DIM: UPDATE/UP

Menu: **Modify ➤ Edit Dimensions ➤ Update Dimension**

Changes old dimensions to new Dimension variable settings. Update works only on associative dimensions that have not been exploded.

To Use Update:

Issue the command, then provide the following information:

• Select objects: Pick the associative dimensions to be updated.

DIM: VARIABLES/VA

Lists the dimension variable settings of a dimension style.

To List the Dimension Variable Settings:

Issue the command, then provide the following information:

- Current dimension style: <current style name>?:

  Enter dimension style name or RETURN to select dimension: Enter **?** to view available dimension styles, enter the name of a known dimension style (wildcards are accepted), or press ↵ to pick a dimension whose dimension style you wish to list.

Notes   The tilde (~) can also be used to compare styles. To find the differences between the current dimension style and another style, enter a dimension style name preceded by a tilde (~) at the prompt Dimension style(s) to list <*>:. Differences are displayed in a list of dimension variable settings.

See Also   Restore, Save.

DIM: VERTICAL/VE

Menu: **Draw ➤ Dimensions ➤ Linear ➤ Vertical**

Forces a dimension to be displayed vertically, regardless of the orientation of the object picked or where the extension line origins are placed.

Sequence of Steps:

Issue the command, then provide the following information:

1. First extension line origin or RETURN to select: Pick one end of object to be dimensioned or press Return.

2. If you pressed Return, you will be prompted to select an object. If you entered coordinates for an extension

line, you will be prompted for the following:

> Second extension line origin: Pick the other end of the object.

3. Dimension line location (Text/Angle): Drag your cursor and pick a point, or enter a coordinate for the location of the dimension line as the extension line with text appears.

4. Dimension text <default dimension>: Press ↵ to accept the default dimension, or enter dimension value.

● OPTIONS

Text   This option will allow you to override the default value specified at the prompt Dimension text <default text>:

Angle   Text will be placed horizontally (0 degrees) unless you specify a dimension text orientation to the prompt Enter text angle:.

DIR

Dir displays a list of the files in any specified drive or directory. If you give no specifications, you will get a list of the current drive.

To List Files:

Issue the command, then provide the following information:

*   File specification: Press ↵ to see a list of files on the current drive, or enter standard DOS file names. Drive letters, directory names, wildcard characters, and DOS **DIR** command switches such as /P and /W are accepted.

See Also   Catalog, Files.

DIST

Transparent: **'Dist**

Menu: **Assist ➤ Inquiry ➤ Distance**

Dist gives the distance between two points in two-dimensional or three-dimensional space. It also gives the angle in the current XY plane, the angle *from* the current XY plane, and the distance in X, Y, and Z coordinate values.

To Find the Distance between Two Points:

Issue the command, then provide the following information:

1. **First point:** Pick the beginning point of the distance.
2. **Second point:** Pick the end point of the distance.

DIVIDE

Menu: **Construct ➤ Divide**

Divide marks an object into equal divisions. You specify the number of divisions, and AutoCAD marks the object into equal parts.

To Divide an Object:

Issue the command, then provide the following information:

1. Select object to divide: Pick a single object.
2. <Number of segments>/Block: Enter the number of segments to be marked or enter the name of the block to use for marking.

• OPTIONS

<Number of segments>   A marker or point is located at specified intervals using the *Pdmode* and *Pdsize* variables for point size and type.

Block   Allows you to use an existing block as a marking device. You receive the prompt Block name to insert: and are asked whether you want to align the block with the object.

If you respond **Y** to the Align block with object: prompt, the block will be aligned either along the axis of a line or tangent to a selected polyline, circle, or arc. The Block option is useful for drawing a series of objects that are equally spaced along a curved path.

Notes   By default, Divide uses a point entity as a marker. Often, a point is difficult to see when placed over a line or arc. You can set the *Pdmode* system variable using the 'Ddptype' command transparently to change the appearance of the points, or you can use the Block option. The point marker can be picked with the **Node** object snap mode.

See Also   Point, Block, Measure, Ddptype. *System Variables:* Mode, Pdsize.

DONUT/DOUGHNUT

Menu: **Draw ➤ Donut**

Donut draws a circle whose line thickness you specify by entering its inside and outside diameters (see FIGURE 21). To create a solid dot enter **0** at the Inside diameter: prompt. The most recent diameters entered are the default values for the inside and outside diameter. Once you issue the Donut command and answer the prompts, you can place as many donuts as you like. Press ↵ to terminate the command.

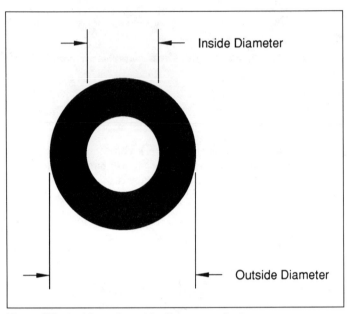

Figure 21: Inside and outside diameters of a donut

To Create a Donut:

Issue the command, then provide the following information:

1. Inside diameter <current default>: Enter the inside diameter of the donut.

2. Outside diameter <current default>: Enter the outside diameter of the donut.

3. Center of donut: Pick a point for the center of the donut.

Notes   Because donuts are actually polylines, you can edit them with the **Pedit** command.

See Also   Fill, Pedit.

DRAGMODE

Transparent: '**Dragmode**

Dragmode controls when the Drag facility is used. The default, Auto, lets you temporarily reposition selected objects by moving them with your cursor.

To Drag an Object:

Issue the command, then provide the following information:

• ON/OFF/Auto <current setting>: Enter the setting.

• OPTIONS

On   Enables the Drag mode, so that objects will be dragged whenever you issue the Drag command modifier.

OFF   Disables the Drag mode, so that no dragging can occur.

Auto   Causes all commands that allow dragging to automatically drag objects, whether you issue the Drag command modifier or not.

Notes   When you are editing large sets of objects, the Drag function can slow you down. It takes time for AutoCAD to refresh a temporary image, especially a complex one. If you set Dragmode on, you can use the Drag function when appropriate by entering **Drag** as a subcommand while performing a operation, and dispense with it when editing large groups of objects.

See Also   *System Variables:* Dragmode.

DTEXT/TEXT

Menu: **Draw ➤ Text ➤ Dynamic**

Dtext allows you to enter several lines of text at once. This command also displays the text on the drawing area as you type. At the first prompt, you can set the justification or set the current text style. Using either the *Fit* or *Align* options, you can tell AutoCAD to fit the text between two points.

To Enter Text Using Dtext:

Issue the command, then provide the following information:

1. Justify/Style/<Start point>: Enter the desired Justify or Style options or pick a start point for your text.

2. If you pick a point to indicate the beginning location of your text, you get the following prompts:

a. Height <default height>: Enter the desired text height, or press ↵ to accept the default. This prompt only appears if the current style has its height set to 0.

b. Rotation angle <default angle>: Enter a rotation angle, or press ↵ to accept the default.

c. Text: Enter the desired text.

These prompts also appear after you have selected a style or set the justification option.

● OPTIONS

Start point   Lets you indicate the location of your text. The text is automatically left-justified.

Justify   Specifies the justification of text. The prompt is:

Align/Fit/Center/Middle/Right/TL/TC/TR/ML/MC/MR/BL/BC/BR:

The two-letter options in this prompt set the justification based on the combination of top, middle, or bottom, and left, center, or right. For example, TL stands for top left and MC stands for middle center.

Align   Forces proportional resizing of text to fit between two points. You are prompted to select the two points. The text height is scaled in proportion to its width in the current text style.

Center   Centers text on the start point, which also defines the baseline of the text.

Fit   Forces text to fit between two points. Unlike *Align*, Fit keeps the default height and either stretches or compresses the text to fit.

Middle   Centers text at the start point. The start point is in the middle of the text height.

Right   Right-justifies the text. The start point is on the right side of the text.

Style   Allows a new text style. The style you enter becomes the current style.

↵   If no option has been selected at the first prompt, pressing ↵ highlights the most recently entered line of text and displays the prompt Text:, allowing you to continue to add text just below that line. The current text style and angle are assumed, as is the justification setting of the most recently entered text.

Notes   If you use Dtext, a box appears showing the approximate size of the text. The text appears on your drawing as you type and the box moves along as a cursor. When you press ↵, the box moves down one line. You can also pick a point anywhere on the screen for the next line of text and still backspace all the way to the beginning line to make corrections.

If you choose a justification option other than Left, the effects will not be seen until you finish entering the text.

The **Text** command works much like Dtext; however, it does not display the text on your drawing as you type. The text you enter appears only in the command-prompt area. Further, once you press ↵, the text appears on the drawing and you are returned to the command prompt. You must press ↵ twice to enter multiple lines of text.

Dtext does not work with Script files. Control codes, like **%%d**, can be entered before or after your text to add diameter, underscores, tolerance symbols, and so on to your text.

See Also   Change, Chtext (AutoLISP), Color, Ddedit, Ddrename, Ptext (AutoLISP), Rename, Style, Qtext. *System Variables:* Texteval, Textsize, Textstyle.

DVIEW

Menu: **View ➤ Set View ➤ Dview**

Dview displays your drawing in perspective and enables you to clip a portion of a view. Unlike the standard **Zoom** and **Pan** commands, Dview allows you to perform zooms and pans on perspective views.

To Display a Drawing with DView:

Issue the command, then provide the following information:

1.   Select object: Pick the objects that will help set up your perspective view.

2.   CAmera/TArget/Distance/Points/PAn/Zoom/TWist/ CLip/Hide/Off/Undo/< eXit>: Select an option from the menu or enter the capitalized letter(s) of the desired option.

3.   The prompts you receive next depend on the option selected in the preceding step.

● OPTIONS

CAmera   Allows you to move the camera location as if you were moving a camera around, while continually aiming at the target point. CAmera prompts you for the vertical and horizontal angles of view. At each prompt, you can either enter a value or select the view by using a slide bar (on the right for vertical, on the top for horizontal). If you enter a value, it will be interpreted in relation to the current UCS. See FIGURE 22.

TArget Allows you to move the target location, as if you were pointing a camera in different directions while keeping the camera location the same. TArget prompts you for the vertical and horizontal angles of view. At each prompt, you can either enter a value or select the view by using a slide bar (on the right for vertical, at the top for horizontal). See FIGURE 23.

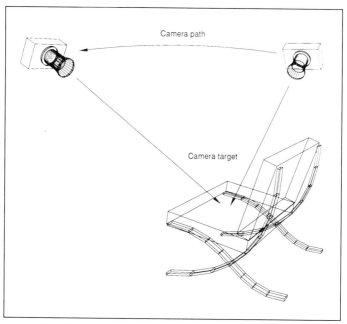

Figure 22: The CAmera option controls the camera location relative to the target.

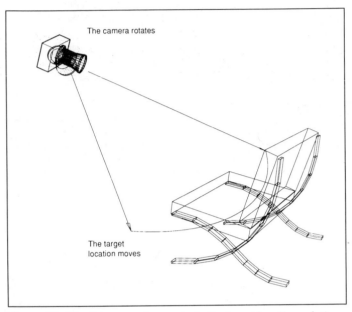

The camera rotates

The target
location moves

Figure 23: The TArget option controls the target location relative to the camera.

Distance   Turns on the Perspective mode and allows you to set the distance from the target to the camera, as if you were moving a camera toward or away from the target point. At the prompt, enter a new distance or move the slide bar at the top of the screen to drag the three-dimensional image into the desired position. See FIGURE 24.

POints   Sets the target and camera points at the same time. The points you pick are in relation to the current UCS. At the prompt, pick a point for the target first, and then pick one for your camera location.

PAn   Moves your camera and target point together, as if you were pointing a camera out the side window of a moving car. You cannot use the standard Pan command while viewing a drawing in perspective. See **Pan** for more information.

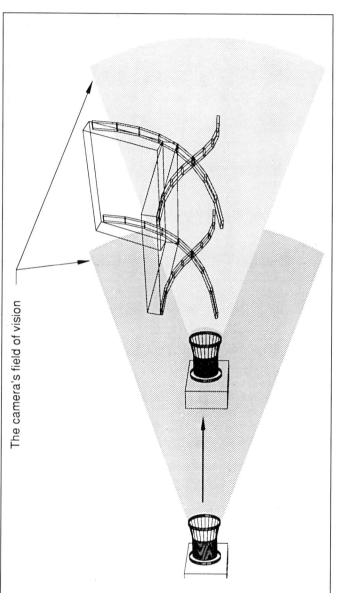

The camera's field of vision

Figure 24: The Distance option controls the distance between the camera and the target.

Zoom Zooms in and out when you are viewing a drawing in parallel projection. Provides the lens focal length when you are viewing a drawing in perspective. You cannot use the standard Zoom command while viewing a drawing in perspective.

If your three-dimensional view is a parallel projection, enter a new scale factor or use the slide bar at the top of the screen to visually adjust the scale factor at the **Dview/Zoom** prompt. If your three-dimensional view is a perspective, enter a new lens length value or use the slide bar at the top of the screen to determine the new lens length at the Dview/Zoom prompt. If you use the slide bar to adjust the focal length, the coordinate readout on the status line will dynamically display the focal length value.

Twist Rotates the camera about the camera's line of sight, as if you were rotating the view in a camera frame. At the **Dview/Twist** prompt, enter an angle or use the cursor to visually twist the camera view. If you use the cursor, the coordinate readout on the status line dynamically displays the camera twist angle.

CLip Hides portions of a three-dimensional view. For example, it removes foreground objects that may interfere with a view of the background (see FIGURE 25). CLip displays the prompt Back/Front/<Off>:. Enter **B** to set Back Clip Plane, **F** to set Front Clip Plane, or **O** or ↵ to turn off the Clip Plane function. If you select Back or Front, a prompt allows you to either turn the selected clip plane on or off or to set a distance to the clip plane. You can use the slide bar at the top of the screen to visually determine the location of the clip plane, or enter a distance value. A positive value places the clip plane in front of the target point; a negative number places it behind the target point.

Hide Removes hidden lines from the objects displayed, turning a wire-frame view into a planar view.

eXit Returns you to the AutoCAD command prompt. Any operation you performed while in the Dview command prompt will affect the entire drawing, not just the selected objects.

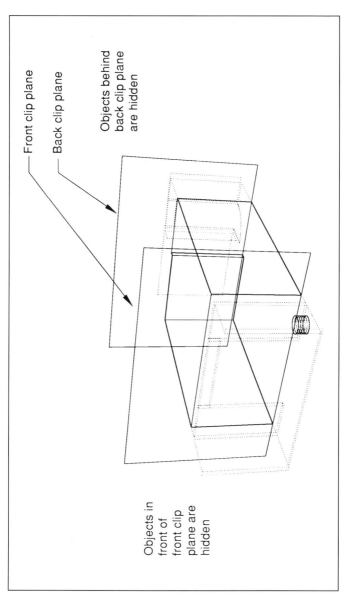

Front clip plane

Back clip plane

Objects behind
back clip plane
are hidden

Objects in
front of
front clip
plane are
hidden

Figure 25: The CLip option allows you to hide foreground or background portions of your drawing.

Notes Because a large drawing slows down the drag function, you are prompted to select objects for dragging at the beginning of the Dview command. This limits the number of objects to be dragged. You should select objects that give the general outline of your drawing and sufficient detail to indicate the drawing's orientation. If you do not pick any objects, a default three-dimensional house image appears to help you select a view. You can create your own block image and use that as the default. The block should be named *Dviewblock*.

See Also UCS. *System Variables:* Backz, Frontz, Lenslength, Target, Viewctr, Viewdir, Viewmode, Viewsize, Viewtwist.

DXBIN

Menu: **File ➤ Import/Export ➤ DXB In**…

Dxbin opens the Select DXB File dialog box to import files in the DXB file format. DXB is a binary file format that contains a limited amount of drawing information. It is the main format used by AutoShade to export files to AutoCAD.

To Import a DXB File:

The Select DXB File dialog list box displays path and filenames of .DXB files in your current directory. Pick a file from the *Files:* list box or enter the name in the *File:* edit box. You can also enter the filename at the command prompt by selecting the *Type it* pick box.

Notes You can use Dxbin to convert AutoCAD three-dimensional views, both perspective and orthogonal, into two-dimensional drawings. Dxbin configures AutoCAD's plotter option to an ADI plotter that produces DXB files. This allows you to generate DXB plot files of any three-dimensional view and import these files into AutoCAD as two-dimensional images. PageMaker accepts DXB files.

See Also Dxfin, Dxfout.

DXFIN

Menu: **File ➤ Import/Export ➤ DXF In**...

Dxfin imports drawing files in the AutoCAD DXF format. These are ASCII files (extension .DXF) that contain a code that allows AutoCAD to import complete drawing information. Many microcomputer and minicomputer CADD programs have a DXF converter so that you can export files to AutoCAD.

To Import a DXF File:

The Select DXF File dialog list box displays path and filenames of .DXF files in your current directory. Pick a file from the *Files:* list box or enter the name in the *File:* edit box. You can also enter the filename at the command prompt by selecting the *Type it* pick box.

Notes   To import a DXF file, open a new file that does not contain any nameable variable definitions such as layers, line types, text styles, or views. Then issue the Dxfin command. (If the current file already contains nameable variables, only the drawn objects in the imported file are imported. Line types, layers, and so on are not imported.)

When you enter the name of the DXF file you wish to import, do not include the .DXF extension.

See Also   Dxfout, Dxbin.

DXFOUT

Menu: **File ➤ Import/Export ➤ DXF Out**...

Dxfout opens the Create DXF File dialog box to create a copy of your current file in the DXF file format for export to other programs. It can also create a binary version of the DXF format, which is highly compressed compared with the ASCII version.

To Export a DXF File:

Issue the command, then provide the following information:

1. Enter the name of the file you wish to export. The Create DXF File dialog list box displays path and filenames of .DXF files in your current directory. Pick a file from the *Files:* list box or enter the name in the *File:* edit box. You can also enter the filename at the command prompt by selecting the *Type it* pick box.

2. Enter decimal places of accuracy (0 to 16) /Entities/ Binary <6>: Enter a value representing the decimal-place accuracy of your DXF file or press ↵ to accept the default.

● OPTIONS

(0 to 16)   Controls the decimal accuracy of the DXF file to be created. The default value is 6.

Entities   Allows you to select specific objects or a portion of the current drawing to be exported. You are then prompted to select objects.

Notes   Many programs use DXF files. Some are converters that translate DXF files for desktop publishing programs, paint programs, or other CADD programs. There are even programs that use DXF files for analysis or for generating database information.

See Also   Dxbin, Dxfin.

EDGESURF

Menu: **Draw ➤ 3D Surfaces ➤ Edge Defined Patch**

Edgesurf draws a three-dimensional surface based on four objects. These objects can be lines, arcs, polylines, or three-dimensional polylines, but they must join exactly end-to-end.

To Create a 3D Surface Using Edgesurf:

Issue the command, then provide the following information:

1. Select edge 1: Pick the first object defining an edge.

2. Select edge 2: Pick the second object defining an edge.

3. Select edge 3: Pick the third object defining an edge.

4. Select edge 4: Pick the fourth object defining an edge.

Notes   The type of surface drawn by Edgesurf is called a *Coons surface patch* (see FIGURE 26).

The first edge selected defines the M direction of the mesh, and the edges adjoining the first define the N direction. The end point closest to the point selected becomes the origin of the M and N directions.

The *Surftab1* and *Surftab2* system variables control the number of facets in the M and N directions, respectively. Increasing the number of facets gives a smoother mesh, but increases the file size of the drawing considerably. This increases file-opening, redrawing, and regeneration times. Increasing the values of *Surftab1* and *Surftab2* after creating the edgesurf will not smooth the 3D surface. Only edgesurfs created after, with the new values, will reflect the changes. See **Setvar** for details.

See Also   Pedit, Pface. *System Variables:* Surftab1, Surftab2.

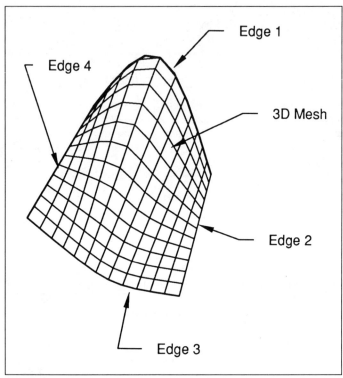

Figure 26: A Coons surface patch

EDIT

Edit opens a specified text file using the DOS EDLIN line editor. The *Edlin.COM* file must be in the default drive and directory or can be accessed through the DOS path. (See your DOS manual for details on EDLIN.)

To Edit a Text File:

Issue the command, then provide the following information:

• File to edit: Enter the DOS or ASCII filename.

Notes Use this command to create an ASCII file for the **Attext** or **Script** commands, or edit existing ASCII files like the Acad.PGP file and LISP files.

You can edit the line Edit,Edlin, 0,File to edit:,4 in your *Acad.PGP* file to start a different text editor within AutoCAD (see **Acad.PGP**) by replacing the **EDLIN** command.

See Also Acad.PGP, Attext, Script.

ELEV

Menu: **Settings ➤ Entity Modes... ➤ Elevation/Thickness**

Elev allows you to set the default Z-axis elevation and thickness of objects being drawn. Normally, objects will be placed at a 0 elevation. Once you enter an elevation or thickness with Elev, all objects drawn afterwards will be given the new Z-axis value; objects you drew before using the Elev command are not affected. You can also change the elevation of an existing object with the **Move** command.

To Set Elevation and Thickness:

Issue the command, then provide the following information:

1. New current elevation <current default>: Set a new default starting plane elevation in the Z-axis.

2. New current thickness <current default>: Set a new default extrusion thickness in the Z-axis.

Notes 3D polylines, faces, and meshes, as well as viewports and dimensions ignore Elev settings, since these entities cannot be extruded.

Text and attribute definition entities are always given a zero thickness, regardless of the Elev values used during initial creation. These, however can be modified with a nonzero thickness using change.

See Also   Ddemodes, Dducs, Move. *System Variables:* Elevation.

ELLIPSE

Menu: **Draw ➤ Ellipse ➤ Axis, Eccentricity/Center, Axis, Axis**

Ellipse draws an ellipse for which you specify the major and minor axes, a center point and two axis points; or the center point and the radius or diameter of an isometric circle. It also allows you to define a second projection of a three-dimensional circle by using the *Rotation* option.

To Draw an Ellipse:

Issue the command, then provide the following information:

1.   If your isometric snap mode is active, the following prompt appears:

- <Axis endpoint 1>/Center/Isocircle: Enter **I**, then pick a point defining one end of the ellipse or **C** to enter a center point.

    If your **Isometric** Snap mode is not active, the prompt is:

- <Axis endpoint 1>/Center: Pick a point defining one end of the ellipse or enter **C** to enter the center point.

2.   For either of the above, the following prompts appear if you select the default option by picking a point:

   a.   Axis endpoint 2: Pick a point defining the opposite end of the ellipse.

   b.   <Other axis distance>/Rotation: Pick a point defining the other axis of the ellipse or enter **R** to enter a rotation value.

● OPTIONS

Axis endpoint   Allows you to enter the endpoint of one of the ellipse's axes (see FIGURE 27).

Center   Allows you to pick the ellipse center point.

Other axis distance   Appears after you have already defined one of the ellipse's axes. Enter the distance from the center of the ellipse to the second axis endpoint.

Isocircle   Appears when you set the Style option for the **Isometric** command to *Isometric*. This option prompts you to select a center and a diameter or radius for the ellipse. AutoCAD draws an isometric circle based on the current **Isoplane** setting.

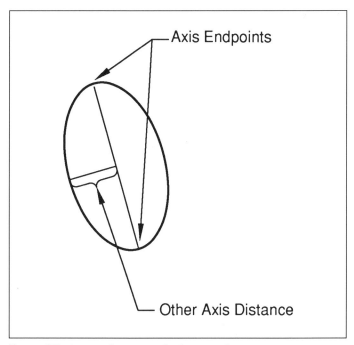

Axis Endpoints

Other Axis Distance

Figure 27: Axis endpoints and other axis distance

Rotation   Allows you to enter an ellipse rotation value between 0 and 89.4 degrees. Imagine the ellipse to be a two-dimensional projection of a three-dimensional circle rotated on an axis. As the circle is rotated, its projection turns into an ellipse. The rotation value determines the rotation angle of this circle. A 0-degree value displays a full circle; an 80-degree value displays a narrow ellipse (see FIGURE 28).

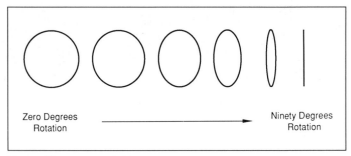

Figure 28: A rotated ellipse

Notes   Because an ellipse is actually a polyline, you can edit it using the **Pedit** command.

See Also   Snap/Style, Isoplane. *System variables:* Snapisopair.

END

End simultaneously exits and saves a file. Edits made prior to the End command are saved. The previous copy of the drawing is changed to a .BAK file.

Notes   For unnamed drawings in which you opened a new drawing and never entered the **Save** command during your editing session, the Create Drawing File dialog box appears. Enter the drawing name in the *Files:* edit box.

When the *Filedia* system variable is set to 0, the command-line prompt requests a File name:. The End command will fail if the current drawing was set to read-only. In this case, you can use the **Saveas** command to save the drawing to another name before quitting.

See Also   Save, Saveas, Qsave, Quit.

ENVIRONMENT SETTINGS

Menu: **File ➤ Preferences**... **Environment**...

There are a variety of AutoCAD settings that control its memory use and tell it where to find support files. Make these settings either through command switches in the Windows Program Manager, through the **Preferences** command, or through the *DOS environment* (a small portion of memory used to store data). When AutoCAD starts up, it looks in the DOS environment for any information that is specifically set aside for AutoCAD.

● OPTIONS

TABLE 6 gives a listing of the environment settings and their uses. It also shows the command switches used to make some of the settings, and the names of the settings as they appear in the File ➤ Preferences... ➤ Environment dialog box. The command switches are used in the Command Line edit box of the Program Item Properties dialog box. To open this dialog box, highlight the AutoCAD program item icon in the AutoCAD program group, then click on **Files ➤ Properties** from the Program Manager menu.

Table 6: The AutoCAD Environment Settings

Environment Setting	Command Line Switch	Environment Dialog Name	Purpose
ACAD	/S	Support Dirs:	Indicates the directory or directories for support files.
NA	/C	NA	Indictates where configuration files *Acad.cfg* and *Acad.ini* are found
ACADALTMNU	NA	Alt. Menu File:	Indictates where to find alternate tablet menu files, if you have a digitizing tablet
ACADDRV	/D	Drivers Dir:	Indictates where to find the Protected mode ADI drivers
ACADHELP	NA	Help File:	Indicates where to find the AutoCAD help files
ACADLOGFILE	NA	Log File:	Indicates where AutoCAD is to place the command prompt log file.
ACADMAXMEM	/M	Max. Memory	Indicates the maximum amount of memory in bytes that AutoCAD requests from the operating system.
ACADPAGEDIR	NA	Page File Dir:	Indicates the directory where page files are stored

Table 6: The AutoCAD Environment Settings (continued)

Environment Setting	Command Line Switch	Environment Dialog Name	Purpose
ACADMAXPAGE	NA	Max. Bytes in Page	Indicates the maximum number of bytes to be sent to the first page file
ACADPLCMD	NA	Plotting:	Indicates the shell command AutoCAD is to use for plot spooling
AVECFG	NA	Rendering Env… ▶ Config. File Dir:	Indicates where to store the renderer's configuration files
RDPADI	NA	NA	Indicates the location and name of the protected mode ADI rendering drive for the renderer
RHPADI	NA	NA	Indicates the location and name of the protected mode ADI hard copy rendering driver for the renderer
AVEFACEDIR	NA	Rendering Env… ▶ Face File Dir:	Indicates the location and name for storing the renderer's temporary files
AVEPAGEDIR	NA	Rendering Env… ▶ Page File Dir:	Indicates the location and name for the renderer's RAM page files
AVEDFILE	NA	Rendering Env… ▶ AVERDFILE:	Indicates where .RND rendering hard copy files are displayed

Notes To set these variables at the DOS prompt, use the **DOS Set** command before starting Windows. For example, to direct AutoCAD to look in *Acadwin\Support* and *Acadwin\font* directories for support files, at the DOS prompt enter:

    SET ACAD=C:\ACAD\SUPPORT;C:\ACAD\FONTS

To set the environment before you run AutoCAD, you can include this line in a batch file that starts Windows.

You can also control these settings from within AutoCAD by clicking on **File ➤ Preferences** and then on **Environment**... at the Preferences dialog box. When the Environment dialog box appears, you can enter values for the settings in the appropriate edit boxes.

AutoCAD looks for environment settings in the following order: first, it looks for the command switch settings made from the Program Manager. If no command switches are used, it looks for settings made from the Preferences command. If neither of these were used, AutoCAD uses settings made from the DOS Set command.

ERASE

Menu: **Modify ➤ Erase ➤ Select/Single/Last/Oops**

Erase deletes one or several objects from the drawing by picking or using any selection method.

To Erase Objects:

Issue the command, then provide the following information:

- Select objects: Select the objects to be erased.

• OPTIONS

These options are available when you have issued the command from the pull-down menu:

Select   Lets you pick each object to be erased or use a selection set option, and continues the Select objects: prompt until you press ↵ twice. (See **Select**). This is also the standard method used from the keyboard.

Single   Lets you pick a single object only. From the keyboard you can also enter **Si** at the Select objects: prompt.

Last   Lets you erase the last entity drawn. From the keyboard you can enter **L** at the Select objects: prompt. You can also enter Previous or **P** from the keyboard to erase the previous selection set.

Oops   Lets you unerase the last erase. (See **Oops**).

Notes   To erase an object that is overlapped by another, use a crossing window to select both objects, then use **R** or the *Remove selection* option and remove the object on top from the selection set with a single pick. If you change your mind, use *Add* or **A** to add an object into your selection option. The Remove and Add modes will remain active only during that specific selection set.

See Also   Select/Si, Multiple, Oops.

EXIT AUTOCAD

Menu: **Files ➤ Exit AutoCAD**

Exit AutoCAD ends the AutoCAD session and returns to the DOS prompt. **Quit** is the command-line equivalent of this selection.

Notes   If any work was done during the drawing session and the drawing was never saved or named, a Drawing Modification dialog box is displayed to indicate that "The current drawing has been changed" and requests you to pick the *Save Changes...*, *Discard Changes*, or *Cancel Command* button.

If no work was done to the drawing, the drawing session is terminated immediately without any warning message.

See Also   Quit, End.

EXPLODE

Menu: **Modify ➤ Explode**

Reduces a block, polyline, associative dimension, or three-dimensional mesh to its component objects. If a block is nested, Explode only "unblocks" the outermost block.

To Explode an Object:

Issue the command, then provide the following information:

- Select objects: Select block reference, polyline, dimension, or mesh to be exploded by picking or specifying any window selection set, including *window*, *wpolygon*, and *fence*.

Notes   Blocks inserted with **Minsert** and blocks with unequal X, Y, or Z insertion scale factors cannot be exploded. You can't explode Xrefs and their dependent blocks. AutoCAD provides an AutoLISP file called *Xplode.LSP* that will explode mirrored blocks. (See **Appload** for loading LISP files. See also **AutoLISP** table.)

Wide polylines lose their width properties when exploded.

See Also   Select, Undo.

EXTEND

Menu: **Modify** ➤ **Extend**

Lengthens an object to meet another object.

To Extend an Object:

Issue the command, then provide the following information:

1. Select boundary edge(s)... tells you to pick one or more objects to which to extend other objects by selecting the entity or using fence selection to designate the boundary objects at the next prompt.

2. Select objects: Select the entity or use fence selection to designate the boundary objects.

3. <Select objects to extend>/Undo: Select objects to be extended by picking an entity, using fence selection, or entering U to undo the last extend operation.

Notes You cannot extend objects within blocks or use blocks as boundary edges. Also, boundary edges must be in the path of the objects to be extended.

You can only extend objects that lie in a plane parallel to the current user coordinate system (UCS).

If you are not viewing the current UCS in plan, you may get an erroneous result. It is best to use the **Plan** command to view the current UCS in plan, and then proceed with the Extend command.

At times, objects will not extend properly even when all conditions are met. If this problem occurs, use the **Zoom** or **Pan** command to change your view, then reissue the Extend command.

See Also Change, Trim.

FILES

Transparent: **'Files**

Menu: **File ➤ Utilities**

When the *Filedia* system variable is set to 0, Files allows you to manipulate files at the command line on your disk without having to exit AutoCAD. You can list all or specified files, as well as delete, rename, or copy them.

To Access the File Utility Menu:

Issue the command, then provide the following information:

If you are in the Drawing editor and the *Filedia* system variable is set to 0, the screen switches to Text mode and the File Utility menu below appears. Enter the number corresponding to the desired option:

```
0. Exit File Utility Menu
1. List Drawing files
2. List user specified files
3. Delete files
4. Rename files
5. Copy file
6. Unlock files
Enter selection (0 to 6) <0>:
```

If the *Filedia* system variable is set to 1, the File Utilities dialog box appears with the following choices:

- List files…   Opens the File List subdialog list box to display the directory you specify.

- Copy file…   Opens the Source File subdialog box to locate and assign the file you want to copy to the Destination File subdialog box so that you can name the new file.

- Rename file… Opens an Old File Name subdialog box to reassign its directory or name to a New File Name subdialog box.

- Delete file… Opens the File(s) to Delete subdialog box in order to rearrange files into other directories, accepting wildcard specifications. *Select All* and *Clear All* button boxes assist in deleting files.

- Unlock files… Opens the File(s) to Unlock subdialog box to unlock files that have been locked due to another user's instructions or by an aborted AutoCAD session. A list is displayed showing which user locked the file and when it was locked. *Select All* and *Clear All* button boxes assist in unlocking groups of files.

- Exit Closes the File Utilities dialog box.

● OPTIONS

The following edit boxes and buttons appear for each File Utilities subdialog box:

Pattern Edit box that lets you specify the type of file you want displayed in the list of files. You can use the standard DOS wildcard characters to filter filenames. Only the Delete and Unlock Files dialog boxes accept wildcards.

Directories Picking from the directory list box positions the *Directory* drive and path.

Files: List box displaying the list of files in the current directory. Highlighting a file with your cursor places it in the *File:* edit box.

File: Edit box for entering filename.

Type it Dimmed button indicates it is disabled.

Default Dimmed button indicates it is disabled.

Notes When entering filenames, you must include the file extension. For the *Unlock Files* option, give the .DWG filename.

The *File Utilities* option on the opening **Main** menu works in the same way as the **Files** command.

When deleting files, take care not to delete files AutoCAD needs for its internal operation. If you or someone on your network is currently editing a file, do not delete AutoCAD temporary files with the extension .$AC, .AC$, or .$A. TABLE 7 lists other AutoCAD file extensions and their purposes.

Table 7: AutoCAD File Extensions and Their Meanings

Standard Extension	Lock File Extension	File Description
.ADS		ADS applications file
.ADT	.ADK	Audit report file
.BAK	.BKK	Drawing backup file
.BDF		VESA font file (video card support)
.CFG	.CFK	AutoCAD configuration file
.DCC		Dialog box color control
.DCE		Dialog box error report
.DCL		Dialog Control Language description file
.DFS		Default file settings file
.DWG	.DWK, .DWL	Drawing file
.DXB	.DBK	Binary data exchange file
.DXF	.DFK	Drawing interchange file
.DXX	.DXK	Attribute data in DXF format
.EPS		Encapsulated PostScript file
.ERR		AutoCAD error report
.EXP		ADS executable file (for DOS)
.FLM	.FLK	AutoShade filmroll file
.HLP		AutoCAD help file
.HDX		AutoCAD help index
.IGS	.IGK	IGES drawing interchange file

Table 7: AutoCAD File Extensions and Their Meanings (continued)

Standard Extension	Lock File Extension	File Description
.LIN	.LIK	Line-type definition file
.LSP		AutoLISP program file
.LST	.LSK	Printer plot file
.MAT		AME Materials file
.MNL		AutoLISP functions related with a menu file
.MNU	.MNK	Menu file
.MNX	.MXK	Compiled menu file
.OLD	.OLK	Backup of a file converted from an early version of AutoCAD
.PAT		Hatch-pattern library file
.PCP	.PCK	Plot-configuration parameter settings file
.PS		PostScript file
.PGP		AutoCAD external program parameter file
.PSF		PostScript support file
.PLT	.PLK	Plot file
.PWD	.PWK	AutoCAD login file
.SCR		Script file
.SHP		Shapte/font definition source file
.SHX	.SHK	Shape or Font compiled file
.SLB		Slide library file
.SLD	.SDK	Slide files

Table 7: AutoCAD File Extensions and Their Meanings
        (continued)

Standard Extension	Lock File Extension	File Description
.TXT	.TXK	Attribute extract or template file (CDF/SDF format)
.UNT		Units file
.XLG	.XLK	External references log file
.XMX		External message file

FILL

Transparent: 'Fill

Menu: **Settings ➤ Drawing Aids ➤ Solid Fill**

Fill turns on or off the solid fills of solids, traces, and polylines. When Fill is off, solid filled areas are only outlined, both on the screen and in prints.

See Also   Pline, Trace, Solid. *System Variables:* Fillmode.

FILLET

Menu: **Construct ➤ Fillet**

Fillet uses an intermediate arc to join two nonparallel lines, a line and an arc, or segments of a polyline.

To Use Fillet:

Issue the command, then provide the following information:

1. Polyline/Radius/<select first object>: Pick the first line to fillet, P, or R. If you enter **P**, the prompt Select 2D polyline: appears; if you enter **R**, you are prompted to Enter fillet radius.

2. Select second object: Pick the second line.

● OPTIONS

Polyline   Fillets all line segments within a polyline. You are prompted to select a two-dimensional polyline. All joining polyline segments are then filleted.

Radius   Allows you to specify the radius of the fillet arc.

Notes   Fillet joins the end points closest to the intersection. The location you use to pick objects determines which part of the fillet is retained. If the lines (or line and arc) already intersect, Fillet substitutes the specified arc for the existing corner. To connect two non-parallel lines with a corner rather than an arc, set the radius to **0**. You can also fillet just a corner of a polyline by picking its adjacent segments. Both segments, however, must be part of the same polyline.

If you are not viewing the current UCS in plan, Fillet may give you the wrong result. Use the **Plan** command to view the current UCS in plan before issuing Fillet.

See Also   Chamfer. *System Variables:* Filletrad.

FILMROLL

Menu: **File►Import/Export►Filmroll …**

Opens the Create Filmroll File dialog box to save files for use with AutoShade.

To Use Filmroll:

Issue the command, then provide the following information:

- Enter filmroll filename <current filename>: Enter the desired filename for the filmroll.

Notes When the *Filedia* system variable is set to 1, the Create Filmroll File list box appears; otherwise, an equivalent command-line prompt appears.

FILTER

Transparent: 'Filter

Menu: **Assist ➤ Object Filters**…

Filter opens the Entity Selection Filters dialog box to generate a selection-set filter based on combinations of entity properties and to save them to a filename.

To Filter Properties:

Issue the command, then apply coordinates, entity type, color, layer, linetype, block name, text style, or thickness to a filter.

● OPTIONS

List Box   Displays a list box (in upper portion of dialog box) of the filtered entities in your current selection set.

Edit Item   Pick box used to transfer the highlighted filter shown in the list box (at the upper portion of the dialog box) to the *Select Filter* area below. Pick *Edit Item* to transfer additional filters from the list box to the *Select Filter* area for editing. You can modify and *Substitute* the filters and their values displayed in the edit boxes below the Select Filter area.

Delete   Pick box to remove the highlighted filter from the list box.

Clear List   Pick box to remove all the filters from the list box.

Select Filter   Area containing X, Y, and Z coordinate edit boxes, and a Select subdialog box listing entity types and relational operators as well as additional pick boxes. The Select subdialog box is specific to the entity type being filtered.

Add to List   Appends entity in *Select Filter* area to the filter list in upper portion of dialog box.

Substitute   Pick box to replace highlighted filter criteria with the one in the *Select Filter* area.

Add Selected Entity   Pick box temporarily exits the dialog box allowing you to select entities from the drawing and add them to the filter list.

Named Filters   Area containing options to save, restore, and delete the current filter list.

Current: Pop-up list displaying names of saved filters.

Save As   Edit box for assigning a name and saving a filter list.

Delete Current Filter List   Pick box for removing the saved filtered names from the *Current:* pop-up list.

Apply   Exits dialog box and executes the filtering procedure.

Notes   Filter is an AutoLISP application. You must have *Filter.LSP* and *Filter.DCL* in the ACAD path to successfully initialize and load the command. Entering Filter transparently (**'Filter**) at the command line allows you to apply the **P** (previous) selection set to access the filtered entities. The following operands must be paired and balanced for filters to operate correctly:

- Begin AND/End AND
- Begin Or/End Or
- Begin XOR/End XOR
- Begin NOT/End NOT

GRAPHSCR/TEXTSCR

Transparent: 'Graphscr/'Textscr

Use Graphscr or Textscr to place instructions in a script file, AutoLISP program, or a menu option to flip the screen to either graphics or text mode respectively. If you have a dual-screen system, these commands are ignored.

Notes These are two separate commands. Use **Graphscr** to switch to graphics mode, **Textscr** to switch to text mode.

GRID

Menu: **Settings ➤ Drawing Aids... ➤ Grid**

Grid sets the grid spacing.

To Use Grid:

Issue the command, then provide the following information:

- Grid spacing(X) or ON/OFF/Snap/Aspect <default value>: Enter the desired grid spacing or other option.

• OPTIONS

Grid spacing(X) Allows you to enter the desired grid spacing in drawing units. Enter **0** to make the grid spacing match the Snap setting.

ON Turns on the grid display. (The F7 key performs the same function.)

OFF Turns off the grid display. (The F7 key performs the same function.)

Snap   Sets the grid spacing to match the Snap spacing. Once set, Grid spacing will dynamically follow every change in the Snap spacing.

Aspect   Specifies a grid spacing in the Y axis that is different from the spacing in the X axis.

Notes   If you follow the grid spacing value with **X** at the Grid spacing... prompt, AutoCAD interprets the value as a multiple of the **Snap** setting. For example, if you enter **2**, the grid points will be spaced two units apart, but if you enter **2X**, the grid points will be twice as far apart as the Snap settings.

At times, a grid setting may obscure the view of your drawing. If this happens, AutoCAD automatically turns off the grid mode and displays the message Grid too dense to display.

If you are using multiple viewports in Paperspace, you can set the grid differently for each viewport.

Grid spacing can also be controlled using the Ddrmodes dialog box.

See Also   Ddrmodes. *System variables:* Gridmode, Gridunit

GRIPS

Entity grips allow you to make quick changes to objects in a drawing. With this feature turned on (using the **Ddgrips** command), you can grab endpoints, centerpoints, and midpoints of objects, and stretch, move, copy, rotate, mirror, or scale them. To reveal the grip points, click on a single object, or select multiple objects at the command prompt. Click on a single grip to edit it, or Shift-click on more than one grip to select several points. If you select multiple grips, you must click on one of the selected grips to begin editing.

When you click on a grip, it becomes a solid color and is called a *hot grip*. The command prompt will change to tell you the current edit option. You can tell you are in a grips edit option by the asterisks that surround the option name, as in **STRETCH** or **MOVE**.

• OPTIONS

Once you select a grip, you see the **STRETCH** prompt along with another prompt showing the options available under **STRETCH**. To switch to the **MOVE**, **ROTATE**, **SCALE**, and **MIRROR** options, press ↵ (the options repeat after **MIRROR**). The hot grip is assumed to be the base point of the edit for all of these options. To specify a new base point, enter **B** ↵ at any of the grips options. You can also copy the selected objects by entering **C** ↵, or undo the last grips option by entering **U**↵.

See Also   Copy, Ddgrips, Mirror, Move, Rotate, Scale, Stretch.

HANDLES

Handles enables and disables the use of unique entity identifiers for every object drawn. The handles assigned to every entity when enabled are internally generated by AutoCAD and will remain unique for each entity in the drawing.

To Disable Handles:

Issue the command. The following prompt appears:

- Handles are disabled ON/DESTROY: Enter the desired option.

• OPTIONS

ON   Enables the Handles function, giving every object drawn an alphanumeric name.

DESTROY   Disables the Handles function, destroying any currently existing handles in the drawing.

Notes   The **List** command displays the selected object's handle in addition to the other information List provides. If you are programming in AutoLISP, you can identify entities using the AutoLISP function *Handent*.

Handle information is written to DXF files and therefore can help you extract database information from a drawing.

Handles are turned off by default, because they add processing overhead.

See Also   List, Dxfout. *System Variables:* Handles.

HATCH/BHATCH

Menu: **Draw ➤ Hatch**…

Hatch fills an area defined by lines, arcs, circles, or polylines with either a predefined pattern or a simple hatch pattern. The equivalent dialog box command is **Bhatch**.

To Select a Hatch:

Issue the command, then provide the following information:

- Pattern (? or name/U,style) <default pattern>: Enter the pattern name or enter **U** to create a simple cross-hatch pattern.

• OPTIONS

U   Defines a simple hatch pattern, including hatch angle, spacing between lines, and whether or not you want a cross-hatch. Cross-hatching occurs at 90 degrees to the first hatch lines.

?   Lists the names of available hatch patterns.

pattern name   Can be entered at the Pattern prompt. Additional prompts then appear:

- Scale for pattern:
- Angle for pattern:

In general, the pattern scale should be the same as the drawing scale. The following modifiers control how the pattern is created. To use these modifiers, enter the pattern name at the Pattern prompt, followed by a comma and the modifier.

N   Fills alternating areas. This is the default option.

O   Fills only the outermost area selected.

I   Causes the entire area within the objects selected to be hatched, regardless of other enclosed areas within the selected area. This option also forces the hatch pattern to avoid hatching over text.

scaleXP   When entered at the scale prompt this modifier lets you specify a hatch scale relative to Paperspace. See **Zoom/XP**.

Notes   There are 53 predefined patterns, illustrated in FIGURE 29. You can create your own hatch patterns by editing the *Acad.PAT* file. This file uses numeric codes to define the patterns.

Selecting **Hatch**... under the Draw pull-down menu activates the **Bhatch** command and opens the Boundary Hatch dialog box. You can use the *Hatch Options*... button for the Hatch Options subdialog box, then pick **Pattern**... for the Choose Hatch Pattern icon boxes. Use the *Next* and *Previous* buttons to scroll through the list, then activate the pattern by picking its icon. The Bhatch command can automatically construct polylines from lines (See **Bhatch**).

Use the **List** command to identify the pattern name, spacing, and scale.

The objects that define the hatch area should be joined end- to-end and be closed. If you use lines and arcs, the endpoints of the objects must meet exactly end-to-end. Polylines should be closed.

To make the hatch pattern begin at a specific point, use the *Rotate* option under the **Snap** command to set the snap origin to the desired beginning point. Hatch uses the snap origin (*Snapbase* system variable) to determine where to start the hatch pattern.

If you need to edit a hatch pattern, use the **Explode** command to break the pattern into its component lines.

See Also   Bhatch, Bpoly, Snap/Rotate, Explode. *System Variables:* Hpname, Hpscale, Hpang, Hpspace, Hpdouble.

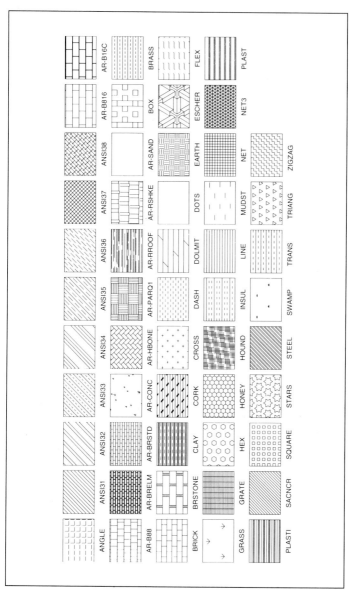

Figure 29: The standard hatch patterns

HELP/?

Transparent: '**Help**/'?

Menu: **Help ➤ Contents/Search for Help on... How to Use Help**

Help or ? opens up the Help dialog box to provide a brief description of how to use a particular command. You can use Help transparently in the middle of another command to get specific information about that command: enter **Help** or **?** preceded by an apostrophe at any prompt in the command.

HIDE

Menu: **Render ➤ Hide**

Hide removes hidden lines on an orthogonal or three-dimensional view when using Vpoint, Dview, or View.

Notes   Once you issue Hide, the message Removing hidden lines appears, followed by a series of numbers that count off the lines as they are hidden. For complex 3D views, you may want to use **Mslide** to save the view with hidden lines removed. In a perspective view, use the *Hide* option under **Dview**.

You can also use **Shade** to get a quick rendering of a 3D model.

Hide is also an option of the **Mview** command.

If you assign HIDDEN as a prefix to a layer name and configure AutoCAD using *Select R11 hidden line removal algorithm* (see **Config**), hidden lines will be drawn on this layer during the Hide command, and thus can appear in a different color instead of being invisible. For example, HIDDENWALL could appear in one color and WALL in another color.

See Also   Config, Dview, View, Mview, Shade.

ID

Transparent: '**Id**

Menu: **Assist ➤ Inquiry ➤ ID Point**...

Id displays the X, Y, and Z coordinate values of a point.

To Display a Point's Coordinates:

Issue the command, then provide the following information:

- Point: Pick a point.

Notes   A point you select with Id becomes the last point in the current editing session (stored in the *Lastpoint* variable).

See Also   Point. *System variable:* Lastpoint.

IGESIN

Menu: **File ➤ Import/Export ➤ IGES In**...

Use Igesin to import files in the Initial Graphics Exchange Standard (IGES) format.

To Import GIF Files:

Issue the command. Depending on the value of the *Filedia* system variable, the Select Iges File list box opens or the following command prompt appears:

- File name: Enter the name of the IGES file to import.

Notes You can import IGES files only to a new, empty drawing file. You cannot add information to an existing AutoCAD file.

See Also Igesout.

IGESOUT

Menu: **File ➤ Import/Export ➤ IGES Out**…

Igesout makes a copy of your current file in the IGES format.

To Copy Files in IGES Format:

Issue the command. Depending on the value of the *Filedia* system variable (1 for enable; 0 for disable), the Create IGES File list box opens or the following command prompt appears:

- File name: Enter the name of the file to save in IGES format.

See Also Igesin.

INSERT

Insert inserts blocks contained within the current file or other drawing files. The equivalent dialog box command is **Ddinsert**.

To Insert Blocks:

Issue the command, then provide the following information:

1. Block name (or ?) <last block inserted>: Enter the block or drawing name or ~ (a tilde) to display the Select Drawing File dialog box.

2. Insertion point: Enter a coordinate value, pick a point with the cursor, or enter a preset option (see "Preset Options" section below).

3. X scale factor <1> / Corner / XYZ: Enter an X scale factor, **C** for corner, **XYZ** to specify the individual X, Y, and Z scale factors, or ↵ to accept the default X scale factor of 1.

If you press ↵ without entering a value or option, the following prompt appears:

- Y scale factor (default=X): Enter a Y scale factor or ↵ to use the scale factor for the Y axis as well.

4. Rotation angle <0>: Enter the rotation angle for the block or pick a point on the screen to indicate the angle. (This last prompt does not appear if you use the *Rotate preset* option.)

● OPTIONS

~ (tilde)   Entered at the Block name... prompt, causes a dialog box to appear. The dialog box lets you select external files for insertion.

=   Replaces a block with an external file. See "Notes" section below.

X scale factor   Scales the block in the X axis. If you enter a value, you are then prompted for the Y scale factor.

Corner   Allows you to enter the X and Y scale factors simultaneously. To scale the block by a factor of 1 in the X axis and 2 in the Y axis, enter **C** at the X scale factor... prompt and then enter **@1,2**. Otherwise, enter a coordinate value or pick a point at the X scale factor... prompt to scale your block.

XYZ   Gives individual X, Y, and Z scale factors. You will be prompted for the factors.

● PRESET OPTIONS

The following options are available at the Insertion point: prompt. They are called Insert *presets* because they allow you to preset the scale and rotation angle of a block before you select an insertion point. Once you select a preset option, the dragged image will conform to the setting used; you will not be prompted for a scale factor after you select the insertion point.

Scale   Allows you to enter a single scale factor for the block. This factor governs X, Y, and Z axis scaling.

Xscale   Sets the X scale factor.

Yscale   Sets the Y scale factor.

Zscale   Sets the Z scale factor.

Rotate   Enters a rotation angle for the block.

PScale   The same as *Scale* but is used only while positioning the block for insertion to "preview" the scaled block. You are later prompted for a scale factor.

PXscale   The same as *PScale* but affects only the X scale factor.

PYscale   The same as *PScale* but affects only the Y scale factor.

PZscale   The same as *PScale* but affects only the Z scale factor.

PRotate   The same as *Rotate* but is used only while positioning the block for insertion. You are later prompted for a rotation factor.

Notes   If a block has previously been inserted, it becomes the default block for insertion (stored in the *insname* variable). Enter **?** to see a list of the blocks in the current file. Coordinate values are in relation to the current UCS.

To insert the individual entities in a block (rather than the block as a single object), type an asterisk before its name at the Block name: prompt. To bring the contents of an external file in as individual entities, insert the file in the normal way and use the **Explode** command to break it into its individual components. To insert a mirror image of a block, enter a negative value at either the X scale factor... or Y scale factor... prompt.

If the inserted block or file contains an attribute and the *Attreq* system variable is set to 1, you are prompted for the attribute information after you have entered the rotation angle. If the system variable *Attdia* is set to 1, a dialog box with the attribute prompts appears. (The default setting for *Attreq* is 1. *Attdia* is normally set to 0.)

You can also use Insert to replace or update a block with an external drawing file. For example, to replace a block named Chair1 with an external file named Chair2, enter **Chair1=Chair2** at the Block name: prompt. If the block and the external filenames are the same (Chair1, for example) enter **Chair1=**. Note, however, that named objects in the current drawing have priority over those in an imported file.

When you attempt to replace blocks containing attributes, the old attributes will remain even though the block has been changed. To avoid them, you must delete the old block, insert the new (external) block, and re-enter the attribute values. You can also use the AutoLISP utility *Attredef* (see **AutoLISP**).

Finally, an external file will be inserted with its WCS (world coordinate system) aligned with the current UCS (user coordinate system). A block will be inserted with its UCS orientation aligned with the current UCS.

See Also   Attdef, Attredef, Base, Block, Ddattdef, Ddatte, Ddattext, Ddinsert, Explode, Xref, Files. *System Variables:* Attreq, Attdia, Filedia, Insname.

ISOPLANE

Transparent: '**Isoplane**

When the snap mode is set to the Isometric style, Isoplane lets you switch the cursor orientation between the left, top, and right isometric planes.

To Change the Cursor Orientation:

Issue the command, then provide the following information:

1.   Left/Top/Right/<Toggle>: Enter your choice or press ↵ to go to the next isoplane.

2.   Current Isometric plane is: Lists the new isoplane.

Notes   Ctrl-E is a toggle control key that selects the next isometric plane in a cycle of isometric planes,

See Also   Ddrmodes, Snap. *System Variables:* Snapisopair

LAYER

Layer creates new layers, assigns colors and line types to layers, sets the current layer, represses editing of layers, and allows you to control which layers are displayed.

To Create and Modify Layers:

Issue the command, then provide the following information:

- ?/Make/Set/New/ON/OFF/Color/Ltype/Freeze/Thaw/ LOck/Unlock: Enter an option.

● OPTIONS

?   Displays the list of existing layers. Wildcards are accepted.

Make   Creates a new layer and makes it current.

Set   Makes an existing layer the current layer.

New   Creates a new layer.

On   Turns on layers.

Off   Turns off layers.

Color   Sets color of a layer.

Ltype   Sets line type of a layer.

Freeze   Freezes one or more layers.

Thaw   Unfreezes one or more layers.

Lock   Prevents editing of visible layers.

Unlock   Releases locked layers to allow editing.

Notes   All Layer options except *Make*, *Set*, and *New* allow you to enter wildcard characters (question marks and asterisks) for input. For example, if you want to turn off all layers whose names begin with G, enter **G∗** at the Layers to turn off: prompt.

The option pairs *Freeze/Thaw* and *On/Off* both control whether or not a layer is displayed. However, unlike Off, Freeze makes AutoCAD ignore objects on frozen layers. This allows faster regenerations. Freeze also affects blocks differently than Off.

Layer 0, the default layer when you open a new file, is white (number 7) and has the continuous line type. Layer 0 also has some unique properties. If you include objects on Layer 0 in a block, they take on the color and line type of the layer on which the block is inserted. The objects created with the *Byblock* option also exhibit this property. (See **Color**).

The dimension layer *Defpoints* is also unique. When it is turned off, objects on this layer are still displayed, and will appear on prints or plots.

See Also   Color, Ddlmodes, Linetype, Regen, Regenauto, Vplayer, Wildcards. *System Variables:* Player, CEColor, CELtype.

LIMITS

Transparent: '**Limits**

Menu: **Settings ➤ Drawing Limits**

Limits determines the drawing boundaries. If you use a grid, it will appear only within the limits.

To Establish Drawing Boundaries:

Issue the command. AutoCAD will indicate which limits are being set:

> Reset Model space limits:

or

> Reset Paper space limits:

Then provide the following information:

1.   ON/OFF/<lower left corner> <0.0000,0.0000>: Enter the coordinate for the lower left corner, or the On/Off option.

2.   Upper right corner <12.0000,9.0000>: Enter the coordinate for the upper right corner.

• OPTIONS

ON   Turns on the limit-checking function. This keeps your drawing activity within the drawing limits.

OFF   Turns off the limit-checking function. This allows you to draw objects without respect to the drawing limits.

<lower left corner>   Allows you to set the drawing limits by entering the coordinates for the lower left corner of the desired limits.

<upper right corner>   Allows you to set the drawing limits by entering the coordinates for the upper right corner of the desired limits.

Notes   To make the virtual screen conform to the limits of the drawing, turn on the limit-checking feature and then perform a Zoom/All operation.

The **Mvsetup** command will set the limits of your drawing automatically according to the sheet size and drawing scale you select.

The limits for Paperspace must be set independently of the Model-space limits.

See Also   Mspace, Mview, Pspace, Regen, Viewres, Zoom.*System Variables:* Limcheck, Limmin, Limmax.

LINE

Menu: **Draw ➤ Line ➤ Segments/1 Segment/Double Lines**

Line draws simple lines—either a single line or a series of lines end-to-end.

To Draw a Line:

Issue the command, then provide the following information:

1.   From point: Select a point to begin the line.

2.   To point: Select the line end point.

3.   To point: Continue to select points to draw consecutive lines or press ↵ to exit the Line command.

● OPTIONS

C   Closes a series of lines, connecting the last start point and the last end point with a line.

↵   At the From point: prompt, lets you continue a series of lines from a previously entered line, arc, point, or polyline. If the last object drawn is an arc, the line is drawn at a tangent from the end of the arc.

U   At the To point: prompt, deletes the last line segment.

To Draw Double Lines:

Issue the command **Dline** or pick **Double Lines** from the Draw ➤ Line menu, then provide the following information:

•   Break/Caps/Dragline/Offset/Snap/Undo/Width/ <start point>: Enter desired option or pick beginning point for double line.

• OPTIONS

Break   Prompts you to break an existing line at the beginning and end of a double line:

Break Dlines at start and end points? OFF/<ON>:

With Break on, any line for which you use the *Snap* option at the beginning or end of a Dline will be broken between the double lines. This automatically joins two double lines in a T-shaped intersection.

Caps   Specifies whether or not to cap either or both endpoints of the double line. An *Auto* option caps a double line at the end that is not located using the *Snap* option.

Dragline   Specifies where the double lines appear relative to the points you pick: to the left, right, or centered. It also specifies the width of the double line.

Offset   Locates the beginning of a double line relative to another existing location, such as the corner of a room. The prompts are as follows:

1.   Offset from:

2.   Offset toward:

3.   Enter the offset distance:

Snap   Begins or ends a double line by snapping to an existing object. Snap controls the range in pixels to which objects will be snapped.

Undo   Backs up a line segment, much like the *U* option under the **Line** command.

Width   Controls the width of the double line.

Arc   Draws double arcs. The arc prompt changes to offer a *Line* option, allowing you to return to drawing straight double lines.

Close   Closes a series of double line segments, much like the Close option under the **Line** command.

Notes   You can convert lines to polylines using the **Pedit** command.

See Also   AutoLISP, Osnap, Pedit, Pline.

LINETYPE

Transparent: **'Linetype**

Linetype enables you to control the type of line you can draw. The default linetype is continuous or solid, but you can choose from several other types, such as a dotted or dashed line or a combination of the two (see FIGURE 30). Several predefined line types are stored in a file called *Acad.LIN*. You can list these line types by entering a question mark at the Linetype prompt.

To Change the Line Type:

Issue the command, then provide the following information:

1.   ?/Create/Load/Set: Enter the option name.

2.   When the *Filedia* system variable is set to 0, the following prompts occur at the command line:

  a. **?**: Specifies linetype file, displaying the message Linetypes defined in C:\ACAD12\SUPPORT \ACAD.LIN.

  b. Create: Prompts for Name of linetype to create:.

  c. Load: Prompts for Linetype(s) to load:. To load all linetypes defined in your *Acad.LIN* file, enter an asterisk at the prompt File to search <ACAD.LIN>:, then press ↵ .

  d. Set: Prompts for New entity linetype (or ?) <BY LAYER>:.

  When the *Filedia* system variable is set to 1, similar command-line prompts open a series of file dialog list boxes. If the *Acad.LIN* file is present in the edit box, pick OK.

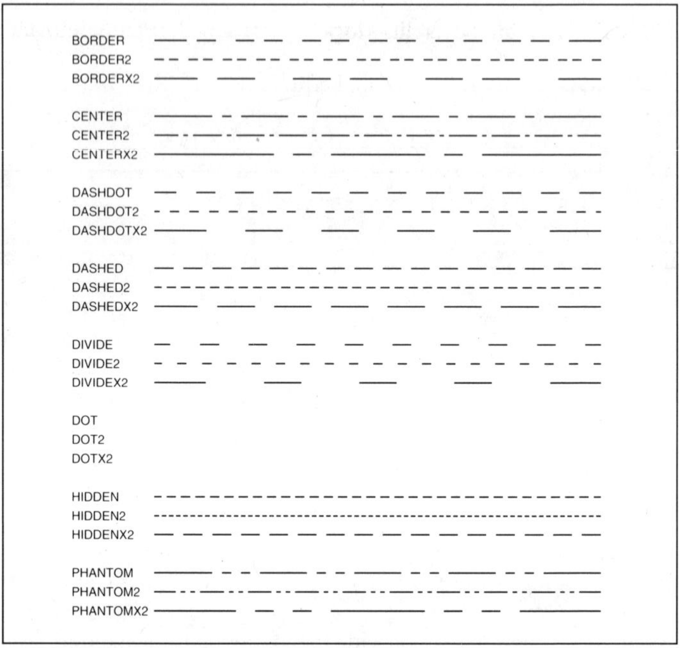

Figure 30: The standard AutoCAD line types

● OPTIONS

?   Lists available line types in a specified external line type file.

Create   Creates a new line type.

Load   Loads a line type from a specified line type file.

Set   Sets the current default line type.

Notes   The *Create* option first prompts you for a line type name. This name can be any alphanumeric string of thirty-one characters or less. (Although the status line will only display the first eight characters). You are then prompted for the name of the file in which to store your line type. Next, you enter a description of the line type. Finally, you enter the line type pattern on the next line, where you will see an *A* followed by a comma and the cursor. Enter a string of

numeric values separated by commas. These values should represent the lengths of lines as they will be plotted. Positive values represent the "drawn" portion of the line; negative values represent the
"pen up," or blank, portion of the line; and a zero indicates a dot.

You can assign line types to layers or to individual objects. Use the
Ltscale command to make the scale of the line types correspond
with the scale of your drawing.

A line type may appear continuous even though it is a noncontinuous type. Several things can affect the appearance of line types.
For example, if the drawing scale is not 1:1, the **Ltscale** must be set
to correspond with your drawing scale. If the drawing scale is ¼"
equals 1', the Ltscale must be set to 48. A low *Viewres* value can also
affect appearance, making line types appear continuous on-screen
even though they plot as a noncontinuous line type. Regenerating
exhibits the true appearance of linetypes.

To display a list of linetypes currently loaded in your drawing, pick
the *Ltype...* button from the Ddlmodes dialog box or use the
Linetype command options *Set*, *?*, then * or click on **Settings... ➤
Entity Modes... ➤ Linetype...**.

See Also   Ddemodes, Ddlmodes, Layer, Viewres. *System Variables:* Ltscale, Plinegen, Psltscale.

LIST

Menu: **Assist ➤ Inquiry ➤ List**

List displays most of the properties of an object, including coordinate location, color, layer, and line type. List informs you if the
object is a block or text. If the object is text, List gives its height,
style, and width factor. If the object is a block, List gives its X, Y, and
Z scale and insertion point. Attribute tags, defaults, and current
values are also listed, if available. If the object is a polyline, the coordinate values for all its vertices are listed. You can also use List to
identify hatch-pattern scale and angle.

To List Properties of an Object:

Issue the command, then provide the following information:

- Select objects: Pick the objects whose properties you wish to see.

Notes   Listing entities causes AutoCAD to flip the screen to text mode and pause when the response is lengthy. Pressing ⏎ continues you through successive screens, then returns you to the command line and the graphics mode.

See Also   Dblist.

LOAD

Use Load to load a shape definition file. Like text and blocks, shapes are single objects made up of lines and arcs.

To Load a Shape:

Issue the command. Depending on the value of the *Filedia* system variable, the Select Shape files dialog list box opens or the following command-line prompt appears:

- Name of shape file to load (or ?): Enter the name of the shape file, excluding the .SHX file extension.

Notes   You can define shapes using the Shape code. Consult your *AutoCAD Customization Manual* for details. You can use shape definitions in place of blocks for frequently used symbols. They draw more quickly and use less file space.

See Also   Shape. *System Variables:* Shpname.

LTSCALE

Transparent: '**Ltscale**

Ltscale controls the scale of line types. Normally, line type definitions are created for a scale of 1:1. For larger scale drawings, 1:20 for example, set Ltscale so that line types fit the drawing scale. Ltscale globally adjusts all line type definitions to the value you give to Ltscale.

To Set the Scale of Linetypes:

Issue the command, then provide the following information:

- New scale factor <current default>: Enter the desired scale factor.

Notes Ltscale forces a drawing regeneration when *Regenauto* is on. If Regenauto is turned off, you won't see the effects of Ltscale until you issue **Regen**.

See Also Linetype. *System Variables:* Ltscale, Psltscale

MEASURE

Menu: **Construct ➤ Measure**

Measure marks an object into divisions of a specified length. Measurement begins at the end of the object closest to the pick point. If the object does not divide evenly by the specified length, the remaining portion will be located at the end farthest from the picked point.

To Measure an Object:

Issue the command, then provide the following information:

1. Select object to measure: Pick a single object.

2. <Segment length>/Block: Enter the length of the segments to mark or the name of the block to use for marking.

● OPTIONS

Block   Establishes an existing, user-defined block as a marking device. You are prompted for a block name and asked if you want to align the block with the object.

Notes   By default, Measure uses a point as a marker. Often, a point is difficult to see when placed over a line or arc. Set the *Pdmode* and *Pdsize* system variables to change the appearance of the points, or select the *Block* option and use a block in place of the point.

The *Block* option is useful if you need to draw a series of objects a specified distance apart along a curved path. For example, to draw identical parking stalls for vehicles, create a block consisting of a line (or stripe) and identify the block name in Step 2.

See Also   Block, Divide, Point, Ddptype

MENU

Menu loads a custom menu file. Once you have loaded a menu into a drawing, that drawing file will include the menu filename. The next time you open the drawing file, AutoCAD will also attempt to load the last menu used with the file.

To Load a Custom Menu:

Issue the command, then provide the following information:

- If the *Filedia* system variable is set to 1, the Select Menu File dialog list box appears. Use this box to select the menu file you want to use.

- If *Filedia* is not set to 1, respond to the following prompt at the command line:

  - Menu filename or . for none <acad>: Enter the menu filename.

Notes You can customize the *Acad.MNU* file using a text editor, then AutoCAD will load a recompiled .MNX version of the same filename. Your first attempt at customizing may be to change the commands assigned to the buttons on your cursor or pointing device. Locked menus create files of the same name with an .MKX extension.

Release 12 also offers a .MNL file which may contain AutoLISP routines specified in the .MNU file.

See Also *System Variables:* Menuctl, Menuecho, Menuname.

MINSERT

Minsert simultaneously inserts a block and creates a rectangular array of that block. You can rotate the array by specifying an angle other than 0 at the Rotation angle: prompt.

To Insert Multiple Objects:

The prompts for Minsert are similar to those for **Insert**, except for the following:

1. Rotation Angle <0>: Enter the array angle.

2. Number of rows (---) <1>: Enter the number of rows in the block array. If the number of rows is greater than 1, one of the following prompts appears:

  - Unit cell or distance between rows (---): Enter the distance between rows. Selecting *Unit cell* requires picking two points with your cursor; after picking the first corner with your cursor, you are prompted for the Other corner:.

3.   Number of columns (| | |) <1>: Enter the number of columns in the block array. If the number of columns is greater than 1, the following prompt appears:

   • Distance between columns (| | |): Enter the distance or select the distance using your cursor.

A row-and-column array of the block will then appear at the specified angle.

Notes   The entire array acts like one block. Unlike **Insert**, Minsert does not permit you to explode a block or use an asterisk option. Listing the Minsert entities will provide such information as number of columns, number of rows, and their spacing. Inserting a block with Minsert groups the entities into a single entity.

See **Insert** for a description of the additional prompts not described here.

See Also   Array, Insert.

MIRROR/MIRROR 3D

Menu: **Construct ➤ Mirror, Construct ➤ Mirror 3D**

Mirror makes a mirror-image copy of an object or a group of objects.

To Mirror Objects:

Issue the command, then provide the following information:

1.   Select objects: Pick the objects to be mirrored.

2.   First point of mirror line: Pick one end of the mirror axis. If you selected Mirror 3D, you see the prompt Plane by Entity/Last/Z axis/View/XY/YZ/ZX/<3points>:. You then define a plane and an axis for the mirror.

3. Second point: Pick the other end of the mirror axis.

4. Delete old objects? <N>: Enter **Y** to delete the originally selected objects or **N** to keep them.

If you have enabled grips for mirroring, the sequence of steps is:

1. Select the object(s) to be mirrored and the grips will appear as the entities are highlighted.

2. Pick one of the grips as your "base" point. (A base, or selected, grip appears as a solid filled rectangle.) The Stretch mode prompt then appears at the command line.

3. Cycle through the grip mode commands pressing ⏎, the space bar, or entering **mirror** or **mi** a sufficient number of times until the following prompt appears:

MIRROR

<Second point>/Base point/Copy/Undo/eXit:

4. To mirror the image *without retaining* the original object(s), and using the selected grip as the base or first point of the mirror line, drag your cursor and pick the second point of the mirror-line axis. To mirror the image while *retaining* the original object(s), and using the selected grip as the base point, enter **C** for *Copy* and pick the second point of the mirror-line axis. (You can hold the Shift key and drag your cursor to pick the second point instead of enter ing **C**.) Then press ⏎ to exit.

- To select a new base point, enter **B** prior to picking the second point or before entering **C**.

● OPTIONS

B or *Base point*   Disengages the cursor from the selected grip so you can assign a new base point for the first point of the mirror-line axis.

C, *Copy*, or *Shift*   Makes a duplicate of original object(s).

U or *Undo*   Allows you to undo the previous operation.

X, eXit, or ↵   Exits the command.

Notes   Normally, text, attributes, and attribute definition entities are mirrored. To prevent this, set the *Mirrtext* system variable to 0.

Mirroring occurs in a plane parallel to the current UCS (user coordinate system).

Use the *Select Settings* area of the Grips dialog box to enable grips.

Select **Construct ➤ Mirror 3D** from the pull-down menu or enter **Mirror3D** to duplicate selected entities about an arbitrary plane. Consult your *AutoCAD Extras Manual* for details.

See Also   Ddgrips. *System Variables:* Mirrtext.

MOVE

Menu: **Modify ➤ Move**

Moves a single object or a set of objects.

To Move Objects:

Issue the command, then provide the following information:

1. Select objects: Select the objects to be moved.

2. Base point or displacement: Pick the reference or "base" point for the move.

3. Second point of displacement: Pick the distance and direction in relation to the base point or enter the displacement value.

If you have enabled grips for moving, the prompts for Steps 1 and 2 and the options are the same as for **Mirror**, except for the following:

• Cycle through the grip mode commands using ↵ or the spacebar, or entering **Move** or **M** a sufficient number of times until you see the following prompt:

MOVE
<Move to point>/Base point/Copy/Undo/eXit:

- To move the object(s) with the selected grip as the base, drag your cursor and pick the second or displacement point. To move the object(s) using a new base point, enter **B** to pick your first reference point or enter coordinate values, then pick the second point of displacement.

Notes   AutoCAD assumes you want to move objects within the current UCS. However, you can move objects in three-dimensional space by entering XYZ coordinates or using the Osnap overrides to pick objects in three-dimensional space.

If you press ⏎ at the Second point: prompt without entering a point value, the objects selected may be moved to a position completely off your drawing area. Use the **U** or **Undo** command to recover.

To make multiple copies of the selected object(s), follow the bulleted steps above to define your base point, then hold the Shift key while picking the first copy point (to set copy mode on), and continue by picking additional points. (Entering **C** after selecting the base point will provide the same results.) Exit the command by pressing ⏎.

Pressing the Shift key in the last step to copy the first object from its source point to a destination point will set an automatic snap mode based on these two points. To apply *Multiple copy* using the snap mode, hold the Shift key down while copying additional objects.

See Also   Ddgrips.

MSLIDE

Mslide saves the current view in a Slide file. (Slide files have .SLD extensions.)

To Save as an .SLD File:

Issue the command. When the *Filedia* system variable is set to 1, the Create Slide File dialog list box is displayed or the following prompt appears:

- File name <current filename>: Enter desired filename, excluding extension.

See Also   Delay, Script, Vslide.

MSPACE

Menu: **View ➤ Model Space**

Mspace lets you move from Paperspace to Modelspace when **Tilemode** is set to 0.

Notes   If the **Tilemode** system variable is set to 0 but no viewports are available in Paperspace, you will receive the message There are no active Modelspace Viewports:.

See Also   Mview, Pspace, Tilemode.

MULTIPLE

Multiple lets you enact multiple repetitions of a command.

Notes At the command prompt, enter **Multiple**, a space, and then the command. The command repeats until you press Ctrl-C.

MVIEW

Menu: **View ➤ Mview**

You will see a cascading menu showing the options described later.

Mview creates Paperspace viewport entities and controls the visibility of viewports. This command works in Paperspace only.

To Create a Paperspace Viewport:

Issue the command, then provide the following information:

- ON/OFF/Hideplot/Fit/2/3/4/Restore/<First point>:
  Pick a point indicating one corner of the new Paperspace viewport or enter an option. If you pick a point, you are prompted for the opposite corner. Mview then creates the viewport.

• OPTIONS

ON/OFF Turns the display of Modelspace on or off within the chosen viewport. When a viewport's Modelspace display is turned off, it no longer regenerates when it is moved or resized. This is helpful when you are rearranging a set of viewports.

Hideplot Controls hidden line removal for individual viewports at plot time. When you select this option, the Select objects: prompt appears. Pick the viewport you wish to have plotted with hidden lines removed. Selecting an entity inside the viewport will not select the viewport, you must pick the edge or border.

Fit   Creates a single viewport that fills the screen.

2/3/4   Lets you create two, three, or four viewports simulta-neously. Once you enter one of these options, different prompts appear, followed by Fit/<first point>:. Selecting **2** prompts for Horizontal/<Vertical>:; selecting **3** prompts for Horizontal/Verti-cal/Above/Below/Left/<Right>:. Pick points to indicate the location of the viewports, or select the *Fit* option to force the viewports to fit in the display area. If you choose Fit, you are further prompted for the orientation of the viewports.

Restore   Translates viewport configurations created using the **Vport** command (Modelspace viewports) into Paperspace viewport entities. You are prompted for the name of a viewport configuration.

Notes   The **Tilemode** system variable must be set to 0 to use Mview. If you are in Modelspace when you issue Mview, you receive the message:

Switching to Paperspace.

Grid and Snap modes as well as layer visibility can be set in-dividually within each Paperspace viewport.

Viewports, like most other entities, can be moved, copied, stretched, or erased. You can hide viewport borders by changing their layer assignments, then turning off their layers. You can also align positions of objects in one viewport with those of another using the **Mvsetup** utility. Viewport scale can be set using the *xp* option under the **Zoom** command.

See Also   Mspace, Mvsetup, Pspace, Tilemode, Vplayer, Vports, Zoom/xp. *System Variables:* Psltscale.

MVSETUP

Menu: **View ➤ Layout ➤ MV Setup**

Sets up the Paperspace of a drawing including viewports, drawing scale, and sheet title block.

To Set up a Paperspace:

Issue the command. On a new drawing with **Tilemode** set to 1, the following prompt appears:

Paperspace/Modelspace is disabled. The pre-R11 setup will be invoked unless it is enabled. Enable Paper/Modelspace?<Y>:

Enter **No** to use the setup method in AutoCAD Releases 9 and 10 (see **Setup**). If you press ⏎ to accept the default **Y**, it sets the Tilemode system variable to 0, and brings up the following prompt:

Align/Create/Scale viewports/Options/Title block/Undo:

• OPTIONS

Align   Aligns locations in one viewport with locations in another viewport. You receive the prompt Angled/Horizontal/Vertical alignment/Rotate view/Undo?:.

Angled   Aligns locations by indicating an angle and distance. You are prompted to pick a base point to which others can be aligned. Next, you are prompted to pick a point in another viewport that you want aligned with the base point. You are then prompted for a distance and angle.

Horizontal/Vertical alignment   Aligns views either horizontally or vertically. You are prompted for a base point (the point to be aligned to) and the point to be aligned with the base point.

Rotate view   Rotates a view in a viewport. You are prompted for a viewport and base point, and then for the angle of rotation.

Create viewports   Creates new viewports. You receive the prompt Delete objects/Undo/<Create viewports>:.

Delete objects   Deletes existing viewport entities.

<Create viewports> displays a list of options for creating viewports:

0: None
1: Single
2: Std. Engineering

3: Array of Viewports

Redisplay/<Number of entry to load>:

0 (None) creates no viewports. *1 (Single)* creates a single viewport for which you specify the area. *2 (Std. Engineering)* creates four viewports set up in quadrants. You can set up these views for top, front, right side, and isometric. *3 (Array of Viewports)* creates a matrix of viewports by specifying the number of viewports in the X and Y axes. The *Add/Delete* option on the prompt adds or deletes options from the list. *Add* provides a title block for the list. *Redisplay* lets you view the list again.

Scale viewports   Sets the scale between Paperspace and the viewport. For example, if your drawing in Modelspace is scaled to ¼" = 1', and your title block in Paperspace is scaled to 1" = 1", you will want the scale factor of your viewport to be 48. When you select this option the prompt Select the viewports to scale: appears. Once you've selected more than one viewport, the prompt Set zoom scale factors for viewports. Interactive/<Uniform>: appears. The Interactive option sets the scale of each selected viewport individually. You are prompted for the Number of paperspace units:, then the Number of modelspace units:. In the ¼" scale example, you would enter **1** for the Paperspace units and **48** for the Modelspace units.

Title block   Produces the prompt Delete objects/Origin/-Undo/<Insert title block>:. *Delete objects* deletes objects from Paperspace. *Origin* sets a new origin point for Paperspace. *<Insert title block>* displays the following:

Available paper/output sizes:

0: None

1: ISO A4 Size (mm)

2: ISO A3 Size (mm)

3: ISO A2 Size (mm)

4: ISO A1 Size (mm)

5: ISO A0 Size (mm)

6: ANSI-V Size (in)

7: ANSI-A Size (in)

8: ANSI-B Size (in)

9: ANSI-C Size (in)

10: ANSI-D Size (in)

11: ANSI-E Size (in)

12: Arch/Engineering (24 X 36)

13: Generic D size Sheet (24 X 36in)

Add/Delete/Redisplay/<Number of entry to load>:

Enter the number corresponding to the title block you want to use. *Add* and *Delete* let you add or delete a title block to the list. Add prompts you for the name you wish to have appear on the list and the name of the file to be used as the title block. *Redisplay* lets you view the list again.

Undo   Undoes an option without leaving the Mvsetup utility.

Notes   When adding a title block to the list in the title block option, you must already have a title block drawing ready and in the current DOS path.

The *Xp* option under the **Zoom** command can also be used to set the scale of a viewport.

Mvsetup saves the current configuration to a file called *Mvsetup.DFS*.

See Also   Mspace, Mview, Pspace, Setup, Tilemode, Zoom

NEW

Menu: **File ➤ New**

Lets you start a new drawing from scratch or use an existing drawing as a template for a new drawing.

To Begin a New Drawing:

Issue the command, then provide information as needed in the dialog or subdialog box(es).

If the *Filedia* system variable is set to 0, and you are working in an unnamed drawing, the Drawing Modification dialog box opens to alert you that the current drawing has been changed. Three options are provided: *Save Changes…*, *Discard Changes*, or *Cancel Command*.

If the *Filedia* system variable is set to 1, and you are working in an unnamed drawing, the Create New Drawing dialog box opens. You can enter the new drawing name in the edit box or pick the *New Drawing Name…* button. This button opens the Create Drawing Files dialog list box.

You can also assign a template or Prototype drawing name when opening a new drawing.

To Use the Current Drawing as a Template:

In the *New Drawing Name…* edit box or at the Enter NAME of drawing: prompt, enter the new filename followed by an equals sign and the name of the file you wish to use as a template. For example, you could enter **new=template**. There should be no spaces between the equal sign and the filenames. Drive and directory specifications can be included.

If *Filedia* is 1, the template name can also be entered in the *Prototype…* edit box.

Notes   Since AutoCAD opens directly to the screen, your drawing session opens to the graphic screen without a name. If no changes were made to your current drawing and you begin a new drawing, the command prompt appears without the Drawing Modification dialog box. The Drawing Modification dialog box is always displayed to save any edited or unsaved drawings before opening a new drawing.

AutoCAD uses a file called *Acad.DWG* as the prototype file for all new drawings. If you want different default settings for your new drawings you can open *Acad.DWG* and set it up the way you want. This file is in the *AutoCAD* directory or in the *Support* subdirectory off the AutoCAD directory.

If you have a nonstandard prototype *Acad.DWG* file and you want to open a file using the standard AutoCAD defaults, type an equals sign after the new filename. If you get the message that AutoCAD cannot find the prototype file, you can create it by entering **ACAD=** in the edit box or at the command prompt.

See Also   Open, Save, Qsave, End, Quit. *System Variables:* Filedia, Dwgname, Dwgtitled, Savename.

OFFSET

Menu: **Construct ➤ Offset**

Offset creates an object parallel to and at a specified distance from its original.

To Offset a Line:

Issue the command, then provide the following information:

1. Offset distance or Through <Through>: Enter a distance value to specify a constant distance to offset, or **T** to specify an offset through-point after each object selection is made.

- Entering a distance value prompts for Side to offset:. Pick the side on which you want the offset to appear. You are then prompted for a Second point:. Pick another point. The distance between the starting point and the second point becomes the default offset distance.

- Selecting *Through* by entering **T** or pressing ↵ prompts you for the Through point:. Pick a point to locate the offset line.

2. Select object to offset: Pick one object.

● OPTIONS

Offset Distance   If you enter a value at the Distance prompt, all the offsets performed in the current command will be at that distance. The prompt will continue offsetting objects at the specified distance until you press ↵.

Through   Identifies a point through which the offset object will pass after you have selected the object to offset. The prompt will continue prompting for the next point until you press ↵.

Notes   Very complex polylines may offset incorrectly or not at all. When this happens it usually means that there is insufficient memory to process the offset or that the offset distance exceeds the command's ability to offset properly.

You cannot perform offsets on objects unless they lie in a plane parallel to the current UCS (user coordinate system). Also, if you are not viewing the current UCS in plan, you may get an erroneous result.

Window, *Crossing*, *Fence*, *WPolygon*, *CPolygon*, and *Last* are not valid selections for Offset.

The offset distance is stored in the system variable *Offsetdist* as the default. If the value is negative, it defaults to Through mode.

See Also   Copy. *System Variables:* Offsetdist.

OLE

Menu: **Edit ➤ Copy Object**

OLE (Object Linking and Embedding) is a Windows feature that lets you link-paste or embed-paste an AutoCAD drawing into another document that supports OLE. An AutoCAD drawing can be link-pasted into a word processor or desktop publishing document. Whenever the AutoCAD drawing changes, the linked application will detect the change and give you the option to update the pasted image. Embed-paste lets you edit a pasted image by double-clicking on it. AutoCAD will start up and the file associated with the image will open.

Notes   To use OLE for a cut and paste operation, use **Edit ➤ Copy Object** to cut AutoCAD images to the clipboard. Consult the manual of the receiving application for information on pasting a linked or embedded document.

OOPS

Menu: **Modify ➤ Erase ➤ Oops!**

Oops restores objects that have been accidentally removed from a drawing.

Notes   Oops retrieves all objects erased by the last **Erase** only.

See Also   Undo, U.

OPEN

Menu: **File ➤ Open**…

Opens an existing drawing.

To Open an Existing Drawing:

Issue the command.

If the *Filedia* system variable is set to 0, and you are working in an unnamed drawing, Open responds the same as **New**, displaying the following command line prompt:

- Enter name of drawing <current default>: Enter the name of your existing drawing. Entering a non-existent drawing will not do anything.

If the *Filedia* system variable is set to 1, the Open Drawing list box displays files and directories for selection. The existing drawing can be retrieved in a *Read Only Mode* or you can *Select Initial View*.

• OPTIONS

Read Only Mode   Drawings that are open in Read Only Mode can be edited and saved to a new name. You can't save changes to the drawing's original name. You are alerted if you try to save changes to a drawing file that is write-protected.

Select Initial View   To open a drawing to a saved view, pick from the Select Initial View dialog box and highlight a view name.

See Also   New, Save, Qsave, End, Quit. *System Variables:* Dwgname, Dwgwrite, Filedia, Savefile, Savename, Savetime.

ORTHO

Transparent: 'Ortho

Menu: **Settings ➤ Drawing Aids, O Button on toolbar**

Ortho forces lines to be drawn in exactly perpendicular directions following the orientation of the crosshairs.

Notes   If you enter Ortho through the keyboard, you are prompted to turn Ortho on or off. Use the F8 function key, the Ctrl-O key combination, or click on the **O** button on the toolbar to toggle between Ortho On and Ortho Off.

If you pick Ortho from the pull-down menu, it retrieves the Ddrmodes dialog box.

To force lines to angles other than 90 degrees, rotate the cursor using the *Snapang* system variable or by setting the *Rotate* option under the **Snap** command.

See Also   Ddrmodes, Snap. *System Variables:* Snapang, Orthmode.

OSNAP

Transparent: '**Osnap**

Sets the current default Object Snap mode, allowing you to pick specific geometric points on an object. You can have several Object Snap modes active at once if you separate their names by commas. For example, to be able to select endpoints and midpoints automatically, enter **END,MID** at the Osnap prompt. AutoCAD knows to select the correct point (MID, END, etc.) according to which point is closer to the target box. The equivalent dialog box command is **Ddosnap**.

To Pick Specific Geometric Points:

Issue the command, then provide the following information:

• Object snap modes: Enter the desired default Object snap mode(s).

● OPTIONS

CENter   Picks the center of circles and arcs.

ENDpoint   Picks the end point of objects.

INSert   Picks the insertion point of blocks and text.

INTersect   Picks the intersection of objects.

MIDpoint   Picks the midpoint of lines and arcs.

NEArest   Picks the point on an object nearest to the cursor.

NODe   Picks a point object. (See *Point*.)

PERpend   Picks the point on an object perpendicular to the end point of the line you are drawing.

QUAdrant   Picks a cardinal point on an arc or circle.

Quick   Shortens the time it takes AutoCAD to find an object snap point. Quick does not work in conjunction with *INTersect*.

Tangent   Picks a tangent point on a circle or arc.

NONE   Disables the current default Object snap mode. Entering **Off** or pressing ↵ at the Object snap modes: prompt does the same.

Notes   You can use the Osnap overrides whenever you are prompted to select a point or object. Enter the first three letters of the name of the override or pick the override from the **Assist Object Snap** pull-down menu, the **Asterisks** side menu, or the **Shift-right Click** popup menu. Unlike the Osnap mode settings, the overrides are active only at the time they are issued.

The *Acad.MNU* file supplied with AutoCAD assigns the third button (blue for some pucks) to the cursor menu on a four-button puck or pointing device. (Pointing devices with two buttons can open the cursor menu by holding the Shift key down while pressing the second button.) Picking this button displays a pull-down menu of osnaps, filters, and a calculator at the cursor's current position on the graphics screen.

See Also   Aperture, Ddosnap. *System Variables:* Osmode.

PAN

Transparent: '**Pan**

Menu: **View ➤ Pan**

Pan shifts the display to reveal parts of a drawing that are offscreen. Retains the same magnification.

To See Offscreen Drawing Areas:

Issue the command, then provide the following information:

1. Displacement: Pick the first point of view displacement.

2. Second point: Pick the distance and direction of displacement.

Notes   You cannot use Pan while viewing a drawing in perspective. Use the **Dview** command's Pan option instead.

See Also   Dview/Pan, View, Zoom.

PEDIT

Menu: **Modify ➤ Polyline Edit**

Pedit edits two- or three-dimensional polylines and three-dimensional meshes, changes the location of individual vertices in a polyline or mesh, and converts a non-polyline object into a polyline. The editing options available depend on the type of object you select. See the following sections for information about individual Pedit operations.

PEDIT FOR 2D AND 3D POLYLINES

Modifies the shape of 2D and 3D polylines. If the object you select is not a polyline, accept the default for the prompt Do you want to turn it into one? <Y>: Y.

To Edit Polylines:

Issue the Pedit command, then select the object you want to edit as a polyline.

- If the object selected is a 2D polyline, the following prompt appears:

  Close/Join/Width/Edit vertex/Fit/Spline/Decurve/Ltype gen Undo/eXit <X>:

- If the object is a 3D polyline, the following prompt appears:

  Close/Edit vertex/Spline curve/Decurve/Undo/eXit <X>:

  (If the polyline is closed, Open appears instead of Close in the prompt above.)

- If the object is a standard line or arc, the following prompt appears:

  Entity selected is not a polyline:

  Do you want it to turn into one: <Y>: Enter Y or N.

● OPTIONS

Close   Joins the end points of a polyline. If the selected polyline is already closed, this option is replaced by *Open* in the prompt.

Open   Deletes the last line segment in a closed polyline.

Join   Joins polylines, lines, and arcs. The objects to be joined must meet exactly end-to-end.

Width   Sets the width of the entire polyline.

Edit vertex   Performs various edits on polyline vertices. See section below on Pedit/Edit vertex.

Fit curve   Changes a polyline made up of straight line segments into a smooth curve.

Spline curve   Changes a polyline made up of straight line segments into a smooth spline curve.

Decurve   Changes a smoothed polyline into one made up of straight line segments.

Ltype gen   Causes the line type to continue uniformly around the vertices of the polyline when turned on.

Undo   Rescinds the last Pedit function issued.

eXit   Exits the Pedit command.

Notes   The *Spline curve* option adjusts the "pull" of the vertex points on the curve by changing the *Splinetype* system variable. The default for *Splinetype* is 6. With *Splinetype* set to 5, the pull is greater. See **System Variables** for more details.

You can view both the curve and the defining vertex points of a Spline curve by setting the *Splframe* system variable to 1.

The *Splinesegs* system variable determines the number of line segments used to draw the curve. A higher value generates more line segments for a smoother curve, but also a larger drawing file.

See Also   Pedit/Edit Vertex, Pedit/3D mesh, Pline, Setvar/ Splframe, Setvar/Splinesegs, Setvar/Splinetype.

PEDIT/EDIT VERTEX

Relocates, removes, moves, or inserts vertices in a polyline. Modifies a polyline's width at a particular vertex and alters the tangent direction of a curved polyline through a vertex.

To Edit a Polyline Vertex:

Issue the Pedit command, then select the polyline object you want to edit.

1.   Close/Join/Width/Edit vertex/Fit/Spline/Decurve/ Ltype gen /Undo/eXit <X>: Enter **E** for *Edit vertex*. An X appears on the first vertex of the selected polyline indicating the vertex currently editable.

2.   Next/Previous/Break/Insert/Move/Regen/Straighten/ Tangent/Width/eXit <N>: Enter the capitalized letter of the function to be used.

● OPTIONS

Next   Moves the X marker to the next vertex.

Previous   Moves the X marker to the previous vertex.

Break   Breaks polyline from the marked vertex. Move the X into the position where you want the break to begin and type **B** for Break. The prompt changes to

   Next/Previous/Go/eXit <N>:

Then move the marker to another vertex to select the other end of the break. Once the X marker is in position, enter **G** to initiate the break.

Insert   Inserts a new vertex. A rubber-banding line stretches from the vertex being edited to the cursor. Enter points either using the cursor or by keying in coordinates.

Move   Allows relocation of a vertex. A rubber-banding line stretches from the vertex being edited to the cursor. You can specify points either using the cursor or by keying in coordinates.

Regen   Regenerates a polyline. This may be required to see effects of some edits.

Straighten   Straightens a polyline between two vertices. Move the cursor to the position where you want the straightening to begin and enter **S**. The prompt changes to

   Next/Previous/Go/eXit <N>:

This allows you to move in either direction along the polyline. Once the X marker (see "Notes" below) is in position, type **G** to straighten the polyline. This removes all vertices between the two markers and creates one segment instead.

Tangent   Allows you to attach a tangent direction to a vertex for later use in curve fitting. A rubber-banding line stretches from the vertex to the cursor, indicating the new tangent direction. Indicate the new tangent angle by picking the direction using the cursor or by keying in an angle value. Tangent only affects curve-fitted or spline polylines.

Width   Varies the width of a polyline segment. When you have entered this function, the prompt changes to Enter starting width <current default width>: This allows you to enter a new width for the currently marked vertex. When you have entered a value, the prompt changes to Enter ending width <last value entered>: This allows you to enter a width for the next vertex.

eXit   Exits from vertex editing.

Notes   When you invoke the *Edit vertex* option, an X appears on the polyline, indicating that the vertex is being edited. Press ⏎ to issue the default N for *Next vertex* and move the X to the next vertex. Type **P** to reverse the direction of the X. When inserting a new vertex or using the *Width* function, pay special attention to the direction the X moves when you select the *Next* function. This is the direction along the polyline in which the new vertex or the new ending width will be inserted.

If you select a 3D polyline, all the edit options except *Tangent* and *Width* are available. Also, point input accepts 3D points.

PEDIT FOR 3D MESHES

Smooths a 3D mesh or moves vertex points in the mesh.

To Edit a 3D Mesh:

Issue the Pedit command, then select a mesh. You will be prompted to choose one of the following options:

    Edit vertex/Smooth surface/Desmooth/Mclose/Nclose/Undo/
    eXit <X>:

● OPTIONS

Edit vertex   Relocates vertices of a selected 3D mesh. When you select this option, you get the prompt:

Vertex (m,n)

Next/Previous/Left/Right/Up/Down/Move/REgen/eXit <N>:
<option>

An X appears on the first vertex of the mesh, marking the vertex to be moved.

Next   Rapidly moves the Edit vertex marker to the next vertex.

Previous   Rapidly moves the Edit vertex marker to the previous vertex.

Left   Moves the Edit vertex marker along the N direction of the mesh.

Right   Moves the Edit vertex marker along the N direction of the mesh opposite to the Left option.

Up   Moves the Edit vertex marker along the M direction of the mesh.

Down   Moves the Edit vertex marker along the M direction of the mesh opposite to the Up direction.

Move   Moves the location of the currently marked vertex.

REgen   Redisplays the mesh after a vertex has been moved.

Smooth surface   Generates a B-spline or Bezier surface based on the mesh's vertex points. The type of surface generated depends on the *Surftype* system variable.

Desmooth   Returns a smoothed surface back to regular mesh.

Mclose   Closes a mesh in the M direction.

Nclose   Closes a mesh in the N direction.

Mopen   Appears when a mesh is closed to open a mesh in the M direction.

Nopen Appears when a mesh is closed to open a mesh in the N direction.

Undo Rescinds the last Pedit option issued.

eXit Exits the Edit vertex option or the Pedit command.

Notes You can use several system variables (see **Setvar**) to modify a 3D mesh. To determine the type of smooth surface generated, use the *Surftype* variable with the *Smooth* option. A value of 5 gives you a quadratic B-spline surface; a value of 6 gives a cubic B-spline surface; and 8 gives a Bezier surface. The default value for *Surftype* is 6.

The *Surfu* and *Surfv* system variables control the accuracy of the generated surface. *Surfu* controls the surface density in the M direction of the mesh, and *Surfv* controls density in the N direction. The default value for these variables is 6.

The *Splframe* system variable determines whether the control mesh of a smoothed mesh is displayed. If it is set to 0, only the smoothed mesh is displayed. If it is set to 1, only the defining mesh is displayed.

See **Bpoly** for automatically grouping lines together into a single entity by picking the internal region.

See Also Bpoly, Splframe, Surftype, Surfu, Surfv, *System Variables:* Setvar.

PFACE

Draws a polygon mesh by first defining the vertices of the mesh then assigning 3dfaces to the vertex locations.

To Draw a Polygon Mesh:

Issue the command, then provide the following information:

1. Vertex 1: Pick a point for the first vertex to be used in defining the mesh. The vertex prompt repeats after each point is selected. The vertex number increases by 1 each time you pick a point. Remember the location of each vertex; you will need to know the number for the next step. When you have finished selecting points, press ↵.

2. Face 1, Vertex 1: Enter the number of the vertex from Step 1 that you want to correspond to the first vertex of the first face. When you enter a number, the same prompt appears with the vertex number increased by 1. You can define one face with as many of the points as you indicated in Step 2. When you have defined the first face, press ↵.

3. Face 2, Vertex 1: Enter the number of the vertex that you want to correspond to the first vertex of the second face. When you have finished, press ↵.

● OPTIONS

–(number)   Makes a face edge invisible when entered at the **Face** n, Vertex n: prompt. You must use a negative value for each overlapping edge.

Layer   Specifies the layer for the face you are currently defining. Enter Layer at the Face n, Vertex n: prompt.

Color   Specifies the color of the face you are currently defining. You can enter Color at the Face n, Vertex n: prompt.

Notes   Pface was designed for programmers who need an entity type that can easily create 3D surfaces with special properties. Pfaces cannot be edited using Pedit. However, you can use **Array**, **Chprop**, **Copy**, **Erase**, **List**, **Mirror**, **Move**, **Rotate**, **Scale**, **Stretch**, and **Explode** on Pfaces.

See Also   Edgesurf, Mesh, Mface, Revsurf, Rulesurf, Tabsurf. *System Variables:* Pfacemax.

PLAN

Menu: **View** ➤ **Set View** ➤ **Plan View** ➤ **Current UCS/World/ Named UCS**

Plan displays a user coordinate system "in plan"—that is, a view perpendicular to the UCS. This allows you to create and manipulate objects in 2D more easily. Plan affects only the active viewport. You can set the *Ucsfollow* system variable so that whenever you change to a different UCS, you get a plan view of it.

To View in Plan:

Issue the command, then provide the following information:

- <Current UCS>/Ucs/World: Enter the capitalized letter of the desired option or press ↵ for the current UCS.

● OPTIONS

↵   Gives you a plan view of the current UCS. This is the default option.

Ucs   Gives you a plan view of a previously saved UCS. You are prompted for the name of the UCS you wish to see in plan. Enter a question mark to get a list of saved UCS's.

- ?/Name of UCS: Enter ? for a list or the name of your saved UCS.

- UCS name(s) to list <*>: Press ↵ to view names.

World   Gives you a plan view of the world coordinate system. This option is automatically issued when you pick **PlanView (world)** from the **Display** pull-down menu.

See Also   UCS. *System Variables:* Ucsfollow.

PLINE

Menu: **Draw ➤ Polyline ➤ 2D**

Pline creates lines having properties such as thickness and curvature. Unlike standard lines, polylines can be grouped together to act as a single object. For example, a box you draw using a polyline will act as one object instead of four discrete lines.

To Create a Polyline:

Issue the command, then provide the following information:

1.   From point: Pick the start point of the polyline.

2.   Arc/Close/Halfwidth/Length/Undo/Width/<Endpoint of line>: Enter the desired option or pick the next point of pline.

● OPTIONS

Arc   Draws a polyline arc. You can enter either the second point, angle, center, direction, radius, or endpoint of the arc. See the **Arc** command for the use of the Arc options. The Arc option are then listed in the prompt:

Angle/CEnter/CLose/Direction/Halfwidth/Line/Radius/Second pt/Undo/Width/<Endpoint of arc>:

Close   Draws a line from the current polyline end point back to its beginning, forming a closed polyline.

Halfwidth   Specifies half the polyline width at the current point. You are first prompted for the starting half-width, which is half the width of the polyline at the last fixed point. Next, you are prompted for the ending half-width—half the width of the polyline at the next point you pick.

Length   Draws a polyline in the same direction as the last line segment drawn. You are prompted for the line segment length. If an arc was drawn last, the direction will be tangent to the end direction of that arc.

Undo   Allows you to step backward along the current string of polyline or polyarc segments.

Width   Determines the whole width of the polyline. Subsequent polylines will be of this width unless you specify otherwise.

Notes   To give a polyline a smooth curve shape, you must use the **Pedit** command after you create the polyline.

The **Explode** command reduces a polyline to its line and arc components. Polylines with a width value lose their width once exploded.

To control the uniformity of a line type that is not continuous around the vertices, set the *Plinegen* system variable to 1.

3DPoly creates a three-dimensional Polyline. Such polylines cannot have width or curvature.

See Also   Bpoly, Explode, Offset, Pedit. *System Variables:* Plinegen, Plinewid.

PLOT

Menu: **File ➤ Print/Plot**

Plot opens up the Plot Configuration dialog box (FIGURE 31) for sending your drawing to a printer or plotter. You can control the plotter pen selection and speed as well as where to preview the drawing on the plotter media. Plot also allows AutoCAD to reduce a scale drawing to fit on the media. Once you change any of the plotter settings, they become the default settings. Several plot configurations can be saved and recalled from the dialog box.

To Print or Plot a Drawing Using the Dialog Box:

Issue the command. When the *Cmddia* system variable is nonzero, the Plot Configuration dialog box opens to display various plotting default parameters and conditions.

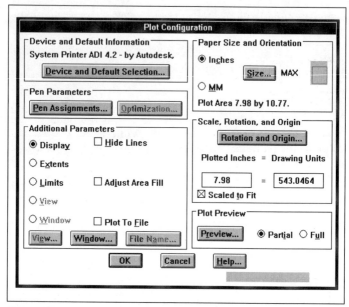

Figure 31: The Plot Configuration dialog box

● OPTIONS

Device and Default Information   This section with the Device and Default Selection… pick box opens a subdialog list box with descriptions of current plot devices assigned during configuration. Additional pick boxes allow you to *Save Defaults To File…*, *Get Defaults From File…*, *Show Device Requirements…*, and *Change Device Requirements…*.

Pen Parameters…   This section with the *Pen Assignment…* pick box opens a subdialog list box for specifying color, pen, line type, speed, and pen width. Highlighting one or more entries in the list box allows you to edit their values in the *Modify Values* edit boxes. The *Feature Legend…* pick box opens a subdialog box displaying line types available for your selected plotting device.

Optimization…   This pick box opens the Optimizing Pen Motion subdialog box for fine-tuning plot performance.

Additional Parameters   This section of the dialog box contains radio buttons for selecting different area configurations: plotting your current *Display* screen, the drawing *Extents*, and *Limits*. You can also save a *View* or create a *Window* to define the drawing area to plot. *View…* and *Window…* pick buttons allow you to retrieve saved images or pick points from the screen. A *Hide Lines* check box removes hidden lines from objects drawn in paper space assigned with the **Mview** command. A *File Name…* pick box lets you specify a specific name or type of file if you instead opt to check *Plot to File*. The *Adjust Area Fill* check box causes AutoCAD to compensate for pen width on Solid fill areas. With this option checked, AutoCAD will offset the borders of a filled area by a pen width so that the area will plot accurately.

Paper Size and Orientation   Button boxes let you specify plotted units by *Inches* or *MM* (Millimeters). Use the *Size…* pick box to open the Paper Size subdialog box in order to select from predefined measurements or set user-defined proportions.

Scale, Rotation, and Origin   A *Rotation and Origin…* pick box opens the Plot Rotation and Origin subdialog box to set the *Plot Rotation* angle and *Plot Origin*. Enter *Plotted Inches = Drawing Units* in the edit boxes when you are working with an explicit scale or pick *Scaled to Fit* your drawing sheet.

Plot Preview   Select the *Preview…* button after picking the *Partial* radio button to preview the placement and paper size (in red) with the effective plotting area in blue, or select the *Full* radio button to see the drawing on screen as it would appear on the paper. Full preview lets you zoom and pan for closer plot inspection.

To Plot a Drawing at the Command Line:

Issue the command, then provide the following information:

When the *Cmddia* system variable is zero, the Plot command prompts are as follows:

1.   What to plot—Display, Extents, Limits, View or Window <default>: Enter the desired option. If *View* is chosen, you are prompted for a view name. Selecting the *Window* option prompts you to pick lower left as First corner: and upper right as the Other corner:. You can also simply enter the corresponding coordinates.

2.   A description similar to the following list will appear on the text screen identifying your current plot settings:

Plotter port time-out = 30seconds

Plot device is Hewlett-Packard (HP-GL) ADI 4.2 - by Autodesk

Description: HP Draftmaster I

Plot optimization level = 4

Plot will NOT be written to a selected file

Sizes are in Inches and the style is landscape

Plot origin is at (0.00, 0.00)

Plotting area is 43.20 wide by 33.81 high (MAX size)

Plot is NOT rotated

Area fill will NOT be adjusted for pen width

Hidden lines will NOT be removed

Scale is 1=1

Do you want to change anything? (No/Yes/File/Save) <N>:

Enter **Y** if you want to change the default plotter settings shown above, then proceed to Step 3. If you enter **N**, prompts similar to those in Step 15 appear.

3.   Do you want to change plotters? <N>: To change the plotter, enter **Y** and AutoCAD identifies the configured plotters, similar to the following example:

1. Hewlett-Packard (HP-GL) ADI 4.2 - by Autodesk:

Description: HP Draftmaster

2. PostScript device ADI 4.2 - by Autodesk

Description: LaserWriter II

Enter selection (number or description) <1>:

Enter the number of the plotter you want.

4.   AutoCAD returns you to the What to plot -- Display, Extents, Limits, View or Window <E>: prompt, displaying the changes. You can assign any description label to your specific plotting device during configuration.

5. Prompts vary depending on the output device selected. If your plotter supports multiple pens, hardware line types, line widths or software-controlled pen speeds, then Auto-CAD displays a list of Entity colors, Pen Number, Line Type, Pen Speed, and Pen Width when you enter **Y** to the following prompt:

Do you want to change anything? (No/Yes/File/Save) <N>:

Changes can be entered globally by preceding each with an asterisk, or individually as prompts appear for Pen number <1>:, Line type <0>:, Pen speed <36>:, and Pen width: <0.010>:.

Pressing ↵ advances through list; entering **C** with the specific color number moves you directly to that assignment; **S** shows the updated colors; and **X** exits the procedure.

6. Write the plot to a file? <N>: Enter **Y** to create a plot file or press ↵ to plot the drawing. The Create Plot File dialog list box opens when the *Filedia* system variable is nonzero or the Enter file name for plot <default>: prompt appears just prior to processing the plot.

7. Size units (Inches or Millimeters) <I>: Enter the unit equivalent of your drawing.

8. Plot origin in Inches <0.00,0.00>: Enter the location of the drawing origin in relation to the plotter origin in X and Y coordinates. The coordinate values should be in final plot size, not in drawing scale sizes.

9. Enter the Size or Width, Height (in Inches) <MAX>: Enter the desired sheet size (see TABLE 8). You can specify and save up to five nonstandard user-defined sizes by entering them in X and Y coordinates.

10. Rotate plot clockwise 0/90/180/270 degrees <0>: Enter the orientation of the plot if other than 0 degrees rotation.

11. Pen width <0.010>: :Enter the pen width used for solid fills.

Table 8: Standard Values in Inches for Plotting Size

Size	Width	Height
A	10.50	8.00
B	16.00	10.00
C	21.00	16.00
D	33.00	21.00
E	43.00	33.00
F	40.00	28.00
A4	11.20	7.80
A3	15.60	10.70
A2	22.40	15.60
A1	32.20	22.40
MAX	*	*

The MAX value is hardware dependent.

12. Adjust area fill boundaries for pen width? <N>. : Enter **Y** if you want the plotter to compensate for pen width on solid filled areas. If you respond **Y** to this prompt, AutoCAD will offset the border of a filled area by half the pen width so that the area will accurately plot.

13. Remove hidden lines? <N>: Enter **Y** if you want a 3D view to be plotted with hidden lines removed.

14. Specify scale by entering: Plotted Inches=Drawing Units or Fit or ? <F>: Enter a scale factor for plot or **F** to force drawing to fit entirely on the selected sheet size.

15. Effective plotting area: A value appears showing you the width and height of the final plotted image:

Specified plot size (44.70, 35.31) exceeds actual paper size (43.20, 33.81). Proceed with plot anyway? <N>:

The size of the image will depend on the sheet size entered at the Standard values for plotting size: prompt, plus the scale factor. Entering **Y** accepts the current information and begins processing the plot output.

16. Enter file name for plot <JUNK>: If this prompt appears, as mentioned in Step 5, enter the desired plot filename.

17. A percentage value for Regeneration done will appear as AutoCAD sends information to the plotter.

18. Autocad responds with Plot complete when the output commences. Then the following prompt appears:

Press RETURN to continue:

Press ⏎ to return to the drawing editor.

Notes Since some plotters do not have built-in line types, the *Select linetype* option may not appear on your plotter.

The Pen width prompt works with the Adjust fill prompt, allowing your plotter to compensate for the pen width during area fills. If you respond with a **Y** at the Adjust fill prompt, AutoCAD uses the *Pen width* value to offset the outline of any filled areas to half the pen width. This causes the edge of filled areas to be drawn to the center line of the fill outline.

If you are using a laser printer, the *Pen width* value determines the thickness of a typical line.

At times, even though all of your plotter settings are correct, your plot may not appear in the proper location on your sheet, or the drawing may not be plotted at all. This often occurs when you are plotting the extents of a drawing. AutoCAD often does not recognize changes to the extents of the drawing when major portions of a drawing have been removed or edited. If you have this problem with a plot, open the file to be plotted and issue **Zoom** *Extents*. Let the drawing complete the regeneration process (it will probably regenerate twice), and try plotting again. If the problem persists, double-check your size units, plot origin, plot size, and plot scale settings.

If you have problems rotating a plot, use the **UCS** command to create a UCS that is rotated the way you want, and the **View** command to save a view of your drawing in the new UCS. Then use the *View* option under the What to plot: prompt.

When plotting from Paperspace, such plots include all viewports and layer settings.

See Also Acad -p, Config. *System Variables:* Filedia, Cmddia, Plotter, Plotid.

POINT

Menu: **Draw ➤ Point**

Point draws a point entity. Points can be used as unobtrusive markers that you can snap to using the **Node** *Osnap* override. Use the Ddptype dialog box to select a point type.

To Draw a Point Entity:

Issue the command, then provide the following information:

- Point: Enter the point location.

● OPTIONS

You can set the *Pdmode* system variable to change the appearance of points. You must set Pdmode before drawing points. 0 is the default setting. When Pdmode is changed, all existing points are updated to reflect the new setting. The setting values are as follows:

Pdmode Value	Entity
0	A dot
1	Nothing
2	A cross

Pdmode Value	Entity
3	An x
4	A vertical line upward from the point selected
32	A circle
64	A square

Notes   You can combine the different *Pdmode* variables to create 20 different types of points. For example, to combine a cross (2) with a circle (32), set Pdmode to **34** (2 + 32).

See Also   Ddptype, Divide, Measure. *System Variables:* Pdmode, Pdsize.

POINT SELECTION

You can enter a point by picking it with your cursor, keying in an absolute or relative coordinate value, or keying in a relative polar coordinate. You can also use modifiers called filters to align points in an X, Y, or Z axis.

● OPTIONS

Absolute coordinate   Specifies points by giving the X, Y, and Z coordinate values separated by commas, as follows:

   Select point: **6,3,1**

The X value is 6, the Y is 3, and the Z is 1. If you omit the Z value, AutoCAD assumes the current default Z value (see the **Elev** command to set the current Z default value). Absolute coordinates use the current UCS's origin as the point of reference.

Relative coordinates: Entered like absolute coordinates, except that an *at* sign (@) precedes the coordinate values, as follows:

Select point: **@6,3,1**

If you omit the Z value, AutoCAD assumes the current default Z value (see the **Elev** command for setting the current Z default value). Relative coordinates use the last point entered as the point of reference. To tell AutoCAD to use the last point selected, simply enter the *at* sign by itself at a point selection prompt.

Relative polar coordinates   Specify points by giving the distance from the last point entered, preceded by an *at* sign and followed by a *less-than* sign and the angle of direction, as follows:

Select point: **@6<45**

This entry calls for a relative distance of 6 units at a 45- degree angle from the last point entered.

Filters   Align a point along an X, Y, or Z axis by first specifying the axis on which to align, then selecting an existing point on which to align, and then entering the new point's remaining coordinate values. The following example aligns a point vertically on a specific X location:

1.   Point: Enter **.x** or select a known point to which you want to align vertically. For precision, use the Osnap overrides.

2.   (need yz): Select a Y-Z coordinate. Again, you can use Osnap overrides to align to other geometries.

You can also enter **.xy**, **.yz**, or **.xz** at the Point: prompt. For example, you can first pick an X-Y location and then enter a Z value for height.

Notes   To override the current angle units, base, and direction settings (set using the **Units** command) use double or triple *lesser-than* signs (<):

<<   Enters angles in degrees, default angle base (east), and direction (counterclockwise) regardless of the current settings.

<<<   Enters angles based on the current angle format
         (degrees, radians, grads, etc.), default angle base
         (east), and direction (counterclockwise), regardless
         of the base and direction settings.

You can enter fractional units regardless of the unit style setting.
This means you can enter **5.5"** as well as **5'6"** when using the architectural format.

See Also   Osnap, Units, Filter.

POLYGON

Menu: **Draw ➤ Polygon ➤ Edge/Circumscribed/Inscribed**

Polygon allows you to draw a regular polygon of up to 1,024 sides.
To define the polygon, you can specify the outside or inside radius,
or the length of one side. The polygon is actually a polyline that can
be exploded into its individual component lines.

To Draw a Polygon:

Issue the command, then provide the following information:

1.   Number of sides: Enter the number of sides.

2.   Edge/<Center of polygon>: Enter **E** to select *Edge* option
         or pick a point to select the polygon center. If you select
         the default center of a polygon, the following prompts
         appear:

         Inscribed in circle/Circumscribed about circle (I/C):
         Enter the desired option.
         Radius of circle: Enter the radius of circle defining
         polygon size.

● OPTIONS

Edge　　Determines the length of one face of the polygon. You are prompted to select the first and second end point of the edge. AutoCAD then draws a polygon by creating a circular array of the edge you specify.

Inscribed　　Forces the polygon to fit inside a circle of the specified radius; the end points of each line lie along the circumference.

Circumscribed　　Forces the polygon to fit outside a circle of the specified radius; the midpoint of each line lies along the circumference.

Radius of circle　　Sets the length of the defining radius of the polygon. The radius will be the distance from the center to either an endpoint or a midpoint, depending on the *Inscribed/Circumscribed* choice.

Notes　　Use the *Pedit* command to edit a polygon's width.

See Also　　Pedit, Pline. *System Variables:* Polysides.

PREFERENCES

Menu: **File ➤ Preferences**…

Preferences lets you control AutoCAD's appearance. You can turn various parts of the AutoCAD screen on or off, set the number of lines that appear on the command prompt, make adjustments to your digitizing tablet and output devices, and make Environment settings here.

● OPTIONS

AutoCAD Graphics Window group　　lets you control the various parts of the AutoCAD window. The four check boxes, *Screen Menu*, *Scroll Bars*, *Toolbar*, and *Toolbox* turn these features on and off. Scroll Bars are only active when you install the nonaccelerated display driver. The *Command Prompt* popup list lets you control the number of text lines displayed in the command prompt area. Set this value to **none** to hide the command prompt entirely.

Window Repair radio buttons let you set the way the window image is repaired. *Bitmap* is best for super-high resolution displays (1280 × 1024 or greater). *Fastdraw* is best for VGA and Super VGA resolutions. Experiment with these settings to see which offers the fastest redraw times for your system.

AutoCAD Settings group lets you store or recall the Preference settings.

- *AutoCAD Defaults* restore the standard AutoCAD settings.

- *Restore from Acad.INI* restores the settings found in the *ACAD.INI* configuration file.

- *Save to Acad.INI* saves the current settings to the *Acad.INI* file. These settings then become the default for later sessions.

- *Current Session* tells AutoCAD to use the current preference settings for the current session only.

Click on **OK** to make these options take effect.

AutoCAD Text Window group lets you control the properties of the text window, which is accessed by pressing **F2**. The *Number of scroll lines* input box lets you control how many lines of text AutoCAD displays in the text window at one time (use the scroll bar to view earlier lines). The *Log File Open* check box lets you store data from the text window in a text file that can be viewed, edited, and printed with any word processing application. When this item is checked, a log file is opened and anything that appears in the command prompt will be written to the file. Note that when the log file is opened, you cannot access it with any other application. When the Log File Open box is unchecked, the log file is closed. You are then able to view the log file using any word processing application. To set the location and name of the log file, use the Environment… dialog box described later in this section.

Digitizer Input radio buttons let you control the way AutoCAD works with your digitizer (if you have one installed). When **Digitizer Only** is selected, AutoCAD will only respond to digitizer movement and input. When **Digitizer/Mouse Arbitration** is selected, AutoCAD will respond to both the digitizer and the mouse, whichever pointing device is moving. If you are using the Digitizer Mole Mode, AutoCAD will only respond to the mouse while the digitizer is in the Digitizer Mode.

Color... button opens the Color dialog box and allows you to set the color for the different parts of the AutoCAD Graphics and Text windows. Click on the graphic on the left to select the part of the screen to set, then use the RGB sliders or the basic color samples to set the color. The System Colors button will set the windows to the settings found in the Windows Control Panel.

Font... button opens the Font dialog box and allows you to set the font, font style, and size of the text in the command prompt, screen menu, and text window.

Environment... button opens the Environment dialog box and allows you to determine where AutoCAD should look for or place resource files. See Environment Settings for more information.

See Also Acad.INI, Environment Settings.

PSDRAG

Psdrag allows you to drag the PostScript image as a boundary with the **Psin** command.

To Display the PostScript Image:

Issue the command, then provide the following information:

- PSIN drag mode <0>: Enter the default value to drag a simple boundary.

See Also Psin, Psfill *System Variables:* Psquality.

PSFILL

Psfill fills two-dimensional polyline outlines with any PostScript pattern defined in the *Acad.PSF* PostScript support file. The pattern is not visible on the screen but is output with the **Psout** command.

To Use a PostScript Fill Pattern:

Issue the command, then provide the following information:

1. Select polyline: Pick the two dimensional polyline outline.

2. PostScript fill pattern (.=none)<.>/?: Enter a pattern name.

Entering **?** displays the following list of available patterns:

- Grayscale RGBcolor Allogo Lineargray Radialgray Square Waffle Zigzag Stars Brick Speck

The prompt is then repeated with the pattern name displayed in the brackets.

3. Scale <1.0000>: Enter a scale factor.

4. Grayscale <50>: Prompts vary for each PostScript pattern. For example, you may be requested for a Foreground-Gray and BackgroundGray value. Values ranging from 0 to 100 represent white to black.

See Also Psin, Psout, Psdrag.

PSIN

Menu: **File ➤ Import/Export ➤ PostScript In**...

Psin imports a raster-image file into your drawing.

To Import an EPS file:

Issue the command, then provide the following information:

1. Psin opens the Select PostScript File dialog box when the *Filedia* system variable is set to 1, displaying an .EPS extension for Postscript files. Enter a filename into the *File:* box for importing into your drawing.

2. Insertion point <0,0,0>: Enter a location for the lower left corner of your box image.

3. Scale factor: Enter a scale factor or drag the image with your cursor.

Notes   When the *Filedia* system variable is set to 0, the PostScript **file name:** prompt appears at the command line. Enter the name without the .EPS extension.

See Also   Psdrag, Psout, Psfill.

PSOUT

Menu: **File ➤ Import/Export ➤ PostScript Out**...

Psout exports your drawing as an EPS file for use in desktop publishing programs or output to a PostScript device.

To Create an EPS File:

Issue the command, then provide the following information:

1. Psout opens the Create PostScript File dialog box when the *Filedia* system variable is set to 1, displaying an .EPS extension for Postscript files. Enter a filename into the *File:* box for exporting into your drawing.

2. What to export -- Display, Extents, View or Window <D>: Enter an option.

3. Include a screen preview image in the file? (None/EPSI/TIFF)<None>: Enter an option. If you wish to include an image in the EPSI or TIFF format, the following prompt appears: Screen preview image size(128x128 is standard)? (128/256/512)<128>:

4. Effective plotting area: Enter width and height in your current size units as inches or millimeters.

5. Size units(Inches or Millimeters) <current value>: Enter a size for the exported image.

6. Output units=Drawing units or Fit or ? <default>: Enter values in one of the following format examples to set the scale for the EPS output: **F** to fit the maximum paper size, **1/4"=1'** for drawing scale proportions, or ? to select from a predefined output size.

● OPTIONS

Display   Exports the drawing based on your current modelspace or paperspace viewport.

Extents   Exports the drawing based on your current modelspace or paperspace drawing extents.

Limits   Exports the drawing based on your drawing limits.

View   Exports the drawing based on a view saved with the **View** command.

Window   Exports the drawing based on a user-defined window by prompting for the first corner and then for the other corner.

See Also   Psdrag, Psin, Psfill. *System Variables:* Psprolog.

PSPACE

Menu: **View ➤ Paperspace**

Pspace lets you move from Modelspace to Paperspace.

To Change Working Areas:

Issue the command. If the **Tilemode** system variable is set to 0, AutoCAD will switch to Paperspace. If it isn't, you receive the message:

** Command not allowed unless tilemode is set to 0 **

Notes   Paperspace is an alternative work space that lets you arrange views of your Modelspace drawing. Paperspace is a "paste up" area, independent from the main drawing (Modelspace).

You can create viewports in Paperspace that are like windows into Modelspace. Layers, Snap, and Grid modes can be set independently for each viewport. You can also accurately control the scale of a viewport for plotting purposes.

To get into Paperspace in a new drawing, set Tilemode to 0, then issue Pspace. Your screen will go blank and the UCS icon will change to a triangle. Use **View ➤ Layout ➤ MVsetup** to set up Viewports so you can display your Modelspace drawing in Paperspace. Use the *Xp* option under the *Zoom* command to set the scale of a viewport display.

Viewports in Paperspace can be resized, moved, copied, and even overlapped using standard AutoCAD editing commands.

See Also   Mvsetup, Mview, Mspace, Tilemode, Vplayer, Vports, Zoom/xp.

PURGE

A drawing may accumulate unneeded blocks, layers, line types, dimension styles, Shape files, or Text styles. These objects and settings can increase the size of the drawing file, making the drawing slow to load and difficult to transport. Purge allows you to eliminate these elements.

To Purge Elements from the Drawing File:

Issue the command, then respond to the following:

Purge unused Blocks/Dimstyle/LAyers/LTypes/SHapes/STyles/All:

When you enter the name of the variable type at the Purge prompt, AutoCAD displays each variable name of the type specified. Enter a **Y** to purge the variable or **N** to keep it. The *All* option purges all variables regardless of type.

Notes You can use Purge in an editing session as long as you haven't made any changes to the drawing's database during that session. You can use commands that affect the display of the drawing and still use Purge afterward, but if you use a drawing or editing command, Purge is no longer accessible. You must close the file and reopen it to use the Purge command.

The layer 0, the continuous line type, the standard text style, User Coordinate Systems, views, and viewport configurations cannot be purged. Nested blocks are removed only by repetitious purging and exiting of the drawing. The *Wblock* command describes an alternative and more effective method for purging.

See Also Wblock.

QSAVE

Menu: **File ➤ Save**…

Quickly saves a named drawing without asking for a filename. If saving an unnamed drawing, Qsave works like **Saveas**, enabling you to name the drawing before saving it.

See Also Save, Saveas. *System Variables:* Dwgtitled, Savename.

QTEXT

Menu: **Settings ➤ Drawing Aids ➤ Qtext Text**

Qtext helps reduce drawing regeneration and redraw times by making text appear as a rectangular box instead of readable text. The rectangle approximates the height and length of the text.

To Assign Text as a Rectangular Box:

Issue the command, then provide the following information:

- ON/OFF <Off>: Enter the desired option.

Notes   You do not see the effects of Qtext until you issue a **Regen** command.

See Also   Dtext, Regen, Text. *System Variables:* Qtextmode.

QUIT

Menu: **File ➤ Exit AutoCAD**

Quit exits a drawing without saving the most recent edits. The file reverts to the condition it was in following the last **Save** or **End** command.

To Exit without Saving:

Issue the command, then provide the following information:

- If no changes were made to the current drawing, AutoCAD exits the program.

- If changes were made and not saved, the Drawing Modification dialog box opens to Save *Changes…*, *Discard Changes*, or *Cancel Command*. If the drawing is unnamed and you pick *Save Changes…*, the Save Drawing As list dialog box will open, giving you an opportunity to name the drawing.

See Also End, Save, Qsave, Saveas. *System Variables:* Dbmod.

RASTERIN

Rasterin imports a raster-image in a TIFF, GIF, or PCX format.

To load the Rasterin ADS application, enter

(xload "rasterin")

To Import a TIFF, GIF, or PCX Raster File:

Load the Rasterin ADS application, enter **Tiffin** ↵, **Gifin** ↵, or **Pcxin** ↵, and provide the following information:

1. *Raster file* name: Enter the name of the imported file without the .TIF, .GIF, or .PCX extension.

2. Insertion point <0,0,0>: Enter a location.

3. Scale factor: Enter a scale factor or drag the image with your cursor.

● OPTIONS

Riaspect sets the aspect ratio of the imported image. You must use an integer for this setting.

Ribackg sets the background color for the imported image. To set the color, use the integer color value (see TABLE 3). For example, 0 is equal to black, 7 is equal to white.

Riedge   sets the edge detection feature. When Riedge is on, only the edges between color patches are drawn. When Riedge is off, the entire color patch is drawn. Use **0** to turn this feature off, or **1** to turn it on.

Rigamut   sets the range of colors used in the imported image. Reducing the color range can reduce the size of the AutoCAD file after import. The default range is 256 colors.

Rigrey   lets you import an image in greyscale instead of in color. Use **0** to turn this feature off, **1** to turn it on.

Rithresh   lets you control importing an image on the basis of its brightness. Use **0** to turn this feature off. Use any non-zero integer to set the brightness threshold.

RECOVER

Menu: **File ➤ Recover**...

A drawing may become corrupted because of problems with your hard disk drive or floppy disk. Corrupted files cannot be opened by AutoCAD. Recover salvages as much of a file as possible and allows AutoCAD to read the file.

To Recover Corrupted Files:

Issue the command, then provide the following information:

1. If the *Filedia* system variable is set to 1, the Open Drawing File list box is displayed to enter the drawing name that you wish to recover. Otherwise, the following command line prompt appears:

   Recover<current filename>: Enter filename to recover.

2. A series of messages appears indicating the action AutoCAD is taking to recover the file. An AutoCAD Alert dialog box opens after recovery to report whether the audit detected any errors in the recovered database. If so, the recovery is processed and reported to the screen.

Notes   AutoCAD Release 12 will not recover damaged files from earlier releases of AutoCAD.

See Also   Audit. *System Variables:* Auditctl.

REDEFINE/UNDEFINE

Undefine suppresses any standard AutoCAD command. For example, if you load an AutoLISP Copy command you have written and then enter **Copy** at the command prompt, you will still get the standard Copy command. However, if you use Undefine to suppress the standard Copy command, you can use the AutoLISP Copy *program*. Redefine reinstates a standard command that has been suppressed.

To Suppress or Reinstate a Standard Command:

Issue the command, then provide the following information:

• Command name: Enter the command name.

Notes   To enter the standard AutoCAD **Copy** command when an AutoLISP version might already be defined, precede the command with a period at the command prompt, as follows:

Command: **Copy**⏎
Select objects:

.

.

.

This is the only way to issue an undefined command with the AutoLISP Command function.

REDO

Menu: **Edit ➤ Redo**

Redo restores a command you have undone using **U** or **Undo**. You are allowed only one Redo per command. If you enter a series of three U's (that is, three Undo 1's), only the last U can be restored.

To Undo Your Undo:

Here is the most effective approach for restoring undo's:

   undo 6

If this undoes too much, then try

   redo

If this undoes too much, then try

   undo 4

Otherwise, enter

   u

See Also   U, Undo. *System Variables:* Undoctl.

REDRAW AND REDRAWALL

Transparent: **'Redraw** and **'Redrawall**

Menu: **View ➤ Redraw/Redraw All**

During the drawing and editing process, an operation may cause an object to partially disappear. Often, the object was previously behind other objects that have since been removed. Redraw and Redrawall refresh the screen and restore such obscured objects.

These commands also clear the screen of blips that may clutter your view.

Redraw will act only on the currently active viewport. Redrawall, on the other hand, refreshes all viewports on the screen at once. These commands affect only the virtual screen, not the actual drawing database.

See Also   Regen, Viewres.

REGEN AND REGENALL

These two commands update the drawing editor screen to reflect the most recent changes in the drawing database.

Notes   If you make a global change in the drawing database and Regenauto is turned on, a regeneration is issued automatically.

If you have Regenauto turned off, regeneration will not occur automatically, so changes to the drawing database are not immediately reflected in the drawing you see. If you need to see those changes, use Regen to update the display.

If you are using multiple viewports, Regen affects only the active viewport. To regenerate all viewports at once, use Regenall.

See Also   Regenauto, Viewres.

REGENAUTO

Transparent: **'Regenauto**

Regenauto automatically regenerates screen display to reflect most recent drawing changes. For complex drawings, regeneration can be very time-consuming. Regenauto enables you to turn off automatic regeneration. Regenauto is on by default.

To Control Regeneration:

Issue the command, then provide the following information:

- ON/OFF/ <current status>: Enter the desired status.

• OPTIONS

On   Causes the display to be automatically regenerated when required to reflect global changes in the drawing database. Your display will reflect all the most recent drawing changes.

Off   Suppresses the automatic regeneration of the display. This can save time when you are editing complex drawings. When a command needs to regenerate the drawing, a prompt allows you to decide whether or not to regenerate the display.

See Also   Regen, Viewres. *System Variables:* Regenmode.

REGIONAL MODELER

The Regional Modeler is an application that allows you to apply Boolean operations to 2D objects. Start by drawing the outline of the object using closed polylines, circles, or polygons; then use the **Solidify** option to turn the outline into 2D regions. These solidified polylines, circles, and polygons are called *region primitives*. Once these primitives are created, you can apply the *Union*, *Subtract*, *Intersect*, or *Modify Boolean* options to them to create new regions (such as a notched plate or a plate with a hole in it).

• OPTIONS

The following options appear in the Model pull-down menu. Their command equivalents are shown in parentheses.

Solidify (solidify)   turns a polyline outline of an object into a region that can be modified using the Regional Modelers Boolean operations.

Union (solunion)   joins two regions into one.

Subtract (solsub)   subtracts one region from another.

Intersect (solint)   joins two or more regions, leaving only the area where the regions intersect.

Modify ➤ *Move* (solmove)   lets you move a region primitive using one of these motion descriptions:

- r[*xyz*]*degrees* rotates the primitive about the *X*, *Y*, or *Z* axis.

- t[*xyz*]*distance* moves the primitive along the *X*, *Y*, or *Z* axis by a given distance.

- a[*efwu*] aligns the primitive with a coordinate system where

  e = edge of coordinate system
  f = face of coordinate system
  u = user coordinate system
  w = world coordinate system
  o = original position

Modify ➤ *Change Primitive* (solchp)   lets you move, copy (instance), replace, resize, or change the color of a primitive.

Modify ➤ *Separate* (solsep)   lets you separate primitives joined by a Boolean operation.

Setup ➤ *Variables* (ddsolvar)   brings up a dialog box that allows you to make settings to the regional modeler.

Setup ➤ *... Units*   lets you set the unit style for the regions.

Inquiry ➤ *List Objects* (sollist)   lists the drawing properties of a region.

Inquiry ➤ *Mass Property* (ddsolmassp)   lists the mass properties of a region.

Inquiry ➤ *Area Calculation* (solarea) lists the area of a region.

Display ➤ *Mesh* (solmesh) sets the regional modeler to show regions as surface meshes.

Display ➤ *Wireframe* (solwire) sets the regional modeler to show regions as wire frames.

Display ➤ *Set Wire Density* (solwdens) sets the number of lines used to indicate curved surfaces.

Display ➤ *Copy Feature* (solfeat) copies a surface or outline of a region.

Utility ➤ *SolUCS* (solucs) sets the UCS to a region.

Utility ➤ *Purge Objects* (solpurge) purges an erased region or region primitive.

Utility ➤ *Unload Modeler* (ai_unloadame) unloads the Regional Modeler.

REINIT

Reinit opens the Re-initialization dialog box to reinitialize the Input/Output ports, digitizer, display, and *Acad.PGP* file.

● OPTIONS

I/O Port Initialization This section contains check boxes for resetting the I/O port for your *Digitizer* and *Plotter*.

Device & File Initialization This section contains check boxes to reinitialize your *Digitizer*, *Display*, and *PGP File*.

Notes If your cursor does not appear on the screen to permit you to select the check boxes, you can use the *Re-init* system variable and specify the sum of several reinitialization values. For example, enter **Re-init** and enter a value of **5** (1 = Digitizer + 4 = Digitizer reinitialization) for a digitizer analog failure. See system variables for additive values.

See Also   *System Variables:* Re-init.

RENAME

Rename renames any nameable drawing element, such as a block, dimstyle, layer, line type, text style, etc.

To Assign a New Entity Name:

Issue the command, then provide the following information:

1.   Block/Dimstyle/LAyer/LType/Style/Ucs/VIew/VPort: Enter the type of drawing element to be renamed.

2.   Old (object) name: Enter old name of entity or object.

3.   New (object) name: Enter new name of entity or object.

RENDER

Menu: **Render ➤ Render**

Render uses light sources and surface settings to render a 3D model. Surfaces can be adjusted for reflectance, shininess, and smoothness. Multiple light sources can be added to the drawing to enhance the rendering, and the intensity of these light sources is adjustable.

● OPTIONS

The following options are on the Render pull-down menu. Their command equivalents are shown in parentheses.

Lights… (Light)   brings up a dialog box that lets you adjust, delete, or create a light source. You can set the intensity of the Ambient light and set the lighting drop-off to be inverse linear or inverse square.

Scenes… (Scene)   brings up a dialog box that lets you set up a scene you can later recall.

Finishes… (Finish)   brings up a dialog box that lets you create a new finish, or import, delete, export, or modify an existing finish. A preview sphere gives you a sample view of what your finish looks like.

Preferences… (Rpref)   brings up a dialog box that lets you set the renderer's preferences.

Preferences… Reconfigure (Rconfig)   lets you configure the renderer's display options.

Files ➤ Replay Image (Replay)   lets you display an RND, GIF, TGA, or TIFF file on the rendering display.

Files ➤ Save Image (Saveimg)   lets you save a rendered image as an RND, GIF, TGA, or TIFF file.

Statistics… (Stats)   provides information about the last scene rendered.

RESUME

See **Script**.

REVSURF

Menu: **Draw ➤ 3D Surfaces ➤ Surface of Revolution**

Revsurf draws an extruded curved surface that is rotated about an axis, like a bell, globe, or drinking glass (see FIGURE 32). Before you can use Revsurf, you must define both the shape of the extrusion and an axis of rotation. Use arcs, lines, circles, or two-dimensional or three-dimensional polylines to define this shape. The axis of rotation can be a line.

To Draw Extruded Surface:

Issue the command, then provide the following information:

1. Select path curve: Pick an arc line, arc, circle, two-dimensional polyline, or three-dimensional polyline defining the shape to be swept.

2. Select Axis of revolution: Pick a line representing the axis of rotation.

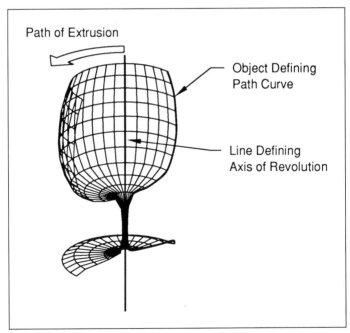

Figure 32: Extruded curved surface drawn by Revsurf

3. Starting Angle <0>: Enter the angle from the object selected as the path curve where the sweep starts.

4. Included angle (+=ccw, -=cw) <Full circle>: Enter the angle of the sweep.

Notes The point you pick on the object in Step 2 determines the positive and negative directions of the rotation. You can use the "right-hand rule" illustrated in FIGURE 33 to determine the positive direction of the rotation. Imagine placing your thumb on the axis line, pointing away from the end closest to the pick point. The rest of your fingers will point in the positive rotation direction. The rotation direction determines the N direction of the surface while the axis of rotation defines the M direction.

You can control the number of facets used to create the revsurf by setting the *Surftab1* and *Surftab2* system variables. *Surftab1* controls the number of facets in the M direction while *Surftab2* controls the facets in the N direction. You can set these variables through the **Setvar** command or by entering the system variable from the command prompt. Resetting a higher value in *Surftab1* or *Surftab2* will not affect already drawn surfaces.

See Also Pedit, 3dmesh. *System Variables:* Splframe, Surftab1, Surftab2.

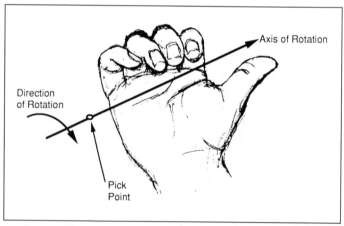

Figure 33: Determining the positive direction of rotation

ROTATE/ROTATE 3D

Menu: **Modify ➤ Rotate**

Rotate rotates an object or group of objects to a specified angle.

To Rotate Objects:

Issue the command, then provide the following information:

1. Select objects: Select as many objects as you like.

2. Base point: Pick the point about which objects are to be rotated.

3. <Rotation angle>/Reference: Enter the angle of rotation or **R** to specify a reference angle.

● OPTIONS

Reference Allows you to specify the rotation angle in reference to the object's current angle. If you enter this option, you get the prompts:

- Reference angle <0>: Enter the current angle of the object or pick two points representing a base angle.

- New angle: Enter a new angle or pick an angle with the cursor.

Notes Rotate is also a grips option.

See Also Ddgrips, Grips.

RSCRIPT

See **Script**.

RULESURF

Menu: **Draw ➤ 3D Surfaces ➤ Ruled Surface**

Rulesurf generates a surface between two curves. Before you can use Rulesurf, you must draw two curves defining opposite ends of the desired surface (see FIGURE 34). The defining curves can be points, lines, arcs, circles, two-dimensional polylines, or three-dimensional polylines.

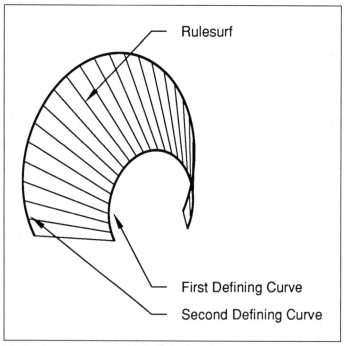

Rulesurf

First Defining Curve

Second Defining Curve

Figure 34: Defining the opposite ends of a surface for Rulesurf

To Use Curves to Define a Surface:

Issue the command, then provide the following information:

1. Select first defining curve: Pick the first curve.

2. Select second defining curve: Pick the second curve.

Notes The location of your pick points on the defining curves affects the way the surface is generated. If you want the surface to be drawn straight between the two defining curves, pick points near the same position on each curve. If you want the surface to cross between the two defining curves, in a corkscrew fashion, pick points at opposite positions on the curves (see FIGURE 35).

The *Surftab1* system variable controls the number of faces used to generate the surface.

See Also Pedit. *System Variables:* Surftab1.

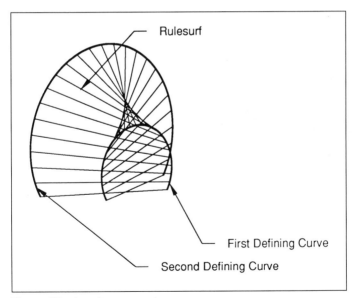

Figure 35: A corkscrew surface

SAVE/SAVEAS

Menu: **File ➤ Save As**…

Stores your currently open file to disk.

To Save Your Current Drawing:

Issue the command, then provide the following information:

- If the *Filedia* system variable is set to 1 and your drawing has not yet been named, the Save Drawing As dialog list box opens. Enter a drawing name in the *File:* edit box. The next time you enter Save, the drawing is saved and no prompt appears.

- If the *Filedia* system variable is set to 0, the following command line prompt appears:

  Save current changes as <Current path and file name>: Enter the filename or press ↵ to accept the default current file name.

Notes   The pull-down menu uses the Saveas command, which is different from the Save command in only one respect: If you enter a name that is different from the current file name for Saveas, you will create a new file with the name you enter and that becomes your current drawing name. Both Save and Saveas make a copy of the current file, i.e., including all changes made up to the time the command was issued.

See **Qsave** for saving your current drawing without being prompted for a drawing name.

AutoCAD lets you set a time interval for saving your drawing during configuration. The current drawing is saved to the default filename *Auto.SV$*. See Automatic-save feature in option 7 of the **Config** command.

See Also   Saveas, Qsave. *System Variables:* Savefile, Savename, Savetime.

SCALE

Menu: **Modify ➤ Scale**

Changes the size of objects in a drawing. You can also scale an object by reference.

To Resize Objects:

Issue the command, then provide the following information:

1. Select objects: Pick the objects to be scaled.

2. Base point: Pick a point of reference for scaling.

3. <Scale factor>/Reference: Enter the scale factor, move the cursor to visually select new scale, or enter **R** to select the *Reference* option.

● OPTIONS

Reference   Allows you to specify a scale in relation to a known length. When using Reference, AutoCAD first prompts for Reference length <1>:, which often requires you to select the same base point. Prompts then appear for Second point: and New length: allowing you to select two new points.

See Also   Block, Ddgrips, Grips, Insert, Select.

SCRIPT

Transparent: **'Script**

"Plays back" a set of AutoCAD commands and responses recorded in a Script file. Script files, like DOS batch files, are lists of commands and responses entered exactly as you would while in AutoCAD.

To Invoke a Script File:

Issue the command, then provide the following information:

- If the *Filedia* system variable is set to 1, the Select Script File dialog list box opens. Enter a script file name in the *File:* edit box.

- If the *Filedia* system variable is set to 0, the following command-line prompt appears:

  Script file <current file name>: Enter the script file name.

● OPTIONS

Delay <milliseconds>   When included in a Script file, makes AutoCAD pause for the number of milliseconds indicated.

Rscript   When included at the end of a Script file, repeats the script continuously.

Resume   Restarts a Script file that has been interrupted using the Backspace or Ctrl-C key.

Backspace or *Ctrl-C*   Interrupts the processing of a Script file.

Notes   You can use Script files to set up frequently used macros to save lengthy keyboard entries or to automate a presentation. Another common use for scripts is to automate plotter and printer setup.

SELECT

Menu: **Edit ➤ Select ➤ (options)**

Provides a variety of options for selecting objects and returns you to the command prompt once you have made your selection. The objects selected become the most recent selection in AutoCAD's memory.

• OPTIONS

Window   Selects objects completely enclosed by a rectangular window. Instead of entering **W** or **Window** at the Select objects: prompt, you can pick two points from left to right and automatically create a window selection set.

Crossing   Selects objects that cross through a rectangular window. Instead of entering **C** or **Crossing** at the Select objects: prompt, you can pick two points from right to left and automatically create a window selection set.

Previous   Selects last set of objects selected for editing. You can use Previous to pick the objects you have picked with Select when a later command prompts you to select objects. The Previous option is useful when you want several commands to process the same set of objects, as in a menu macro.

All   Selects everything in the drawing, including objects in layers that are frozen or turned off.

Last   Selects last object drawn or inserted.

Remove   Removes objects from the current selection of objects.

Add   Adds objects to the current selection of objects. You will usually use this option after you have issued the *R* option. The *Remove* and *Add* modes will remain in effect only during the specific command's execution and can be interchanged as often as necessary.

Multiple   Allows you to pick several objects at one time before highlighting them and adding them to the current selection of objects.

Undo   Removes the most recently added object from the current selection of objects.

BOX   Allows you to use either a crossing or a standard window, depending on the orientation of your window pick points. If you pick points from right to left, you will get a crossing window, but if you pick points from left to right, you will get a standard window.

AUto   Allows you to select objects by picking them or by using a window, as you would with the *BOX* option. After you issue the AUto option, you can pick objects individually, as usual. If no object is picked, AutoCAD assumes you want to use the *BOX* option, and a window appears that allows you to use either a crossing or standard window to select objects.

SIngle   Selects only the first picked object or the first group of windowed objects.

WPolygon   Selects objects that are contained within any shape you define. The shape assumes a closed polyline. There are certain restrictions: For example, you cannot include intersecting rubber-band lines, and you cannot place a vertex on an existing polygon segment.

CPolygon   Similar to *WPolygon*, except it selects objects that cross or enclose any shape you define. The shape assumes a closed polyline. There are certain restrictions: For example, you cannot include intersecting rubber-band lines, and you cannot plac a vertex on an existing polygon segment.

Fence   Similar to *CPolygon*, except it selects intersecting or crossing objects with one or more rubber-band lines you define, including lines that intersect themselves.

Notes   The Select command maintains a selection set only until you pick a different group of objects at another Select object: prompt. Entering the AutoLISP command **(setq set1 (ssget))** at the command prompt allows you to create a selection set that you can return to again and again during the course of the current editing session. Whenever you want to select this group of objects again, enter **!set1** at the Select objects: prompt.

See **Ddselect** for information on Implied Windowing and Entity Sort methods.

See Also   Aperture, Ddselect. *System Variables:* Pickauto.

SHADE

Menu: **Render ➤ Shade**

Produces a quick "Z buffer" shaded view of a 3D model. This command should not be confused with **Render,** which offers more control over your rendered view.

● OPTIONS

The *Shadedge* and *Shadedif* system variables give you some control over the way a model is shaded.

Notes   You can't plot images that were created using Shade. However, you can use the **Slide** command to store them for quick retrieval later.

On systems that support fewer than 256 colors, Shade produces an image with hidden lines removed and 3dfaces in their original color. However, Shade can produce an image faster than the **Hide** command, and might be used where speed is a consideration.

On systems with 256 colors or more, Shade produces a shaded image for which the light source and viewer location are the same.

See Also   *System Variables:* Shadedge, Shadedif.

SHAPE

If you have created a group of custom shapes in an AutoCAD *.SHX* file, you can insert them using the Shape command. First, use the **Load** command to load the *.SHX* file dialog box. (AutoCAD provides a sample *.SHX* file called *PC.SHX*.) Shapes act like blocks, but you can't break them into their drawing components or attach attributes to them.

To Insert Custom Shapes:

Issue the command, then provide the following information:

1. Shape name (or ?) <default>: Enter the name of the shape or a question mark to list available shapes.

2. Start point: Pick the insertion point.

3. Height <1.0>: Enter the height value or select a height using the cursor.

4. Rotation angle <0.0>: Enter or visually select the angle.

Notes Because shapes take up less file space than blocks, you may want to use shapes in drawings that do not require the features offered by blocks.

See Also Compile, Load, Wildcards. *System Variables:* Shpname.

SKETCH

Menu: **Draw ➤ Line ➤ Sketch**

Allows you to draw freehand. (It actually draws short line segments end-to-end to achieve this effect.) The lines Sketch draws are only temporary lines that show the path of the cursor. To save the line, you must use the *Record* and *eXit* options.

To Draw Freehand:

Issue the command, then provide the following information:

1. Record increment: Enter a value representing the distance the cursor travels before a line is fixed along the sketch path.

2. Pen eXit Quit Record Erase Connect: Start your sketch line or enter an option.

• OPTIONS

Pen   As an alternative to the pick button on your pointing device, you can press **P** from the keyboard to toggle between the pen-up and pen-down modes. With the pen down, the short temporary line segments are drawn as you move the cursor. With the pen up, no lines are drawn.

eXit   Saves any temporary sketch lines and then exits the Sketch command.

Quit   Exits the Sketch command without saving temporary lines.

Record   Saves temporary sketched lines during the time you are using the Sketch command.

Erase   Erases temporary sketched lines.

Connect   Allows you to continue from the end of a sketch line.

. (period)   Allows you to draw a long line segment while using the Sketch command. With the pen up, place the cursor at the location of the long line segment, then type a period.

Notes   To draw polylines with Sketch instead of standard lines, use the **Setvar** command to set the *Skpoly* system variable to 1, or select **Skpoly** from the **Sketch** menu before you start your sketch.

The easiest way to use Sketch is with a digitizer equipped with a stylus. You can trace over other drawings or photographs and refine them later. The stylus gives a natural feel to your tracing.

The Record increment: prompt allows you to set the distance the cursor travels before AutoCAD places a line. The *Record increment* value can greatly affect the size of your drawing. If this value is too high, the sketch line segments are too apparent and your sketched lines will appear "boxy." If the increment is set too low, your drawing file becomes quite large, and regeneration and redrawing times increase dramatically. A rule of thumb is to set the Record increment value so that at least four line segments are drawn for the smallest 180-degree arc you anticipate drawing.

When AutoCAD runs out of RAM in which to store the lines being sketched, it must pause for a moment to set up a temporary file on your disk drive before it continues to store additional sketch lines in

RAM. Your computer will then beep and display the message Please raise the pen. If this occurs, press **P** to raise the pen. (You may have to press **P** twice.) When you get the message Thank you. Lower the pen and continue, press **P** again to proceed with your sketch. Setting *Record increment* to a low value increases your likelihood of running out of RAM.

Turn the Snap and **Ortho** modes off before starting a sketch. Otherwise, the sketch lines will be forced to the snap points, or drawn vertically or horizontally. The results of having the Ortho mode on may not be apparent until you zoom in on a sketch line.

If you prefer, you can sketch an object and then use the **Pedit** or **Fit** command to smooth the sketch lines.

See Also   Pedit, Pline. *System Variables:* Sketchinc, Skpoly.

SLIDELIB.EXE

Slidelib.EXE is an external AutoCAD program that runs independently from AutoCAD. Use it to combine several slide files into a slide library file. You use slide libraries to create icon menus and to help organize slide files.

To Build a Slide Library:

To use slidelib.exe, you must be either in DOS or in a DOS window under Windows.

At the DOS prompt, enter the following:

    Slidelib slide-library-name < ascii-list> ↵

Notes   Before you can create a slide library, you must create an ASCII file containing a list of slide-file names to include in the library. Do not include the *.SLD* extension in the list of names. You can give the list any name and extension. You can then issue the Slidelib program from the DOS prompt.

See Also   Mslide, Vslide.

SNAP

Controls the settings for the Snap mode. The Snap mode allows you to accurately place the cursor by forcing it to move in specified increments. The equivalent dialog box option is Ddrmodes.

To Set Snap Mode:

Issue the command, then provide the following information:

- Snap spacing or ON/OFF/Aspect/Rotate/Style <default spacing>: Enter the desired snap spacing or an option.

● OPTIONS

Snap spacing   Allows you to enter the desired snap spacing. The Snap mode is turned on and the new snap settings take effect.

ON   Turns on the Snap mode. Has the same effect as pressing the F9 function key or Ctrl-B.

OFF   Turns off the Snap mode. Has the same effect as pressing the F9 function key, Ctrl-B, or clicking on the **S** button on the toolbar.

Aspect   Enters a Y-axis snap spacing different from the X-axis snap spacing.

Rotate   Rotates the snap points and the AutoCAD cursor to an angle other than 0 and 90 degrees.

Style   Allows you to choose between the standard orthogonal snap style and an isometric snap style.

Notes   You can use the *Rotate* option to rotate the cursor; the Ortho mode will conform to the new cursor angle. This option also allows you to specify a snap origin, allowing you to accurately place hatch patterns. The *Snapang* system variable also lets you rotate the cursor.

If you use the **Isometric** *Style* option, you can use the **Isoplane** command to control the cursor orientation. Also, the **Ellipse** command allows you to draw isometric ellipses.

You can set many of the settings available in the Snap command using the **Ddrmodes** dialog box.

See Also   Ddrmodes, Ellipse, Hatch, Isoplane. *System Variables:* Snapang, Snapbase, Snapisopair, Snapmode, Snapunit.

SOLID

Solid allows you to fill an area solidly. You determine the area by picking points in a crosswise, or "bow-tie" fashion. Solid is best suited to filling rectilinear areas. Polylines are better for filling curved areas.

To Fill an Area:

Issue the command, then provide the following information:

1. First point: Pick one corner of the area to be filled.

2. Second point: Pick the next, adjacent corner of the area.

3. Third point: Pick the corner diagonal to the last point selected.

4. Fourth point: Pick the next, adjacent corner of the area.

Continue to pick points until you have defined the filled area.

Notes   In large drawings that contain many solids, you can reduce regeneration and redrawing times by setting the Fill command to *Off* until you are ready to plot the final drawing.

See Also   Fill, Pline, 3dface, Trace.

STATUS

Menu: **Assist ➤ Inquiry ➤ Status**

Displays the current settings of a drawing, including the drawing limits and the status of all drawing modes. It also displays the current memory usage.

To Display Current Drawing Settings:

Issue the command. You will see the display shown in FIGURE 36.

Modelspace limits and *Modelspace uses* change to *Paperspace limits* and *Paperspace uses* when you are in the Paperspace mode.

See Also   Layers, Settings, Time.

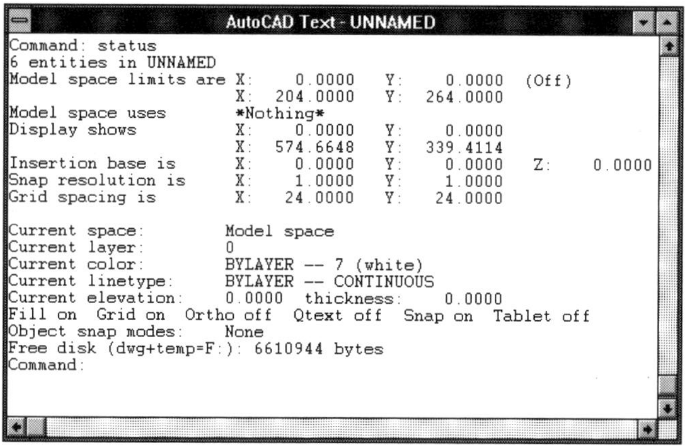

```
                        AutoCAD Text - UNNAMED
Command: status
6 entities in UNNAMED
Model space limits are X:     0.0000    Y:     0.0000   (Off)
                       X:   204.0000    Y:   264.0000
Model space uses       *Nothing*
Display shows          X:     0.0000    Y:     0.0000
                       X:   574.6648    Y:   339.4114
Insertion base is      X:     0.0000    Y:     0.0000    Z:     0.0000
Snap resolution is     X:     1.0000    Y:     1.0000
Grid spacing is        X:    24.0000    Y:    24.0000

Current space:         Model space
Current layer:         0
Current color:         BYLAYER -- 7 (white)
Current linetype:      BYLAYER -- CONTINUOUS
Current elevation:     0.0000   thickness:     0.0000
Fill on  Grid on  Ortho off  Qtext off  Snap on  Tablet off
Object snap modes:     None
Free disk (dwg+temp=F:): 6610944 bytes
Command:
```

Figure 36: The Status display screen

STRETCH

Menu: **Modify ➤ Stretch**

Moves vertices of objects while maintaining the continuity of connected lines.

To Stretch an Object:

Issue the command, then provide the following information:

1. Select objects: Enter **C** to use a crossing window.

2. Select objects: Enter **R** to remove objects from the set of selected objects or press ↵ to confirm your selection.

3. Base point: Pick the base reference point for the stretch.

4. New point: Pick the second point in relation to the base point indicating the distance and direction you wish to move.

Notes You can select vertex locations separately from the objects to be stretched. Indicate the vertices with a window, then select the objects individually with a pick. If there are several lines or other objects connected at the same vertex, you can use the same method to stretch a selection of them.

Another way to use Stretch is to enter **C** (for Crossing window) at the Select objects: prompt. You can then deselect objects with the *Remove object selection* option. Do not use a window to deselect an object.

You cannot stretch blocks or text. If a block's or text's insertion point is included in a crossing window, the entire block will be moved.

See Also Copy, Ddgrips, Grips, Move.

STYLE

Menu: **Draw** ➤ **Text** ➤ **Set Style**...

Allows you to create a text style by specifying the AutoCAD font on which it is based, its height, its width factor, and the obliquing angle. You can change a font to be backwards, upside down, or vertical. See FIGURE 37 for a list of the standard AutoCAD fonts and FIGURE 38 for tables of the symbol, Greek, and Cyrillic fonts. You can also use Style to modify an existing text style.

AutoCAD Font	Font Description
This is Txt	
This is Monotxt	
This is Simplex	(Old version of Roman Simplex)
This is Complex	(Old version of Roman Complex)
This is Italic	(Old version of Italic Complex)
This is Romans	(Roman Simplex)
This is Romand	(Roman double stroke)
This is Romanc	(Roman Complex)
This is Romant	(Roman triple stroke)
This is Scripts	(Script Simplex)
This is Scriptc	(Script Complex)
This is Italicc	(Italic Complex)
This is Italict	(Italic triple stroke)
Τηισ ισ Γρεεκσ	(This is Greeks — Greek Simplex)
Τηισ ισ Γρεεκχ	(This is Greekc — Greek Complex)
Узит ит Вшсиллив	(This is Cyrillic — Alphabetical)
Тхис ис Чйрилтлч	(This is Cyriltlc — Transliteration)
This is Gothicr	(Gothic English)
Thif if Gothicg	(Gothic German)
Uhis is Gothiri	(Gothic Italian)

Figure 37: The AutoCAD script fonts

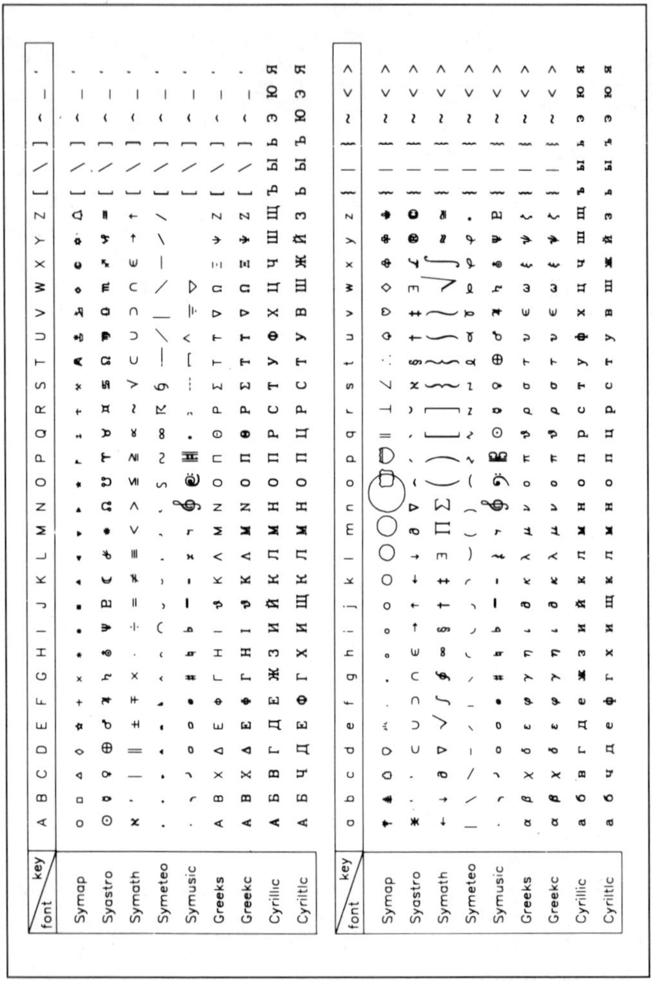

Figure 38: The AutoCAD symbol fonts

To Create a Text Style:

Issue the command, then provide the following information:

1. Text style name (or ?) <current style>: Enter a style name or a question mark for a list of available styles. Wildcards are accepted. (Setting the *Filedia* system variable to 1 displays the Select Font File list dialog box. Selecting **Set Style** from the pull-down menu displays icon boxes to pick from available styles.)

2. Font file <default font file>: Enter a font file name, or ↵ to accept the default.

3. Height <default height>: Enter the desired height, or ↵ to accept the default.

4. Width factor <default width factor>: Enter the desired width factor, or ↵ to accept the default.

5. Obliquing angle <default angle>: Enter the desired width obliquing angle, or ↵ to accept the default.

6. Backwards? <N>: Enter **Y** if you want the text to read backward, or ↵ to accept N, the default.

7. Upside-down? <N>: Enter **Y** if you want the text to read upside-down, or ↵ to accept N, the default.

8. Vertical? <N>: Enter **Y** if you want the text to read vertically, or ↵ to accept N, the default.

• OPTIONS

Text style name Allows you to enter either a new name to define a new style or the name of an existing style to redefine the style.

Font file Allows you to choose from several fonts. You can select from a set of predefined fonts from the **Select Font File** dialog box. You can also use PostScript Type 1 fonts.

Height Allows you to determine a fixed height for the style being defined. A value of 0 allows you to determine text height as it is entered.

Width factor Allows you to make the style appear expanded or compressed.

Obliquing angle   Allows you to "italicize" the style.

Backwards   Allows you to make the style appear backwards.

Upside down   Allows you to make the style appear upside-down.

Vertical   Allows you to make the style appear vertical.

Notes   If you modify a style's font, text previously entered in that style is updated to reflect the modification. If any other style option is modified, previously entered text is not affected. Once you use the Style command, the style created or modified becomes the new current style.

A 0 value at the Height: prompt causes AutoCAD to prompt you for a text height whenever you use this style with the **Dtext** or **Text** commands.

At the Width factor: prompt, a value of 1 generates normal text. A greater value expands the style; a smaller value compresses it.

At the Obliquing angle: prompt, a value of 0 generates normal text. A greater value slants the style to the right, creating italics. A negative value slants the style to the left.

If you pick Draw ➤ Text ➤ Set Style… from the pull-down menu, a set of icon menus appear. These display the various standard fonts available (see FIGURE 39). When you pick a font from an icon menu, AutoCAD automatically enters a style name and font at the first two prompts. You enter the style height, width factor, obliquing angle, and so on.

You can also set the current text style by clicking on Settings ➤ Entity Modes… ➤ Text Style…

See Also   Change, Ddedit, Dtext, Qtext, Text, Wildcards.

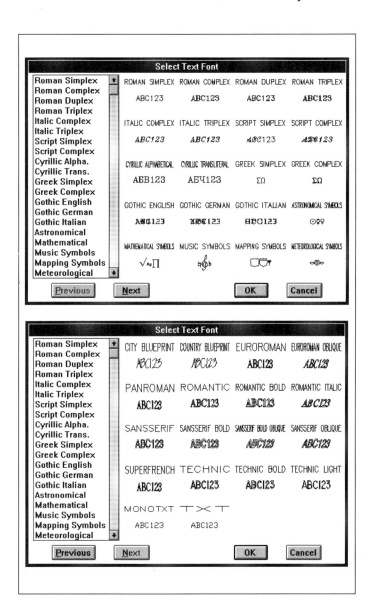

Figure 39: The Fonts icon menus

SYSTEM VARIABLES

Transparent: **System_Variable_Name**

The system variables control AutoCAD's many settings. Many of these variables are accessible through the commands they are associated with. You can also set system variables using the AutoLISP interpreter with the *Setvar* and *Getvar* AutoLISP functions.

To Set a System Variable:

Enter the System Variable name, then provide the following information:

- **Variable name or ?:** Enter the desired system variable name or a question mark for a list of variables.

● OPTIONS

TABLE 9 lists all of the system variables. They fall into three categories: adjustable variables, read-only variables, and variables accessible only through Setvar. You can set an adjustable variable by issuing the Setvar command and the name of the desired variable. A prompt then asks for an integer value. The meaning of that value depends on the nature of the variable.

If you already know the system variable name, in most cases you can enter it directly instead of using the Setvar command.

Table 9: System Variables

Variable	Explanation
Acadprefix	Read-only. Displays the name(s) of the directory path or paths saved in the DOS environment variable *Acad*, using the DOS command **SET**.
Acadver	Read-only. Displays the AutoCAD version number.
Aflags	Controls the attribute mode settings: 1 = invisible, 2 = constant, 4 = verify, 8 = preset. For more than one setting, use the sum of the desired settings. See **Attdef**.
Angbase	Controls the direction of the 0 angle. Can also be set with the **Units** command.
Angdir	Controls the positive direction of angles: 0 = counterclockwise, 1 = clockwise. Can also be set with the **Units** command.
Aperture	Controls the Osnap cursor target height in pixels. Can also be set with the **Aperture** command.
Area	Read-only. Displays the last area computed. See the **Area** command.
Attdia	Controls the attribute dialog box for the **Insert** command: 0 = no dialog box, 1 = dialog box.
Attmode	Controls the attribute display mode: 0 = off, 1 = normal, 2 = on. Can also be set with the **Attdisp** command.
Attreq	Controls the prompt for attributes. 0 = no prompt or dialog box for attributes. Attributes use default values. 1 = normal prompt or dialog box upon attribute insertion. Can also be set with the **Units** command.

Table 9: System Variables (continued)

Variable	Explanation
Auditctl	Controls the creation of Audit log files. 0 = create, 1 = do not create. See **Audit**.
Aunits	Controls angular units: 0 = decimal degrees, 1 = degrees- minutes-seconds, 2 = grads, 3 = radians, 4 = surveyors' units.
Auprec	Controls the precision of angular units determined by decimal place. Can also be set with the **Units** command.
Backz	Displays the distance from the Dview target to the back clipping plane. See **Dview**.
Blipmode	Controls the appearance of blips: 0 = off, 1 = on. See **Blipmode**.
Cdate	Read-only. Displays calendar date/time read from DOS. See **Time**.
Cecolor	Displays/sets current object color. See **Color**.
Celtype	Displays current object line type. See **Linetype**.
Chamfera	Stores first chamfer distance. See **Chamfer**.
Chamferb	Stores second chamfer distance. See **Chamfer**.
Circlerad	Sets a default value for circle radius. Enter 0 for no default.
Clayer	Displays/sets current layer. See **Layer** and **Ddlmodes** .
Cmdactive	Read-only. Shows status of commands, scripts and dialog boxes: 1 = ordinary command is active, 2 = ordinary and transparent commands are active, 4 = script is active, 8 = dialog box is active. If more than one setting is active, the variable shows the active sum.

Table 9: System Variables (continued)

Variable	Explanation
Cmddia	Controls dialog box for commands other than file dialogs: 1 = use dialog box, 0 = use command-line prompts only.
Cmdecho	Used with AutoLISP to control what is displayed on the prompt line. 0 = not echoed to screen, 1 = echoed. See the AutoLISP manual for details.
Cmdnames	Displays in English current active command name, including transparent command.
Coords	Controls coordinate readout: 0 = coordinates are displayed only when points are picked. 1 = absolute coordinates are dynamically displayed as cursor moves. 2 = distance and angle are displayed during commands that accept relative distance input. Also controlled by the F6 function key.
Cvport	Shows/sets ID number for current viewport.
Date	Read-only. Displays Julian date/time. See **Time**.
Dbmod	Read-only. Identifies drawing database modification status: 0 = drawing database not modified, 1 = entity database modified, 2 = symbol table modified, 4 = database variable modified, 8 = window modified, 16 = view modified.
Diastat	Read-only. Dialog box exit method: 0 = via Cancel, 1 = via OK.
Distance	Read-only. Displays last distance read using **Dist**. See **Dist**.

Table 9: System Variables (continued)

Variable	Explanation
Donutid	Sets inside diameter default value for **Donut** command.
Donutod	Sets outside diameter default value for **Donut** command.
Dragmode	Controls dragging: 0 = no dragging, 1 = on if requested, 2 = automatic drag. See **Dragmode**.
Dragp1	Controls regen-drag input sampling rate.
Dragp2	Controls fast-drag input sampling rate. Higher values force the display of more of the dragged image during cursor movement, and lower values display less.
Dwgcodepage	Current drawing code page.
Dwgname	Read-only. Displays drawing name. See **Status**.
Dwgprefix	Read-only. Displays drive and directory prefix or path for the current drawing file.
Dwgtitled	Read-only. Drawing name status: 0 = drawing is unnamed, 1 = drawing is named.
Dwgwrite	Controls drawing's read-only status: 0 = drawing open as read-only, 1 = drawing open for reading and editing.
Elevation	Controls current three-dimensional elevation. See **Elev**.
Errno	Displays/sets code for errors from AutoLISP and ADS applications.

Table 9: System Variables (continued)

Variable	Explanation
Expert	Controls prompts, depending on level of user's expertise. 0 issues normal prompts. 1 = suppresses the *About to Regen* and *Really want to turn the current layer off?* prompts and the *Verify Regenauto OFF* setting. 2 = suppresses previous prompts plus *Block already defined…Redefine it?* and *A drawing with this name already exists*. 3 = suppresses previous prompts plus line type warnings. 4 = suppresses previous prompts plus **UCS** and **Vports** *Save* warnings. 5 = suppresses previous prompts plus DIM Save and DIM Override warnings.
Extmax	Read-only. Displays upper right corner coordinate of drawing extent.
Extmin	Read-only. Displays lower left corner coordinate of drawing extent.
Filedia	Controls file dialog box: 0 = off unless requested by ~ (tilde), 1 = on
Filletrad	Stores current fillet radius. See **Fillet**.
Fillmode	Controls fill status: 0 = off, 1 = on. See **Fill**.
Flatland	Controls AutoCAD's handling of three-dimensional functions and objects as they relate to Object snaps, DXF formats, and AutoLISP. 0 = functions take advantage of version 10's advanced features, 1 = functions operate as they did prior to release 10.
Frontz	Displays the distance from the Dview target to the front clipping plane. See **Dview**.
Gridmode	Controls grid: 0 = off, 1 = on. See **Grid**.
Gridunit	Controls grid spacing. See **Grid**.

Table 9: System Variables (continued)

Variable	Explanation
Gripblock	Sets the appearance of grips in blocks: 0 = grip appears at block insertion only (default value), 1 = grips assigned to all entities within blocks.
Gripcolor	Sets color for nonselected grips.
Griphot	Sets color for selected grip.
Grips	Displays grips for **Stretch**, **Move**, **Rotate**, **Scale**, and **Mirror**: 0 = grips off, 1 = grips on.
Gripsize	Sets grip box size. Default value is 3.
Handles	Read-only. Displays the status of the Handles command. 0 = off, 1 = on. See **Handles**.
Highlight	Controls object-selection ghosting: 0 = no ghosting, 1 = ghosting.
Hpang	Sets default hatch pattern angle.
Hpdouble	Sets default double hatch for user-defined pattern: 0 = single hatch, 1 = double hatch.
Hpname	Sets default hatch pattern name and style.
Hpscale	Sets default hatch pattern scale.
Hpspace	Sets default line spacing for user-defined hatch pattern.
Insbase	Controls insertion base point of current drawing. See **Base**.
Insname	Default block name for **Ddinsert** or **Insert** command.
Lastangle	Read-only. Displays the end angle of last arc or poly arc.

Table 9: System Variables (continued)

Variable	Explanation
Lastpoint	Displays coordinates of last point entered. Same point referenced by at sign (@).
Lenslength	Displays the current lens focal length used during the **Dview** command *Zoom* option.
Limcheck	Controls limit checking: 0 = no checking, 1 = checking. See **Limits**.
Limmax	Stores the coordinate of drawing's upper right limit. See **Limits**.
Limmin	Stores the coordinate of drawing's lower left limit. See **Limits**.
Loginname	Read-only. Displays user's login name set during configuration.
Ltscale	Stores the line type scale factor. See **Ltscale**.
Lunits	Controls unit styles: 1 = scientific, 2 = decimal, 3 = engineering, 4 = architectural, 5 = fractional. See **Units**.
Luprec	Stores unit accuracy by decimal place or size of denominator. See **Units**.
Macrotrace	Debugging tool for diesel expressions: 0 = disabled, 1 = enabled.
Maxactvp	Maximum number of viewports to regenerate at one time.
Maxsort	Sets the maximum number of symbol or file names to be sorted by any listing command.
Menuctl	Controls swapping of the screen menus whenever a command is entered: 0 = doesn't switch, 1 = switches.

Table 9: System Variables (continued)

Variable	Explanation
Menuecho	Controls the display of commands and prompts issued from the menu. A value of 1 suppresses display of commands entered from menu (can be toggled on or off with Ctrl-P); 2 suppresses display of commands and command prompts when command is issued from AutoLISP macro; 3 is a combination of options 1 and 2; 4 disables Ctrl-P menu echo toggle; 8 enables the printing of all input and output strings to the screen for debugging DIESEL macros.
Menuname	Stores the current menu file name. See **Menu**.
Mirrtext	Controls text mirroring: 0 = no text mirroring, 1 = text mirroring.
Modemacro	Allows display of text or special strings like current drawing name, time, date, or specials modes at the status line. See DIESEL macro language in AutoCAD Customization manual.
Offsetdist	Stores offset default distance.
Orthomode	Controls the Ortho mode: 0 = off, 1 = on. See **Ortho**.
Osmode	Sets the current default Osnap mode: 0 = none, 1 = end point, 2 = midpoint, 4 = center, 8 = node, 16 = quadrant, 32 = intersection, 64 = insert, 128 = perpendicular, 256 = tangent, 512 = nearest, 1024 = quick. If more than one mode is required, enter the sum of those modes. See **Osnap**.
Pdmode	Sets the type of symbol used as a point during the Point command. Several point styles are available. See **Point**.

Table 9: System Variables (continued)

Variable	Explanation
Pdsize	Controls the size of the symbol set by **Pdmode**.
Perimeter	Read-only. Displays the perimeter value currently being read by Area, List, or Dblist. See **Area**, **List**, or **Dblist**.
Pfacevmax	Read-only. Defines maximum number of vertices for mesh entity faces.
Pickadd	Controls ability to add or remove entities from a selection set using the Shift key. 0 = disabled, 1 = enabled.
Pickauto	Controls automatic windowing for *Select objects:* prompt: 0 = disabled, 1 = enabled
Pickbox	Controls the size of the Select Object cursor.
Pickdrag	Controls how a selection window is drawn: 0 = Click mouse at each corner, 1 = Click mouse at one corner, hold mouse down while dragging, then release at other corner.
Pickfirst	Lets you select first, then use an edit/inquiry command: 0 = disabled, 1 = enabled.
Platform	Read-only. Message indicating AutoCAD version, such as Microsoft Windows, 386 Dos Extended, Apple Macintosh.
Plinegen	Controls linetype pattern to adjust its appearance between vertices. 0 = linetype displays dash at vertices, 1 = linetype continuous around vertices.
Plinewid	Default polyline width.
Plotid	Changes default plotter based on text description.
Plotter	Changes default plotter based on its assigned configuration number.

Table 9: System Variables (continued)

Variable	Explanation
Polysides	Stores **Polygon** command's default for number of sides.
Popups	Read-only. Displays the availability of the Advanced User Interface based on the display driver. 0 = not available, 1 = available.
Psltscale	Sets linetype scale for paper space. 0 = no specific scale factor, 1 = adjust linetype scale based on viewport.
Psprolog	Assigns a name for the prologue section for **Psout** command.
Psquality	Sets rendering quality of importing PostScript file into a drawing.
Qtextmode	Controls the Quick text mode: 0 = off, 1 = on. See **Qtext** command.
Regenmode	Controls the Regenauto mode: 0 = off, 1 = on. See **Regenauto**.
Re-init	Resets I/O ports, digitizer, display, plotter, and *Acad.PGP* file.
Savefile	Read-only. Displays current auto-save filename.
Savename	Read-only. Filename assigned to the currently saved file.
Savetime	Automatic-save time interval: 0 = disabled.
Screenboxes	Read-only. Number of boxes displayed on screen menu of graphics area.
Screenmode	Read-only. Controls grpahics/text screens: 0 = text screen, 1 = graphics mode, 2 = dual screen. Values are additive.
Screensize	Read-only. Reads the size of the graphics screen in pixels.

Table 9: System Variables (continued)

Variable	Explanation
Shadedge	Sets shading parameters: 0 = faces shaded, edges not highlighted, 1 = faces shaded with edges drawn using background color, 2 = faces unfilled with edges in entity color, 3 = faces in entity color, edges with background color.
Shadedif	Sets the ratio (in percent) of diffuse reflective light to ambient light.
Shpname	Stores default shape name.
Sketchinc	Sets the sketch record increment. See **Sketch**.
Skpoly	Controls whether the **Sketch** command uses regular lines or polylines. 0 = line, 1 = polyline.
Snapang	Controls snap and grid angle. See **Snap**.
Snapbase	Controls snap, grid, and hatch pattern origin. See **Snap**.
Snapisopair	Controls isometric plane: 0 = left, 1 = top, 2 = right. See **Snap** command.
Snapmode	Controls snap toggle: 0 = off, 1 = on. See **Snap** command.
Snapstyl	Controls snap style: 0 = standard, 1 = isometric. See **Snap**.
Snapunit	Sets snap spacing given in X and Y values. See **Snap**.
Sortents	Controls entity sorting order: 0 = disabled, 1 = object selection, 2 = object snap, 4 = redraws, 8 = Mslide slide creation, 16 = regens, 32 = plotting, 64 = PostScript output. Values are additive.

Table 9: System Variables (continued)

Variable	Explanation
Splframe	Controls the display of spline vertices, surface-fit three- dimensional meshes, and invisible edges of 3dfaces. 0 = no display of Spline vertices of invisible 3dface edges. Displays only defining mesh or surface-fit mesh. 1 = display of Spline vertices or invisible 3dface edges. Displays only surface-fit mesh.
Splinesegs	Controls the number of line segments used for each spline patch.
Splinetype	Controls the type of curved line generated by the **Pedit Spline** command. 5 = quadratic B-spline, 6 = Cubic B-spline.
Surftab1	Controls the number of mesh control points for the **Rulesurf** and **Tabsurf** commands and the number of mesh points in the M direction for the **Revsurf** and **Edgesurf** commands.
Surftab2	Controls the number of mesh control points in the N direction for the **Revsurf** and **Edgesurf** commands.
Surftype	Controls the type of surface fitting generated by the **Pedit Smooth** command. 5 = quadratic B-spline, 6 = cubic B-spline, and 8 = Bezier surface.
Surfu	Controls the accuracy of the smoothed surface models in the M direction.
Surfv	Controls the accuracy of the smoothed surface models in the N direction.
Syscodepage	Read-only. Indicates system code page of *Acad.XMF*.
Tabmode	Sets tablet mode: 0 = disabled, 1 = enabled.

Table 9: System Variables (continued)

Variable	Explanation
Target	Read-only. Displays the coordinate of the target point used in the **Dview** command.
Tdcreate	Read-only. Displays time and date of drawing creation. See **Time**.
Tdindwg	Read-only. Displays total editing time. See **Time**.
Tdupdate	Read-only. Displays time and date of last save. See **Time**.
Tdusrtimer	Read-only. Displays user-elapsed time. See **Time**.
Tempprefix	Read-only. Displays the name of the directory where temporary AutoCAD files are saved.
Texteval	Controls whether prompts for text and attribute input to commands are taken literally or as an AutoLISP expressions. 0 = literal, 1 = text you input with left parens and exclamation points will be interpreted as AutoLISP expression. **Dtext** takes all input literally, regardless of this setting.
Textsize	Controls default text height except for styles with an assigned fixed height. See **Dtext**, **Text**, and **Style**.
Textstyle	Sets the current text style. See **Style**.
Thickness	Controls three-dimensional thickness of objects being drawn. See **Elev**.
Tilemode	Toggle between paperspace and modelspace: 0 = enables paper space and viewport entities, 1 = release-10 mode.
Tracewid	Sets default trace width. See **Trace**.

Table 9: System Variables (continued)

Variable	Explanation
Treedepth	Lets you set a four-digit integer coding that ultimately affects AutoCAD's quickness for searching a database to execute commands. Changing the value of this variable forces a drawing regeneration regardless of the **Regenauto** setting.
Treemax	Limits the number of nodes in the spacial index created by Treedepth. This option limits memory consumption during regeneration.
Ucsfollow	Controls whether changing the current UCS automatically displays the plan view of the new current UCS. 0 = displayed view does not change, 1 = automatic display of new current UCS in plan.
Ucsicon	Controls ucsicon display: 0 = off, 1 = on, 2 = origin, when displayed.
Ucsname	Read-only. Displays the name of the current UCS. See **UCS**.
Ucsorg	Read-only. Displays the current UCS origin point. See **UCS**.
Ucsxdir	Read-only. Displays the X direction of the current UCS. See **UCS**.
Ucsydir	Read-only. Displays the Y direction of the current UCS. See **UCS**.
Undoctl	Read-only. Displays state of **Undo**: 1 = set if Undo enabled, 2 = set for one undo, 4 = set if Auto-group mode enabled, 8 = set if group currently active.
Undomarks	Read-only. Desplays the number of Undo's by *Mark* and *Back* options placed in the current drawing.

Table 9: System Variables (continued)

Variable	Explanation
Unitmode	Sets how fractional, feet-and-inches, and surveyors' angles are displayed on the status line. 0 = normal (for example, 1'–6~~FS1/2"). 1 = same as input format (for example, 1'6–1/2").
Useri1-5	Five variables for storing integers for custom applications.
Userr1-5	Five variables for storing real numbers for custom applications.
Users1-5	Five variables for storing text strings for custom applications.
Viewctr	Read-only. Displays the current UCS coordinates of the center of the current viewport.
Viewdir	Read-only. Displays the view direction of the current view port. This also describes the camera point as a 3D offset from the TARGET point.
Viewmode	**Controls** view mode for current viewport: 1 = perspective on, 2 = front clipping plane on, 4 = back clipping plane on, 8 = UCS follow mode on, 16 = front clipping plane not at eye level.
Viewsize	Read-only. Displays the height of the current view in drawing units.
Viewtwist	Read-only. Displays the view twist angle for the current viewport. See **Dview**.
Visretain	Controls **Xref** layering status: 0 = current drawing's layering status takes precedence over the Xref's layer definition, 1 = doesn't take precedence (this is the default value).

Table 9: System Variables (continued)

Variable	Explanation
Vsmax	Read-only. Displays the three-dimensional coordinate of the upper right corner of the current viewport's virtual screen relative to the current UCS.
Vsmin	Read-only. Displays the three-dimensional coordinate of the lower left corner of the current viewport's virtual screen relative to the current UCS.
Worlducs	Read-only. Displays the status of the World Coordinate System. 0 = WCS is not current, 1 = WCS is current. See **UCS**.
Worldview	Controls whether point input to the **Dview** and **Vpoint** commands is relative to the WCS or the current UCS. 0 = commands use the current UCS to interpret point value input, 1 = commands use WCS to interpret point value input.
Xrefctl	Controls creation of external *.XLG* files: 0 = not written, 1 = written.

TABLET

Tablet is useful only if you have a digitizing tablet. Use it to set up your tablet for accurate tracing.

To Set Up a Tablet:

Issue the command, then provide the following information:

- Option (ON/OFF/CAL/CFG): Enter an option. If you do not have a digitizing tablet, you will get the message Your pointing device cannot be used as a tablet.

• OPTIONS

ON/OFF   Toggles the *Calibrated* mode on or off. When on, you cannot access the screen menus. The F4 function key performs the same toggling function.

CAL   Allows you to *Calibrate* a tablet so distances on the tablet correspond to actual distances in your drawing. The calibration is effective only for the space (Paper/Modelspace) in which it is performed.

CFG   Allows you to *Configure* your digitizing tablet for a tablet menu like the one provided by AutoCAD.

Notes   The CAL or Calibrate option allows you to set specific distances on the tablet to correspond to actual distances in your AutoCAD drawing. You are prompted to pick a first known point on the tablet and enter its corresponding coordinate in your AutoCAD drawing. This point should be at the lowest left corner of a known origin—for example, one corner of a property line. Then you are prompted to pick a second known point on your tablet and enter its corresponding coordinate in your drawing. This second point should be the upper right end of the line of known length. For best results, this line should be as long as possible and should be horizontal or vertical, not diagonal. You may want to include a graphic scale in your drawing to be digitized just for the purpose of calibrating your tablet.

You may not be able to calibrate your tablet if you have configured it to have menus and a small screen pointing area. If this is the case, you may have to reconfigure it so that its entire surface is designated for the screen pointing area.

The *CFG* or Configure option allows you to control the location and format of tablet menus as well as the pointing area on your tablet. You are first prompted for the number of tablet menus you want.

The AutoCAD tablet menu contains four menus. Then you are prompted to pick the upper left, lower left, and lower right corners of the tablet menus. The AutoCAD template shows a black dot at these corners. Next, you are prompted for the number of columns and rows that each menu contains. Finally, you are asked if you want to specify the screen pointing area. This is the area on the tablet used for actual drawing. If you answer yes to this prompt, you are prompted to pick the lower left and upper right corners of the pointing area.

TABLET MENU

Allows you to use a pointing device to activate commands from a digitizing tablet.

To Use the Tablet Menu:

Issue the command to bring up the tablet menu. You can activate a command from the tablet by moving your pointing device to a box that represents the desired command and pressing the pick button. Commands you pick from the tablet menu often display a corresponding screen menu to allow you to pick the command options. The blank area at the top of the tablet menu is reserved for additional custom menu options.

See Also   Sketch, Tablet Mole Mode.

TABLET MOLE MODE

If you are using a digitizing tablet, you will be asked a series of questions about the *mole mode* feature during configuration. If you do not use the mole mode feature, you can only use your digitizing tablet to select points in the drawing area and to pick menu options from the screen menu. The toolbar, pull-down menus, and any other window outside of AutoCAD are not accessible. To get to these other areas, you must use your standard Windows pointing device. With the Mole Mode feature activated, you will be able to access the toolbar and pull-down menus with your digitizer, though you will still be restricted to using the digitizer within AutoCAD.

● OPTIONS

The following list shows you the questions you will be asked when you configure your digitizing tablet:

1. Do you want to configure your digitizer as a mole?
<Y>: allows you to activate the mole mode.

2. Do you want an audible mole/context state in-dicator? <N>: lets you turn on an audible indicator to notify you when you enter mole mode.

3. Do you want a visible mole/context state indicator?
<Y>: lets you turn on a visual indicator to notify you when you enter digitizer or mole mode.

4. Do you want to assign a CURSOR BUTTON to toggle modes? <N>: lets you assign a button on your digitizer puck to turn mole mode on and off.

5. Do you want a PRIMARY MOLE area? <Y>: lets you set up a primary mole mode area. If you answer yes, you are prompted to pick the lower left corner and upper right corner for the primary mole area.

6. Do you want a SECONDARY MOLE area? <N>: lets you set up a secondary mole mode area. If you answer yes, you are prompted to pick the lower left corner and upper right corner for the primary mole area.

7. Do you want a PRIMARY TOGGLE area? <N>: lets you set up an area on your digitizing tablet to act as a switch to turn mole mode on and off. If you answer yes, you are prompted to pick the lower left corner and upper right corner for the primary toggle area. You don't need to select a large area for this option.

8. Do you want a SECONDARY TOGGLE area? <N>: lets you set up a second area on your digitizing tablet to act as a switch to turn the mole mode on and off. If you answer yes, you are prompted to pick the lower left corner and upper right corner for the primary toggle area. You don't need to select a large area for this option.

FIGURE 40 illustrates possible locations for primary and secondary mole and toggle areas.

Notes   If you are using a single primary mole area, you cannot use the mole area for tracing, nor can you use the mole area to select commands from a tablet overlay menu. If you need to use the entire tablet for an overlay menu, use a *toggle area* in conjunction with a *secondary mole* area to make a tablet area serve two functions.

If you choose to use a toggle area, make it very small and place it near the mole area, since it is used only to switch the mole area on and off. This way, you can use an area on your digitizer for both a mole area and for selecting commands. If you choose to use a toggle area and

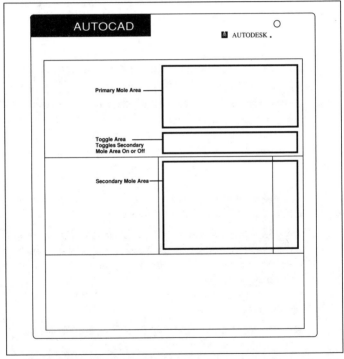

Figure 40: Sample locations for primary and secondary mole and toggle areas.

a secondary mole area, you may want the screen pointing area to double as the mole area.

If you chose the visible mole indicator, the AutoCAD Window title bar displays the word **Mole** or **Digitizer**, depending on the digitizer's current mode. The sound option beeps each time you toggle from mole to digitizer mode.

If you have both a mouse and a digitizer connected to your computer, you can still use both devices for AutoCAD.

TABSURF

Menu: **Draw ➤ 3D Surfaces ➤ Tabulated Surface**

Draws a surface by extruding a curve in a straight line (see FIGURE 41). Before using Tabsurf, you must draw a curve defining the extruded shape and a line defining the direction of the extrusion (the direction vector).

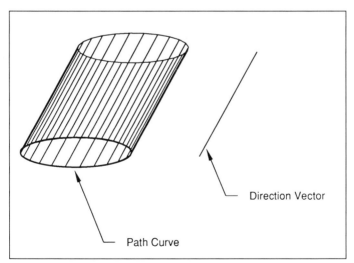

Direction Vector

Path Curve

Figure 41: A curve extruded in a straight line

To Straighten a Curved Surface:

Issue the command, then provide the following information:

1. Select path curve: Pick a curve defining the surface shape.

2. Select direction vector: Pick a line defining the direction of the extrusion.

Notes The point at which you pick the direction vector at the Select direction vector: prompt determines the direction of the extrusion. The end point nearest the pick point will serve as the base of the direction vector, and the other end indicates the direction of the extrusion.

You can draw the curve with a line, arc, circle, two-dimensional polyline, or three-dimensional polyline. The direction vector can be a three-dimensional line. Tabsurf has an effect similar to changing the thickness of an object, but extrusions using Tabsurf are not limited to the Z axis.

See Also Pedit. *System Variables:* Surftab1.

TEXT

See **Dtext**.

TEXTSCR

See **Graphscr/Textscr**.

3DFACE

Menu: **Draw ➤ 3D Surfaces ➤ 3D Face**

Allows you to draw a 3dface in three-dimensional space. 3dfaces are surfaces defined by four points in space picked in circular fashion. Although they appear transparent, 3dfaces are treated as opaque when you remove hidden lines from a drawing. After the first face defined, you are prompted for additional third and fourth points, which allow the addition of adjoining 3dfaces.

To Draw a 3dface:

Issue the command, then provide the following information:

1. First point: Select the first corner.

2. Second point: Select the second corner.

3. Third point: Select the third corner.

4. Fourth point: Select the fourth corner.

5. Third point: Continue to pick pairs of points defining more faces or press ↵ to end the command.

● OPTIONS

Enter **Invisible** or **I** at the point prompt to make an edge of the 3dface invisible.

Notes Use the *Invisible* option if you want to hide the joint line between joined 3dfaces. Do this by entering **I** just before you pick the first defining point of the side to be made invisible.

Make invisible edges visible by setting the *Splframe* system variable to an nonzero value. See **Setvar** for more on *Splframe*.

All meshes are composed of 3dfaces. If you explode a 3dmesh, each facet of the mesh will be a 3dface.

AutoCAD provides the *Edge.LSP* AutoLISP file for changing edges to invisible.

See Also   *System Variables:* Pfacevmax, Splframe.

3DMESH

Menu: **Draw ➤ 3D Surfaces ➤ 3D Objects...➤** Mesh

Draws a three-dimensional surface using coordinate values you specify. 3dmesh can be used when drawing three-dimensional models of a topography or performing finite element analysis. 3dmesh is designed for programmers who want control over each node of a mesh.

To Draw with 3dmesh:

Issue the command, then provide the following information:

1. Mesh M size: Enter the number of vertices in the M direction.

2. Mesh N size: Enter the number of vertices in the N direction.

3. Vertex (0,0): Enter the XYZ coordinate value for the first vertex in the mesh.

4. Vertex (0,1): Enter the XYZ coordinate value for the next vertex in the N direction of the mesh.

5. Vertex (0,2): Continue to enter XYZ coordinate values for the vertices.

Notes   To use 3dmesh to generate a topographic model, arrange your XYZ coordinate values in a rectangular array, roughly as they would appear in the plan. Fill any blanks in the array with dummy or neutral coordinate values. Start the 3dmesh command and use the number of columns for the mesh M size and the number of rows for the N size. At the **Vertex:** prompts, enter the coordinate values row by row, starting at the lower left corner of your array and reading from left to right. Include any dummy values.

See Also   Mface, Pedit, Pface. *System Variables:* Surftype, Surfu.

3DPOLY

Menu: Draw ➤ Polyline ➤ 3D

Allows you to draw a polyline in three-dimensional space using XYZ coordinates or object snap points. Three-dimensional polylines are like standard polylines, except that you can't give them a width or use arc segments. Also, you cannot use the **Pedit** command's *Fit curve* option with 3dpoly. To create a smooth curve using three-dimensional polylines, use the **Spline** *Pedit* option.

To Draw a 3dpoly Line:

Issue the command, then provide the following information:

1.   From point: Enter the beginning point.

2.   Close/Undo/<Endpoint of line>: Enter the next point of the line.

3.   Close/Undo/<Endpoint of line>: Continue to pick points for additional line segments or press ↵ to end the command.

● OPTIONS

Close   Connects the first point with the last point in a series of line segments.

Undo   Moves back one line segment in a series of line segments.

See Also   Pedit, Pline.

TIME

Keeps track of the time you spend on a drawing. The time is displayed in "military" format, using the 24-hour count.

To Display Drawing-Time Data:

Issue the command, and you will be shown the following information:

1. Current time: Enter date and time.

2. Times for this drawing:

- Created: Displays date and time.
- Last updated: Displays date and time.
- Total editing time: Displays days and time.
- Elapsed time (on): Displays days and time.
- Next automatic save in: Displays the time interval until the next automatic save.
- Display/On/Off/Reset: Enter an option.

● OPTIONS

Display   Redisplays time information.

On   Sets elapsed timer on.

Off   Sets elapsed timer off.

Reset   Resets elapsed timer to 0.

See Also   *System Variables:* Tdindwg, Tdupdate, Tdusrtimer, Tdcreate.

TOOLBAR

The toolbar gives you quick access to some of the more common AutoCAD settings. In addition, you can create custom macros using the blank toolbar buttons. FIGURE 42 shows the different parts of the toolbar.

● OPTIONS

Color button   opens the same dialog box as the Ddemodes command. This dialog box lets you set the default color, line type, layer, text style, elevation, and thickness of objects.

Layer button   opens the same dialog box as the Ddlmodes command or the Settings ➤ Layer Control menu selection, and controls all the layering functions.

Layer Popup list   lets you select the current layer from a list.

O button   turns the Ortho mode on and off.

S button   turns the Snap mode on and off.

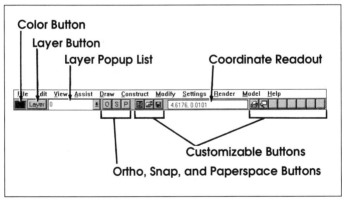

Figure 42: The AutoCAD Toolbar and its components

P button turns paperspace on and off when the Tilemode system variable is set to **0**.

Coordinate display shows the coordinate of your cursor. Click on it to switch between dynamic readout mode and static readout mode.

Blank buttons are customizable. If you right-click on any of these buttons, an *AutoCAD Toolbar Button dialog box* appears allowing you to add the keystrokes you want entered when the button is clicked. The keystrokes are stored in the *ACAD.INI* file. You have the option to use either a predefined icon or an alphabetical character for the toolbar buttons.

Notes You can add more icons to those available in the Toolbar Button dialog box by using a third party program such as Borland's Resource Workshop. You must edit the *Tbar16.DLL* or *Tbar24.DLL* file and include any additions to the resource stringtable.

TOOLBOX

Menu: Icon on Status Line

The Floating Toolbox is a set of icons that gives you quick access to the more common AutoCAD commands and options. As you move the arrow cursor over the buttons, their functions appear in the toolbox title at the top. The toolbox can be customized by right-clicking on any button. You then see the Toolbox Customization dialog box.

● OPTIONS

The following are the options in the Toolbox Customization dialog box:

Insert adds a new button to the toolbox. You can have as many as 128 buttons.

Delete removes a button from the toolbox.

Cancel exits the Toolbox Customization dialog box without making changes.

Toolbox Width/Floating lets you set the number of columns in the toolbox when it is floating.

Toolbox Width/Locked lets you set the number of columns in the toolbox when it is locked.

AutoCAD Command lets you enter the keystrokes you want associated with the button.

Image Name lets you select from a set of predefined icons.

Save to Acad.INI lets you permanently store changes to the toolbox.

The last customizable button on the left end of the toolbar turns the toolbox on and off and changes its status from floating to locked. When the toolbox is floating, you can position it anywhere on the screen. When it is locked, it appears either in the upper left or upper right corner of the drawing.

Notes You can add more icons to those available in the *Image Name* list by using a third party program such as Borland's Resource Workshop. You must edit the *Tbar16.DLL* or *Tbar24.DLL* file and include any additions to the resource stringtable.

TRACE

You can use Trace where a thick line is desired. Alternatively, you can accomplish the same thing using the **Pline** command. If you draw a series of Trace line segments, the corners are automatically joined to form a sharp corner.

To Draw a Thick Line:

Issue the command, then provide the following information:

1. Trace width <default width>: Enter the desired width.

2. From point: Pick the start point for the trace.

3. To point: Pick the next point.

As with the **Line** command, you can continue to pick points to draw a series of connected line segments. Trace lines appear only after the next point is selected.

Notes If you draw a series of Trace line segments, the corners are automatically joined to form a sharp corner. For this reason, traces do not have an Undo option, and the starting and ending segments will not join and bevel properly. To have traces bevel properly for the start and end segments, begin the trace not on the desired corner/endpoint but at any point midway on the desired first segment, then make the end segment complete the actual first segment.

See Also Fill. *System Variables:* Tracewid.

TRANSPARENT COMMANDS

Transparent commands are ones which can be used while AutoCAD is still executing another command. Control is transferred temporarily to the transparent command until it is completed, or until you terminate it by pressing Ctrl-C. Not all commands can be used transparently. Transparent commands are indicated with an apostrophe preceding the command name.

To Issue a Command
While Another Is Executing:

Type an apostrophe preceding the command name. (This only works for commands that are identified as transparent commands in the main entries throughout this book.) See TABLE 10 below for a list of Transparent Commands.

Table 10: AutoCAD Transparent Commands

Transparent Commands		
About	Dragmode	Redraw
Aperture	Fileopen	Redrawall
Attdisp	Files	Regenauto
Base	Fill	Resume
Blipmode	Graphscxr	Script
Color	Grid	Setvar
Ddemodes	Help / ?	Snap
Ddgrips	Id	Style
Ddim	Isoplane	Status
Ddlmodes	Layer	Textscr
Ddosnap	Limits	Time
Ddrmodes	Linetype	Units
Ddselect	Ltscale	View
Ddunits	Ortho	Zoom
Delay	Osmode	
Dist	Pan	

TREESTAT

Displays data (see FIGURE 43) regarding the drawing's current spatial index, allowing you to improve drawing efficiency via the *Treedepth* system variable. Information is provided separately for Modelspace and Paperspace.

To View the Spatial Index:

Issue the command.

Notes The number of nodes being reported is shown in the Model-space branch and Paper-space branch. Each node requires approximately 80 bytes of memory. Setting the *Treedepth* system variable to a large number increases disk swapping, negating performance benefits of the spatial index. The objective is to have fewer entities per node to take advantage of spatial indexing, the optimum number being dependent on the amount of memory your computer has. The more memory you have, the more you can take advantage of spatial indexing. The use of *Treedepth* and *Treestat* is best suited to large drawings in order to optimize performance.

See Also *System Variables:* Maxtreenodes, Treedepth, Treestat.

```
Model-space branch
-------------------
Oct-tree, depth limit = 30
Subtree containing entities with defined extents:
    Nodes: 19  Entities: 12   Maximum depth: 21
    Average entities per node: 0.63
    Average node depth: 12.32   Average entity depth: 11.00
    Entities at depth 5: 1   6: 1   20: 1   21: 1
    Nodes with population 0:  12  1: 5   3: 1   4: 1
Total nodes: 22    Total entities: 12

Paper-Space branch
-------------------
Quad-tree, depth limit = 20
Subtree containing entities with defined extents:
    Nodes: 1    Entities:  0
    Average entities per node: 0.00
    Average node depth: 5.00
    Nodes with population 0: 1
Total nodes: 4    Total entities: 0
```

Figure 43: The Treestat display

TRIM

Menu: **Modify ➤ Trim**

Trim shortens an object to meet another object.

To Trim an Object:

Issue the command, then provide the following information:

1. Select cutting edge(s)...: Pick the objects to which you want to trim other objects.

2. <Select objects to trim>/Undo: Pick the objects you want to trim, one at a time.

Notes At the Select cutting edge: prompt, you can pick several objects that intersect the objects you want to trim. Once you've selected the cutting edges, press ↵ and the Select object to trim: prompt appears, allowing you to pick the sides of the objects to trim. You cannot trim objects within blocks or use blocks as cutting edges. In addition, cutting edges must intersect the objects to be trimmed. If you pick an object that falls between two other "cutting edge" objects, the segment between the "cutting edge" objects will be removed.

You can only use Trim on objects that lie in a plane parallel to the current UCS (user coordinate system). Also, if you are not viewing the current UCS in plan, you may get an erroneous result.

See Also Break, Change.

U

Menu: **Edit ➤ Undo**

Reverses the most recent command. You can undo as many commands as you have issued during any given editing session.

Notes   The *Auto*, *End*, *Control*, and *Group* options under the **Undo** command affect the results of the U command. U is essentially the Undo command with 1 as the parameter.

See Also   Redo, Undo.

UCS

The User Coordinate System, or UCS, is a tool for creating and editing three-dimensional drawings. A UCS can be described as a plane in three-dimensional space on which you can draw. Using the UCS command, you can create and shift between as many UCS's as you like. The dialog box for this command is Dducs.

There are specialized three-dimensional drawing commands for creating three-dimensional surfaces. You can issue these three-dimensional commands independently of the UCS. In general, however, objects are drawn on or parallel to the plane of a UCS.

To Modify a UCS:

Issue the command, then provide the following information:

- Origin/ZAxis/3point/Entity/View/X/Y/Z/Prev/ Restore/Save/Del/?/<World>: Enter an option.

• OPTIONS

Origin   Determines the origin of a UCS.

ZAxis   Defines the direction of the Z-coordinate axis. You are prompted for an origin for the UCS and for a point along the Z axis of the UCS.

3point   Allows you to define a UCS by selecting three points: the origin, a point along the positive direction of the X axis, and a point along the positive direction of the Y axis.

Entity   Defines a UCS based on the orientation of an object.

View   Defines a UCS parallel to your current view. The origin of the current UCS will be used as the origin of the new UCS.

X/Y/Z   Allows you to define a UCS by rotating the current UCS about its X, Y, or Z axis.

Prev   Places you in the previously defined UCS. The *UCS Previous* option under the **Settings** pull-down menu has the same effect.

Restore   Restores a saved UCS.

Save   Saves a UCS for later recall.

Del   Deletes a previously saved UCS.

?   Displays a list of currently saved UCS's. You can use wildcard filter lists to search for specific UCS names.

World   Returns you to the World Coordinate System.

Notes   The World Coordinate System, or WCS, is the base from which all other UCS's are defined. The WCS is the default coordinate system when you open a new file.

When you pick preset UCS options from the **Settings** pull-down menu, an icon menu appears that contains several predefined UCS options.

If you use the *Entities* option, the way the selected entity was created affects the orientation of the UCS. TABLE 11 correlates selected entities with UCS orientation.

See Also   Dducs, Dducsp, Dview, Elev, Plan, Rename, Thickness, Ucsicon, Vpoint, Wildcards. *System Variables:* Ucsfollow, Ucsicon, Ucsname, Ucsorg, Ucsxdir, Ucsydir, Worlducs, Vsmax, Vsmin.

Table 11: UCS Orientation Based on Entities

Object Type	UCS Orientation
Arc	The center of the arc establishes the UCS origin. The X axis of the UCS passes through one of the endpoints nearest to the picked point on the arc.
Circle	The center of the circle establishes the UCS origin. The X axis of the UCS passes through the pick point on the circle.
Dimension	The midpoint of the dimension text establishes the UCS origin. The X axis of the UCS is parallel to the X axis that was active when the dimension was drawn.
Line	The endpoint nearest the pick point establishes the origin of the UCS, and the XZ plane of the UCS contains the line.
Point	The point location establishes the UCS origin. The UCS orientation is arbitrary.
2D Polyline	The starting point of the polyline establishes the UCS origin. The X axis is determined by the direction from the first point to the next vertex.
Solid	The first point of the solid establishes the origin of the UCS. The second point of the solid establishes the X axis.
Trace	The first point of the solid establishes the origin of the UCS. The second point of the solid establishes the X axis.

Table 11: UCS Orientation Based on Entities (continued)

Object Type	UCS Orientation
3Dface	The first point of the 3Dface establishes the origin. The first and second points establish the X axis. The plane defined by the face determines the orientation of the UCS.
Shapes, Text, Blocks, Attributes, and Attribute Definitions	The insertion point establishes the origin of the UCS. The object's rotation angle establishes the X axis.

UCSICON

Menu: **Settings ➤ UCS ➤ Icon ➤ On/Origin**

Controls the display and location of the UCS icon. The UCS icon tells you the orientation of the current UCS. It displays an "L" shaped graphic symbol showing the positive X and Y directions. The icon displays a W when the WCS is the current default coordinate system. If the current UCS plane is perpendicular to your current view, the UCS icon displays a broken pencil to indicate that you will have difficulty drawing in the current view. The UCS icon changes to a cube when you are displaying a perspective view. When you are in Paperspace, it turns into a triangle.

To Modify the UCS Icon:

Issue the command, then provide the following information:

- ON/OFF/All/Noorigin/ORigin <ON>: Enter an option.

• OPTIONS

ON   Turns the UCS icon on.

OFF   Turns the UCS icon off.

All   Forces the Ucsicon settings to take effect in all viewports if you have more than one viewport. Otherwise, the settings will affect only the active viewport.

Noorigin   Places the UCS icon in the lower left corner of the drawing area, regardless of the current UCS's origin location.

ORigin   Places the UCS icon at the origin of the current UCS. If the origin is off the screen, the UCS icon will appear in the lower left corner of the drawing area.

See Also   UCS, Viewports. *System Variables:* Ucsicon.

UNDEFINE

See Redefine.

UNDO

Allows you to undo parts of your editing session. This can be useful if you accidentally execute a command that destroys part or all of your drawing. Undo also allows you to control how much of a drawing is undone.

To Undo Edits:

Issue the command, then provide the following information:

- Auto/Back/Control/End/Group/Mark/<number>:
  Enter an option to use or the number of commands to
  undo.

• OPTIONS

Auto   Makes AutoCAD view menu macros as a single command.
If Auto is set to On, the effect of macros issued from a menu will be
undone regardless of the number of commands the macro contains.

Back, Mark   Allow you to experiment safely with a drawing by
first marking a point in your editing session to which you can
return. Once a mark has been issued, you can proceed with your
experimental drawing addition. Then, you can use Back to undo all
the commands back to the place that Mark was issued.

End, Group   Allow you to mark a group of commands to be undone together. Issue the Undo/Group command and proceed with
your editing until you reach the point where you wish to end the
group. Then, issue the Undo/End command. If you use the **U** command, the commands issued between the Undo/Group and the
Undo/End commands will be treated as a single command and
will all be undone at once.

Control   Allows you to turn off the Undo feature to save disk
space or to limit the Undo feature to single commands. You are
prompted for All, None, or One. *All* fully enables the Undo feature,
None disables Undo, and *One* restricts the Undo feature to a single
command at a time.

Notes   Many commands offer an Undo option. The Undo option
under a main command will act more like the **U** command and will
not offer the options described here.

See Also   Redo, U. *System Variables:* Undoctl, Undomarks.

UNITS

Sets AutoCAD to the unit format appropriate to the drawing. For example, if you are drawing an architectural floorplan, you can set up AutoCAD to accept and display distances using feet, inches, and fractional inches. You can also set up AutoCAD to accept and display angles as degrees, minutes, and seconds of arc rather than the default decimal degrees.

To Change Drawing Units:

Issue the command, then provide the following information:

1. System of Units:

Enter choice, 1 to 5 <2>: Enter the number corresponding to the desired unit system, as described below. With the exception of the Engineering and Architectural modes, you can use these modes with any basic unit of measurement.

2. Number of digits to right of decimal point (0 to8): <4>:

Enter a number to specify the degree of precision.

3. Systems of angle measure:

Enter choice, 1 to 5 <1>: Enter the number corresponding to the desired angle measure system, as described below.

4. Number of fractional places for display of angle (0 to 8) <0>: Enter a number to specify the degree of precision.

5. Direction for angle 0:

Enter direction for angle 0 <0>: Enter the desired angle for the 0 degree direction, as described below.

6. Do you want angle measured clockwise? <N>:

Enter **Y** if you want angles measured clockwise, otherwise press ↵.

● OPTIONS

System of units   Sets format of units that AutoCAD will accept as input:

Report Format	Example
1. Scientific	1.55E+01
2. Decimal	15.50
3. Engineering	1'–3.50"
4. Architectural	1'–3 1/2"
5. Fractional	15 1/2

System of angle measure   Sets format of angle measurement AutoCAD will accept as input:

Measurement Format	Example
1. Decimal degrees	45.0000
2. Degrees/minutes/seconds	45d0'0"
3. Grads	50.0000g
4. Radians	0.7854r
5. Surveyor's units	N 45d0'0" E

Direction for angle 0   Sets direction for the 0 angle:

East	3 o'clock = 0
North	12 o'clock = 90
West	9 o'clock = 180
South	6 o'clock = 270

Notes   You can set decimal or fractional input regardless of the unit format being used. This means you can enter 5.5', as well as 5'6" when using the Architectural format.

Decimal mode is perfect for metric units as well as decimal English units.

See Also   Ddunits, Mvsetup. *System Variables:* Aflags, Angbase, Angdir, Aumits, Luprec, Unitmode.

VIEW

Allows you to save views of your drawing. Instead of using the **Zoom** command to zoom in and out of your drawing, you can save views of the areas you need to edit, and then recall them using the *Restore* option of the View command. The corresponding dialog box command is Ddview.

To Save Views of Your Drawing:

Issue the command, then provide the following information:

- ?/Delete/Restore/Save/Window: Enter an option.

● OPTIONS

?   Lists all currently saved views. Wildcard filter lists are accepted.

Delete   Prompts you for a view name to delete from the drawing database.

Restore   Prompts you for a view name to restore to the screen.

Save   Saves current view. You are prompted for a view name.

Window   Saves a view defined by a window. You are prompted first to enter a view name and then to window the area to be saved as a view.

Notes   AutoCAD provides a *Select Initial View* check box to restore a previously saved view in the Open Drawing dialog box when you open an existing drawing.

View will save three-dimensional orthographic projection views, perspective views, and Paperspace or Modelspace views. View does not save hidden-line views or shaded views.

See Also   Open.

VIEWPORTS

See **Vports**.

VIEWRES

Controls whether AutoCAD's *virtual screen* feature is used, and how accurately AutoCAD displays lines, arcs, and circles.

To Invoke Fast Zoom Mode:

Issue the command, then provide the following information:

- Do you want fast zooms? **<Y>**: Enter **Y** or **N**. If you respond with **Y**, the following prompt appears:

    - Enter circle zoom percent (1-20000) <current setting>: Enter a value from 1 to 20,000 or press ↵ to accept the default.

● OPTIONS

Yes Sets up a large virtual screen within which zooms, pans, and view/restores occur at redraw speeds. You are prompted for a circle zoom percent (based on the current zoom magnification). This value determines how accurately circles and noncontinuous lines are shown.

No Turns off the virtual screen. All zooms, pans, and view/restores will cause a regeneration.

Notes The circle zoom percent value also affects the speed of redraws and regenerations. A high value slows down redraws and regenerations; a low value speeds them up. Differences in redraw speeds are barely noticeable unless you have a very large drawing.

Use a high percent value for circle zoom to display smooth circles and arcs and to accurately show noncontinuous lines. A low value causes arcs and circles to appear as a series of line segments when viewed up close. Noncontinuous lines, however, may appear continuous. This does not mean that prints or plots of your drawing will be less accurate; only the display is affected.

The default value for the circle zoom percent is 100, but at this value dashed or hidden lines might appear continuous, depending on the *Ltscale* setting and how far you are zoomed into the drawing. A value of 2000 (i.e., 20×) or higher reduces or eliminates this problem with little sacrifice of speed.

A low circle zoom value causes object end points, intersections, and tangents to appear inaccurately placed when you edit a closeup view of circles and arcs. Often, this results from the segmented appearance of arcs and circles and does not necessarily mean the object placement is inaccurate. It may also be hard to distinguish between polygons and circles. Setting the circle zoom percent to a high value also reduces or eliminates these problems.

The drawing limits affect redraw speed when the virtual screen feature is turned on. If the limits are set to an area much greater than the actual drawing, redraws are slowed down.

To force the virtual screen to contain a specific area, set your limits to the area you want, set the limit's checking feature to On, and issue a **Zoom**/*All* command. The virtual screen will conform to these limits until another **Regen** is issued or until you pan or zoom outside of the area set by the limits.

See Also   Limits, Redraw, Regen, Regenauto.

VPLAYER

Menu: **View ➤ Mview ➤ Vplayer**

Controls the visibility of layers for each individual viewport and allows display of different types of information in each viewport, even though the views are of the same drawing. You can use Vplayer in conjunction with overlapped viewports to create clipped views. Tilemode must be set to **0**.

To Modify Viewport Layer Visibility:

Issue the command, then provide the following information:

- ?/Freeze/Thaw/Reset/Newfrz/Vpvisdflt: Enter the desired option.

● OPTIONS

?   Displays the names of layers that are frozen in a given viewport. You are prompted to select a viewport. If you are in Modelspace, AutoCAD temporarily switches to Paperspace during your selection.

Freeze   Lets you specify the name of layers you want to freeze in selected viewports. You are first prompted for the names of the layers you wish to freeze, then for the viewport(s) in which to freeze them.

Thaw   Thaws layers in specific viewports. You are prompted for the layer names to thaw, then the viewports in which the layers are to be thawed.

Reset   Restores the default visibility setting for layers in a given viewport. See the *Vpvisdflt* option for information on default visibility.

Newfrz   Creates a new layer that is automatically frozen. You can then turn this new layer on for each viewport individually. The option *Vp Frz* under the **Ddlmodes** dialog box performs the same function.

Vpvisdflt   Presets the visibility of layers for new viewports to be created using *Mview* by prompting:

- Layer name(s) to change default viewport visibility: Enter layer name.

- Change default viewport visibility to Frozen/<Thawed>: Enter an option.

Notes   All options that prompt you for layer names allow use of wildcard characters to select multiple layer names. You can also use comma delimiters for lists of layers with dissimilar names.

See Also   Ddlmodes, Layers, Mview, Mvsetup, Pspace. *System Variables:* Tilemode.

VPOINT

Menu: **View ➤ Set View ➤ Viewpoint ➤ Set Vpoint**

Selects an orthographic, three-dimensional view of your drawing.

To Set a Viewing Point:

Issue the command, then provide the following information:

- Rotate/<View point> <current setting>: Enter a coordinate value, enter **R** for the Rotate option, or press ↵ to set the view with the compass and axes tripod.

● OPTIONS

Rotate   Allows you to specify a view in terms of angles from the XY plane and from the X axis. You are first prompted to enter an angle in the XY plane from the X axis. Next, you are prompted to enter an angle from the XY plane.

View point   Allows you to specify your view point location by entering an X,Y,Z coordinate value.

↵   Allows you to visually select a view by using the compass and axes tripod.

Icon menu   If you pick **3DView** or **Vpoint 3D** from the pull-down menu, an icon menu appears, offering several preset three-dimensional views. You can pick one of these options.

Notes   There are three methods for selecting a view:

- Enter a value in X, Y, and Z coordinates that represents your view point. For example, entering 1,1,–1 will give you the same view as entering 4,4,–4.

- Use the *Rotate* option to specify a view point as horizontal and vertical angles in relation to the last point selected. Use the **ID** command to establish the view target point (the last point selected) before you start Vpoint (see FIGURE 44).

- Press ↵ at the Vpoint prompt, and visually select a view point using the compass and axes tripod. To select a view, move your pointing device until the tripod indicates the desired X, Y, and Z axis orientation. A cross on the compass indicates your location in plan. For example, placing the cross in the lower left quadrant of the compass places your view point below and to the left of your drawing. Your view elevation is indicated by the distance of the cross from the compass center. The closer the cross is to the center, the higher the elevation. The circle inside the

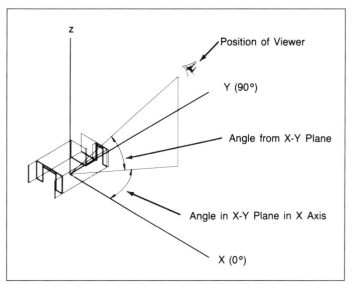

Figure 44: The viewpoint angles and what they represent

compass indicates a 0 elevation. If the cross falls outside of this circle, your view elevation becomes a minus value and your view will be from below your drawing (see FIG-URE 45).

See Also Dview.

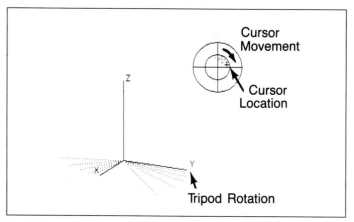

Figure 45: How the tripod rotates as you move the cursor around the target's center

VPORTS/VIEWPORTS

Menu: View ➤ Mview ➤ Create Viewport/Viewport On/Viewport Off/Fit Viewport/2 Viewports/3 Viewports/4 Viewports

Displays multiple views, or viewports, of your drawing at one time. This command is disabled when the *Tilemode* system variable is set to 0. Paperspace and the **Mview** command then take the place of the Vports functions.

To Display Multiple Viewports:

Issue the command, then provide the following information:

- Save/Restore/Delete/Join/SIngle/?/2/<3>/4: Enter the desired option.

● OPTIONS

Save   Saves the current viewport arrangement.

Restore   Restores a previously saved viewport arrangement.

Delete   Deletes a previously saved viewport arrangement.

Join   Joins two adjacent viewports of the same size to make one larger viewport.

SIngle   Changes the display to a single viewport.

?   Displays a list of saved viewport arrangements along with each viewport's coordinate location.

2   Splits the display to show two viewports. You are prompted for a horizontal or vertical split.

3   Changes the display to show three viewports.

4   Changes the display to show four equal viewports.

Notes   Each viewport can contain any type of view you like. For example, you can display a perspective view in one viewport and a plan view of the same drawing in another viewport.

You can only work in one viewport at a time. To change active viewports, pick any point inside the desired viewport. The border around the selected viewport will thicken to show that it is active. The standard cursor appears only in the active viewport. (When you move the cursor into an inactive viewport, it changes into an arrow.) Any edits made in one viewport are immediately reflected in the other viewports.

Each viewport has its own virtual display within which you can pan and zoom at redraw speeds. For this reason, the **Regen** and

Redraw commands affect only the active viewport. To regenerate or redraw all the viewports at once, use the **Regenall** and **Redrawall** commands.

You can pick from several predefined viewport arrangements by selecting the one you want from the pull-down menu.

See Also Mview Redraw, Redrawall, Regen, Regenall, Viewres. *System Variables:* Cvports, Maxactvp, Viewctr, Viewdir, Viewtwist, Vsmax, Vsmin.

VSLIDE

Displays slide files. Slides are individual files with the extension .SLD. You may combine individual slide files into a slide library file by using the extension .SLB.

To Display Slide Files:

Issue the command, then provide the following information:

> File name <current file name>: Enter the name of the slide file to be displayed.

See Also Mslide, Script, Slidelib.EXE.

WBLOCK

Lets you create a new file from a portion of the current file or from a block of the current file.

To Write a Block to Disk:

Issue the command, then provide the following information:

1. File name: Enter the filename.

2. Block name: Enter the block name or press ⏎ to select objects.

The block or set of objects will be written to your disk as a drawing file.

Notes If you are exporting a block from your drawing and you want the filename to be the same as the block name, enter an equals sign at the Block name: prompt, or enter the same block name again.

If you enter the name of an existing file at the File name: prompt, you receive the prompt:

A drawing with this name already exists.

Do you want to replace it? <N>:

You can replace the file or return to the command prompt to restart Wblock.

To write a portion of the current drawing view to a file, press ⏎ without entering anything at the Block name: prompt. You receive the following two prompts:

- Insertion base point: Enter a coordinate or pick a point.

- Select objects: Select objects using the standard AutoCAD selection options.

The objects you select are written to your disk as a drawing file. The point you select at the Insertion base point: prompt becomes the origin of the written file. The current UCS (user coordinate system) becomes the WCS (world coordinate system) in the written file. When you save a block to disk, the UCS active at the time you create the block becomes the WCS of the written file.

Entering an asterisk (*) at the Block name: prompt writes the entire current file to disk, stripping it of all unused blocks, layers, line types, and text styles. This can reduce a file's size and access time. (See **Purge**).

Objects are placed in the Modelspace of the output file unless the asterisk is used. In that case, objects are placed in the space they are in.

See Also   Base. *System Variables:* Insbase, Handles.

WILDCARD CHARACTERS

Wildcard characters allow you to list filenames by using a filter to include or exclude files according to similarities in their names. AutoCAD wildcard characters are extensions of the standard DOS wildcard characters.

To Create Lists of Names:

At any prompt that asks for names to list, enter a name containing wildcard characters (listed below).

• OPTIONS

Matches any number. For example, **C#D** selects all names that begin with C, end with D, and have a single-digit number between.

@   Matches any alphabetical character. For example, **C@D** selects any name that begins with C, ends with D, and has a single alphabetical character between.

. (period)   Matches any character not numeric or alphabetical. For example, **C.D** might select the name C-D.

* (asterisk)   Matches any string of characters. For example, ***CD** selects all names of any length that end with CD.

? (question mark)   Matches any single character. For example **C?D** selects all names of three characters that begin with C and end with D.

~ (tilde)   Matches anything *but* the set of characters that follow. For example, **~CD** selects all names that do *not* include CD.

[ ]   Typing any set of characters between two brackets matches any *one* of the characters enclosed in brackets. For example, **[CD]X**

selects the names CX and DX but not CDX. Brackets can be used in conjunction with other wildcard characters. For example, you could use [~CD]X to find all names except CX and DX.

- (hyphen)   Lets you specify a range of characters when used within brackets. For example, [C-F]X selects the names CX, DX, EX, and FX.

`*(reverse quote)*   Forces the character that follows to be read literally. (The reverse quote is the character that is located to the left of the *1* key on most keyboards.) For example, `*CD selects the name *CD, instead of all names that end in CD.

XBIND

Imports a block, dimension style, layer, line type, or text style from a cross-referenced file.

To Bind Symbols into Your Drawing:

Issue the command, then provide the following information:

1.   Block/Dimstyle/LAyer/LType/Style: Enter the desired option.

2.   You are then prompted for the name of the item to import. Enter a single name, a list of names separated by commas, or use wildcard characters to specify a range of names.

Notes   Named variables from a cross-referenced file are prefixed with their source filename. For example, a block named *Wheel* from a cross-referenced file called *Car* will have the name *Car | wheel* in the file that has the cross-reference assigned to it. When you use Xbind to import the Wheel block, its name will change to *Car0wheel* to reflect its source file. If a block Car0wheel already exists, the 0 is replaced with a 1 as in *Car1wheel*.

See Also   Xref.

XREF

Menu: **File ➤ Xref ➤ Attach…/Detach/Reload/List/Change Path**

Xref lets you attach an external file to your current file for reference purposes.

To Import an External File:

Issue the command, then provide the following information:

- ?/Bind/Detach/Path/Reload/<Attach>: Enter the desired option.

• OPTIONS

?   Displays a list of cross-referenced files in your current drawing. The name of the file as well as its location on your storage device is shown. You can filter the Xref'ed filenames by using wildcard characters.

Bind   Causes a cross-referenced file to become a part of the current file. Once Bind is used, the cross-referenced file becomes an ordinary block in the current file. You are prompted for the name of the Xref'ed file to be bound:

- Xref(s) to bind: Enter name or names separated with commas or wildcard.

Detach   Detaches a cross-referenced file, so it is no longer referenced to the current file:

- Xref(s) to detach: Enter name or names separated with commas or wildcard.

Path   Lets you specify a new DOS path for a cross-referenced file. This is useful if you have moved an Xref'ed file to another drive or directory. You are prompted for the Xref's name:

- Old Path: Enter old path.
- New Path: Enter new path.

Reload Lets you reload a cross-reference without exiting and re-entering the current file. This option is useful if you are in a network environment and you know that someone has just finished updating a file you are using as a cross-reference.

- Xref(s) to reload: Enter name or names separated with commas or wildcard.

Attach Lets you attach another drawing file as a cross-reference. You are prompted for a filename, notified if the file exists, then requested for an insertion point.

- Xref to Attach <default>: Enter name, or a ~ (tilde) to open the Select Drawing File dialog box.
  Xref (filename) has already been loaded.
  Insertion point: Enter location.

Notes Xref'ed files act like blocks; they cannot be edited from the file they are attached to. The difference between blocks and Xref'ed files is that Xref'ed files do not become part of the current file's database. Instead, the current file "points" to the Xref'ed file. The next time the current file is opened, the Xref'ed file is also opened and automatically attached. This has two advantages. First, since the Xref'ed file does not become part of the current file, the current file size remains small. Second, since the Xref'ed file stays independent, any changes made to it are automatically reflected in the current file whenever it is re-opened.

In most of the options, you can enter a single name, a list of names separated by commas, or a name containing wildcard characters.

Named variables from the Xref'ed files will have the filename as a prefix. For example, a layer called *wall* in an Xref'ed file called *house* will have the name *House | wall* in the current file.

At a filename prompt, you can assign a name to an Xref'ed file that is different from its actual filename by appending to the filename an equals sign followed by the new name. For example, at the prompt Xref to Attach:, enter a statement in the form of

    newplan=oldplan

where newplan is the new name and oldplan is the filename of the Xref'ed file.

AutoCAD keeps a log of Xref activity in an ASCII file. This file has the same root name as your current drawing file and has the extension .XLG. You can delete this file with no effect on your drawing.

See Also   Block, Insert, Xbind. *System Variables:* Xrefctl.

ZOOM

Menu: **View ➤ Zoom ➤ Window/Dynamic/Previous/All/Extent/Vmax**

Zoom controls the display of your drawing.

To Use Zoom:

Issue the command, then provide the following information:

- All/Center/Dynamic/Extents/Left/Previous/Vmax/Window/<Scale(X/XP)> : Enter the desired option.

● OPTIONS

All   Displays the area of the drawing defined by the drawing's limits or extents, whichever are greater (see **Limits**).

Center   Displays a view based on a selected point. You are first prompted for a center point for your view and then for a magnification or height. A value followed by an **X** is read as a magnification factor; a lone value is read as the desired height in the display's drawing units.

Dynamic   Displays the virtual screen and allows you to use a view box to select a view. The drawing extents, current view, and the current virtual screen area are indicated as a solid white box, a dotted green box, and red corner marks, respectively. You can pan, enlarge, or shrink the view by moving the view box to a new location, adjusting its size, or both. Whenever the view box moves into an area that will cause a regeneration, an hourglass appears in the lower left corner of the display (see FIGURE 46).

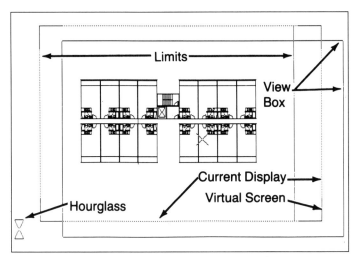

Figure 46: The Dynamic Zoom display

Extents   Displays a view of the entire drawing. The drawing is forced to fit within the display and is forced to the left. The drawing limits are ignored (see **Limits**).

Left   Similar to the *Center* option, but the point you pick at the prompt becomes the lower left corner of the display.

Previous   Displays the last view created by a **Zoom**, **Pan**, or **View** command. AutoCAD will store up to four previous views.

Vmax   Displays an overall view of the current virtual display. Unlike the *Extents* and *All* options, no regen occurs.

Window   Enlarges a rectangular area of a drawing, based on a defined window.

Scale(X)   Expands or shrinks the drawing display. If an **X** follows the scale factor, it will be in relation to the current view. If no X is used, the scale factor will be in relation to the area defined by the limits of the drawing.

Scale(XP)   Sets a viewports scale in relation to the Paperspace scale. For example, if you have set up a title block in Paperspace at a scale of 1" = 1", and your full-scale Modelspace drawing is to be at a final plot scale of 1/4" = 1′, you can enter **1/48xp** at the Zoom prompt to set the viewport at the appropriate scale for Paperspace. You must be in Modelspace to use this option.

Notes   Zoom cannot be used as a transparent command while viewing a drawing in perspective. Use the **Dview** command's Zoom option instead.

See Also   Limits, Mspace, Mview, Mvsetup, Pspace, Redraw, Regen, Regenauto, Viewres. *System Variables:* Viewsize.

Index

Note to the Reader: This index differentiates between mentions of items, listed in regular type, and explanations of items, listed as **bold** page numbers. *Italic* page numbers refer to figures.

E

F

318

AutoCAD pull-down menus

File
New...
Open...
Save...
Save As...
Save DIB
Recover...

Plot...

ASE
Import/Export
Xref

Preferences...
Configure
Compile...
Utilities...
Applications...

Exit AutoCAD

Find File...
1 F:\ACADWIN\SAMPLE\NOZZLE3D
2 F:\ACADWIN\SAMPLE\DASHLINE
3 F:\ACADWIN\SAMPLE\SEXTANT
4 F:\ACADWIN\SAMPLE\TROL1

Edit
Undo
Redo

Copy Image
Copy Vectors
Copy Object
Paste
Paste Command

Text Window
DDE

Select

View Redraw
Redraw All

Zoom
Pan

√ Tilemode
Toggle Viewport   Ctrl+V
Model Space
Paper Space
Mview

Set View

Layout

Assist Cancel   Ctrl+C
Object Filters...
Object Snap

Inquiry

Calculator

Draw Line
Arc
Circle
Point

Polyline
Donut
Ellipse
Polygon
Rectangle

Insert...

3D Surfaces

Hatch...

Text

Dimensions